THIRD EDITION

Rudiments of MUSIC

Robert W. Ottman
Frank D. Mainous

College of Music, University of North Texas

Prentice Hall, Upper Saddle River, New Jersey 07458

Library of Congress Cataloging-in-Publication Data

OTTMAN, ROBERT W.
    Rudiments of music / Robert W. Ottman and Frank D. Mainous.—3rd
ed.
      p.   cm.
    Includes index.
    ISBN 0-13-706740-2
    1. Music—Theory, Elementary.   I. Mainous, Frank D.   II. Title.
MT7.O82 1995
781—dc20
                                        94-41687
                                          CIP
                                          MN

Acquisitions editor: *Norwell F. Therien*
Editorial/production supervision
    and interior design: *Carole R. Crouse*
Copy editor: *Carole R. Crouse*
Cover designer: *Rich Dombrowski*
Buyer: *Robert Anderson*

 © 1995, 1987, 1970 by Prentice-Hall, Inc.
Simon & Schuster Company / A Viacom Company
Upper Saddle River, New Jersey 07458

Printed in the United States of America

10

ISBN 0-13-706740-2

PRENTICE-HALL INTERNATIONAL (UK) LIMITED, *London*
PRENTICE-HALL OF AUSTRALIA PTY. LIMITED, *Sydney*
PRENTICE-HALL CANADA INC., *Toronto*
PRENTICE-HALL HISPANOAMERICANA , S.A., *Mexico*
PRENTICE-HALL OF INDIA PRIVATE LIMITED, *New Delhi*
PRENTICE-HALL OF JAPAN, INC., *Tokyo*
SIMON & SCHUSTER ASIA PTE. LTD., *Singapore*
EDITORA PRENTICE-HALL DO BRASIL, LTDA., *Rio de Janeiro*

Contents

Preface

Should you improvise a tune, either singing or on your instrument, each of the sounds you produce becomes inaudible almost immediately. These sounds are so nebulous that they cannot be captured physically, except by electronic recording. Repeating your tune, therefore, depends upon memory, or, if you wish to make it available to others, upon finding a way to write it on paper.

The object of this text is to discover how musical sounds are represented on paper through the use of graphic symbols and the basic ways in which they relate to each other in a music composition. The procedures are much the same for both language and music. In early human history, people learned to communicate with each other through speech. But because these sounds, like music, are also nebulous, their conversations or stories could be repeated only from memory. Nothing could be exactly and permanently retained until the invention of hieroglyphic symbols that could be inscribed on a suitable surface—in ancient times, on a clay tablet or a sheaf of papyrus, among several possibilities, and today, on paper.

The first representations of speech, dating from about 7000 B.C., were created by the Sumerians, in what is now Iraq. But it was not until about A.D. 800 that in Western civilization we first find written symbols indicating musical sound (excluding the remaining fragments of alphabetical symbols used by the Greeks about 600 B.C.). But we know that between those dates there was much musical activity. Examples are numerous, from sources such as Psalm 150 of the Bible, naming many instruments, images on Greek potteries depicting music performance, and actual trumpets discovered in the tomb of the Egyptian king Tutankhamen (d. 1325 B.C.).

But how did this music sound? Was it all single-line melody only? Did the two instrumentalists on a Greek vase play the same sounds or two different sounds at the same time? Did the horns, reeds, and drum at a festival for Cleopatra play in harmony and in specific rhythmic patterns? These and all similar questions are, of course, unanswerable.

Placing on paper the chants of the medieval Christian church was the motivation for a notation that ultimately would evolve into today's notation. The earliest, about A.D. 800, consists of what appear to be squiggly symbols, called *neumes,* that represent a vague relationship between pitches, used probably as a reminder to someone who was already familiar with the chant. Added later was a single line that represented a single pitch as a point of reference.

Neumes, circa eighth century

One-line staff, circa tenth century

In the years between A.D. 800 and A.D. 1600, these symbols developed into the system of staves, notes, and rests used today to represent pitch and rhythm. With these symbols, we can now easily make a written record of our musical ideas, and read and reproduce those of others.

Knowing this historical background, you are better able to appreciate the efficiency of our modern notation, one that over a period of four hundred years has provided for composers the means to express multitudinous musical ideas, and for the performer an easy and practical way to grasp and to express those ideas.

In this text, we will consider the notation of pitch and of duration and the application of these to the keyboard, to basic devices such as scales, intervals, meter, and rhythmic patterns, and to elementary harmony. The principles of each of the subjects presented are easy enough to understand. If only casual understanding were necessary, this text would be much shorter than it is. In fact, you can easily find that information in a music dictionary. If, however, your study is to aid you in improving performing ability, it is necessary that you be able to apply your knowledge quickly and accurately in a musical situation. To that end, *Rudiments of Music* provides you with enough practice in each lesson that not only will you be able to say, "Yes, I've got the general idea," but more important, you can say, "I can actually do these things quickly and accurately." Then you will receive your dividends, not only in better understanding, but also in quicker learning and more accuracy in your performance of music. In addition, you will have laid the groundwork for more advanced musical studies, perhaps even for music composition, and for increased appreciation and enjoyment of all music.

Robert W. Ottman
Frank D. Mainous

Suggestions for the Use of this Book

Sequence of Chapters

After Chapters 1 and 2 (Pitch), early chapters on *Pitch* and *Time* are found in alternate groupings. It is suggested that the course follow the given sequence of chapters, but other organizations of material are also useful. To that end, a reference at the end of each chapter indicates the next chapter in that subject area.

These are the chapter numbers in each subject area:

Pitch: 1, 2, 4, 5, 6, 10, 11, 14–19
Time: 3, 7, 8, 9, 12, 13
Harmony: 20–23

In another format, a class session may be devoted to the study of both pitch and time. When combined for such a presentation, chapters and their exercises can easily be halved, quartered, or otherwise abridged to fit class time.

Exercises

Rudiments of Music is designed as a combination text and workbook. Each chapter presentation is followed by a group of appropriate exercises. Marginal references throughout the presentation direct the student to an exercise providing practice in the particular material just covered. After each exercise (or group of exercises), a page reference directs the student back to the location in the book where the presentation continues. This procedure, the immediate use of exercises following a presentation, is recommended. Optionally, exercises can be deferred and worked as a group at the end of the chapter.

Most of the exercises can be completed by the student working alone and handed in to the instructor. Notice that the pages are perforated for easy tear-out and are punched for a standard three-ring binder so that the detached pages can be replaced and secured in order.

Some of the exercises, those dealing with aural drills, should be conducted by the instructor (or another qualified person). These are identified by the signal word "(Instructor)" following the exercise number.

CHAPTER ONE

Pitch

As we set out to learn how sound is represented on paper, we should first ask what properties make up the sensation we know as musical sound. There are four such properties:

1. *Pitch.* How high or low is the sound?
2. *Duration.* How long is the sound held?
3. *Intensity.* How loud or how soft is the sound?
4. *Timbre.* What is the quality of the sound? (As an example, we recognize the sound of a violin as a different timbre from that of a saxophone.)

Of the four properties, *intensity* and *timbre* are functions of acoustics and are discussed in Appendix A. Our studies will concentrate for the most part on the remaining two properties, beginning with the notation of *pitch*.

Pitch

When we hear two different sounds produced by a musical instrument such as the piano, we hear one of the sounds as being higher or lower than the other. This property of sound, its seeming highness or lowness, is called *pitch*. To indicate on paper the difference in pitch in musical sound, we use a device called the *staff*.

The Staff

The music *staff* (plural, *staves*) consists of five parallel horizontal lines and four resultant spaces. These lines and spaces represent successively higher pitches when progressing from the lowest to the highest line.

The lines are numbered from the bottom to the top, 1 through 5. Spaces are similarly numbered from the bottom, 1 through 4. The pitches represented by lines and spaces are identified by letters of the *musical alphabet*.

FIGURE 1-1   *The staff*

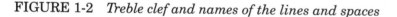

```
                5th line -.                              -. 4th space ⎫
                4th line -. -.  ═══════════════════   -. 3rd space ⎬  higher pitches
              ⎧ 3rd line -. -.  ═══════════════════   -. 2nd space ⎭
lower pitches ⎨ 2nd line -. -.  ═══════════════════   -. 1st space
              ⎩ 1st line -.                           
```

The Musical Alphabet

The first seven letters of the alphabet, A B C D E F G, make up the musical alphabet. These letters are used to name the lines and spaces of the staff, but the particular letter assigned to a specific line or space is determined by a symbol called a *clef,* which appears at the beginning of the staff.

Clefs

The two clefs most commonly used in music are (1) 𝄞, the G clef, in which the lower loop encircles a line of the staff to be designated as G; and (2) 𝄢, the F clef, in which the two dots are found on either side of a line of the staff to be designated as F.

Treble Clef

When the G clef is placed on the staff with the lower loop encircling the second line, it is known as the *treble clef.*

Thus, the second line of the staff receives the designation G. By fixing G on the staff, you can determine the names of the other lines and spaces. Letters of the musical alphabet are employed in order on ascending adjacent lines and spaces (staff degrees). After G, A follows on the next higher staff degree, which is the second space. Notes or letter names following a treble clef may be referred to as "in the treble clef" or "on the treble staff."

FIGURE 1-2   *Treble clef and names of the lines and spaces*

EXERCISES
1-1, 1-2

Bass Clef

When the F clef is placed on the staff with the two dots on either side of the fourth line, it is known as the *bass clef.*

Thus, the fourth line of the staff receives the designation F. By fixing F on the staff, you can determine the names of the other lines and spaces. After F, G follows on the next higher staff degree, which is the fourth space. Notes or letter names following a bass clef may be referred to as "in the bass clef" or "on the bass staff."

FIGURE 1-3 *Bass clef and names of the lines and spaces*

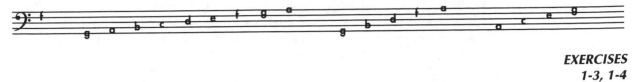

EXERCISES
1-3, 1-4

At times, a musical sound may be either higher or lower than those pitches represented by lines and spaces of the staff. Means of writing such pitches are provided by *ledger lines*.

Ledger Lines

Short lines added above and below the staff are called *ledger (leger) lines*. By extending the staff, ledger lines provide a means for indicating pitches either higher or lower than the limits of the five-line staff. Added ledger lines and resultant ledger spaces are drawn *equidistant* to lines and spaces of the staff. In Figure 1-4, a *note* (o) is used to show a specific pitch more clearly. All note shapes and their values are presented in Chapter Two.

FIGURE 1-4 *Ledger lines*

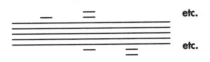

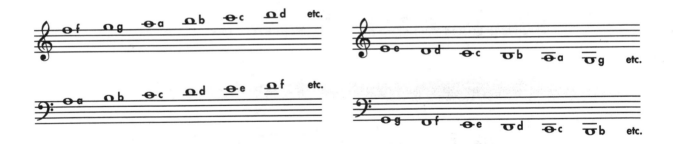

Observe that a note on the space above or the space below the staff does not require a ledger line:

EXERCISES
1-5, 1-6, 1-7

Uses of Treble and Bass Clefs

The treble clef is used by women's voices and by instruments that produce relatively higher pitches. Similarly, the bass clef accommodates men's voices and instruments producing relatively lower pitches.

However, when the staff accommodates only a tenor voice, the treble clef may be written as 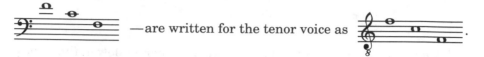, and is used with the understanding that the pitch to be sounded is the next lower pitch with the same letter name. In this way, fewer ledger lines are needed. For example, the sounds of the pitches F C F—

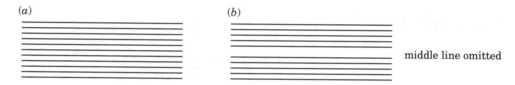

—are written for the tenor voice as

The Great Staff (Grand Staff)

When two staves are used together and are joined by a vertical line and a bracket, called a *brace,* the combination is known as the *great staff,* or *grand staff,* or *piano staff.*

In theory, the great staff is one large staff of eleven lines (Figure 1-5*a*). The middle line is omitted (Figure 1-5*b*) to create a separation, which permits quick visual discrimination of the upper and lower staff degrees.

FIGURE 1-5   *Eleven-line staff*

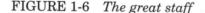

(a)   (b)

middle line omitted

With the brace added, the great staff is usually found with the treble clef placed on the upper five lines and the bass clef on the lower five lines (Figure 1-6).

FIGURE 1-6   *The great staff*

(brace)

If a ledger line were placed between the staves, like the omitted middle line in the eleven-line staff, then this single ledger line would be considered either the first ledger line above the bass or the first ledger line below the treble. See Figure 1-7, in which the pitch found on this ledger line centered between the staves is called *middle C.*

Notice that the space formed between the fifth bass line and the ledger line for middle C is occupied by the pitch B; continuing upward, notice that the space formed between the ledger line for middle C and the first treble line is occupied by the pitch D. Observe the alphabetical order of pitches on successive lines and spaces, from the bass upward through middle C and into the treble.

FIGURE 1-7 *Pitches on the great staff*

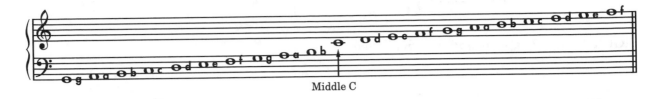

Middle C

Figure 1-7, with the staves placed closely together to show relation of bass to treble, is purposefully a theoretical illustration. Actually, in printed music the distance between the two staves of the great staff is increased to provide sufficient room for several additional ledger lines both above the bass and below the treble. Figure 1-8 shows such a great staff. The series of pitches in the treble clef is identical in sound to the series in the bass clef; this is easily seen by comparing *middle C* in each clef.

FIGURE 1-8 *The great staff with ledger lines above bass and below treble*

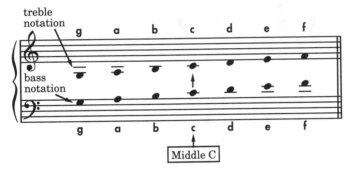

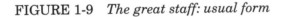

Middle C

EXERCISE
1-8

Remember that in printed music, or when you draw the great staff, the two staves are not close together but are well separated, as in Figure 1-8 and as in the following music excerpts.

FIGURE 1-9 *The great staff: usual form*

Beethoven, Sonata for Piano, Op. 2, No. 1[1]

Allegro

---

[1]*Opus* (Latin, "work"), abbreviated *op.*, together with a number identifies a composition and is usually supplied by the composer.

When necessary, the great staff may display two treble clefs (Figure 1-10), two bass clefs (Figure 1-11), or a change from treble to bass or vice versa (Figure 1-12).

FIGURE 1-10   *The great staff: two treble clefs*

Mozart, Sonata for Piano, K. 279[2]

FIGURE 1-11   *The great staff: two bass clefs*

Chopin, Prelude, Op. 28, No. 20

FIGURE 1-12   *The great staff with change of clef*

Mozart, Sonata for Piano, K. 576

EXERCISES
1-9, 1-10

[2]K.: abbreviation for Ludwig von Köchel, who in 1862 made a chronological listing of Mozart's works. Mozart did not give his works opus numbers.

NAME _Wes Hiller_

EXERCISE 1-1

Treble clef, lines and spaces

On staff *a* draw a treble clef sign and on each line write the correct letter name. On staff *b* draw a treble clef sign and on each space write the correct letter name.

To facilitate drawing the treble clef, think of it as in two separate parts, 1 and 2, and then combined, 3. Observe in 2 and 3 how the loop encircles the second line.

(1)   (2)   (3)

(*a*) Treble clef, names of lines   (*b*) Treble clef, names of spaces

EXERCISE 1-2

Pitches on the staff, treble clef

Next to each note, write the letter name of the pitch.

(*a*)

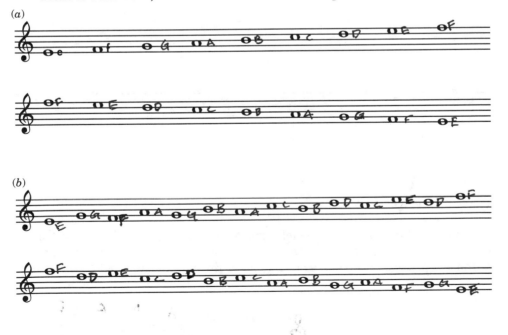

(*b*)

(Upon completion of this exercise, *return* to page 2.)

EXERCISE 1-3
Bass clef, lines and spaces

On staff *a* draw a bass clef sign and on each line write the correct letter name. On staff *b* draw a bass clef sign and on each space write the correct letter name.

(*a*) Bass clef, names of lines

(*b*) Bass clef, names of spaces

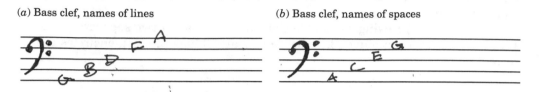

EXERCISE 1-4
Pitches on the staff, bass clef

Next to each note, write the letter name of the pitch.

(*a*)

(*b*)

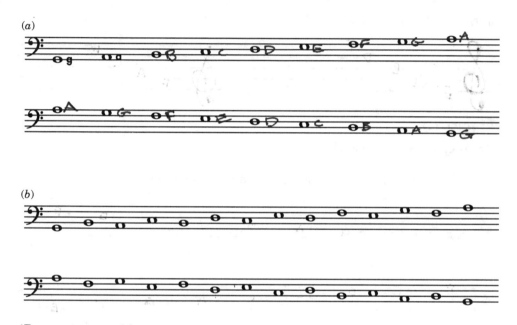

(*Return* to page 3.)

EXERCISE 1-5
Treble clef, ledger lines

On staff *a* draw a treble clef sign. Name the pitches of the notes on the ledger lines and spaces above the staff. On staff *b* draw a treble clef sign and name the pitches of the notes on the ledger lines and spaces below the staff.

(*a*) Treble clef, notes above staff

(*b*) Treble clef, notes below staff

NAME _Wes Hik___

EXERCISE 1-6
Bass clef, ledger lines

On staff *a* draw a bass clef sign. Name the pitches of the notes on the ledger lines and spaces above the staff. On staff *b* draw a bass clef sign and name the pitches of the notes on the ledger lines and spaces below the staff.

(*a*) Bass clef, notes above staff

(*b*) Bass clef, notes below staff

EXERCISE 1-7
Pitches above and below staff

Next to each note, write the letter name of the pitch.

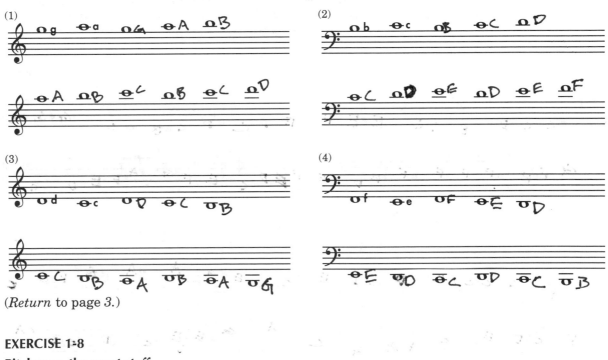

(1)

(2)

(3)

(4)

(*Return* to page 3.)

EXERCISE 1-8
Pitches on the great staff

Next to each note, write the letter name of the pitch.

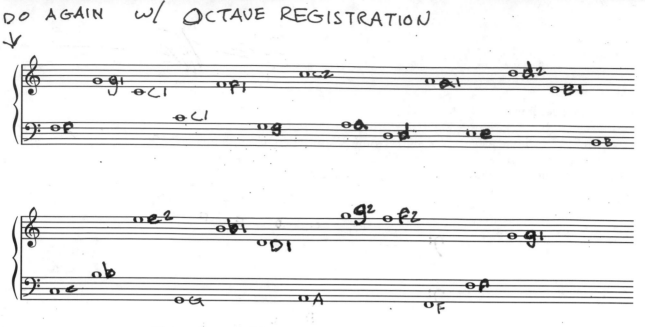

(*Return* to page 5.)

EXERCISE 1-9

Pitches in melody

The examples in this exercise are actual music examples, and as such, they contain notation not yet studied. At this time, we are interested only in naming the line or the space on which the note head o or • is located.[3]

Next to each note, write the letter name of the pitch.

[3]Examples of actual music will be used throughout the text and at times will contain elements not yet studied. These examples have been chosen to illustrate most efficiently the element under study; the remaining elements will not be found essential to the particular study, and they will be covered in later chapters.

NAME _Wes Fife_

[music example (6)]

⁴MSS: *Music for Sight Singing* (fourth edition) by Robert W. Ottman, ©1996 by Prentice-Hall, Inc.

EXERCISE 1-10
Reading notes by letter names

Read aloud the letter names of notes in the following melodies. Read in a normal speaking voice, making no attempt to produce highness or lowness or duration of the actual sounds of pitches. You are merely to recite names of the pitches and not sing them. Read as quickly as possible. Through additional practice, try to increase your speed.

Note to the Instructor: In this exercise, the student should ignore rhythm and any key signature and simply recite the alphabetical names. For example, "America" will be read *ccdbcdeefedcdcbcgggfgefffedefedcefgafedc*. The objective of this reading practice is to develop the ability to instantly recognize lines and spaces and respond by pitch names.

"America"

"Auld Lang Syne"

MSS 121

12

NAME

"America"

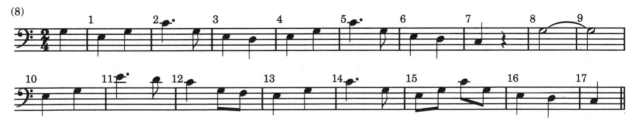

"Auld Lang Syne"

Reminder to the Instructor: In the remaining exercises, the student should ignore rhythm and any key signature and simply recite the alphabetical names (without accidentals).

MSS 129

MSS 210

MSS 111

MSS 103

For optional additional practice, continue the procedure used in Exercise 1-10 by reading letter names of notes in any melodies in Chapters 1 and 3 of *Music for Sight Singing,* third edition, by Robert W. Ottman, Prentice-Hall, Inc., 1986.

CHAPTER SUMMARY

1. The term *pitch* refers to the seeming highness or lowness of a sound.

2. A staff, five parallel lines and the resultant four spaces, is a device used to indicate differences in pitch.

3. The lines of the staff, starting with the bottom line, are numbered consecutively from 1 to 5; the spaces, starting with the bottom space, are numbered consecutively from 1 to 4.

4. Pitches are represented by letters of the musical alphabet, A B C D E F G.

5. Letter names of the lines and spaces of the staff are assigned by a clef sign at the beginning of the staff.

6. The *G clef,* 𝄞, placed on a staff so that its lower loop encircles the second line, indicates that that line is G. In this position, it is known as a *treble clef.*

7. The *F clef,* 𝄢, placed on a staff so that the two dots are on either side of the fourth line, indicates that that line is F. In this position, it is known as a *bass clef.*

8. *Ledger lines,* short lines and spaces above and below the staff, indicate pitches higher or lower than the limits of the five-line staff.

9. The *great staff* consists of two staves joined by a *brace.* Commonly, the upper staff carries a treble clef, and the lower staff a bass clef.

10. Middle C is found on the first ledger line below the treble staff and on the first ledger line above the bass staff.

CHAPTER TWO

Pitch:
The Keyboard

CARDBOARD KEYBOARD

Rudiments of Music, third edition, includes a CARDBOARD KEY-BOARD that can be used in lieu of a piano for studies of pitch, scales, intervals, and chords. A superimposed staff shows the note for each key. Full-sized keys enable the student to develop a sense of fingering and to feel distances between different keys.

Place the CARDBOARD KEYBOARD on a flat surface and simulate playing. For use with a real instrument, insert the card behind matching keys.

The Keyboard

The standard piano keyboard has 88 keys, consisting of 52 white keys and 36 black keys. Black keys are found in alternate groups of two and three. This can easily be seen on the keyboard because one group of black keys is always separated from another by a pair of white keys.

Keys at the left of the keyboard sound the lower pitches, and keys at the right sound higher pitches. Pitches at the extreme left are said to be at the *bottom* of the keyboard; pitches at the extreme right are said to be at the *top* of the keyboard. Accordingly, when looking from right to left, you look *down* the keyboard; when looking from left to right, you look *up* the keyboard.

Each white and black key of the keyboard is identified by name. First, we shall learn the *names of white keys*.

FIGURE 2-1 *Keyboard groups of two and three black keys*

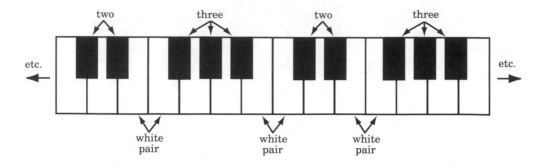

FIGURE 2-2 *The standard piano keyboard*

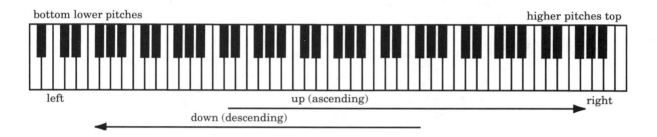

Names of White Keys

White keys are named with the seven letters of the musical alphabet. The white key at the far left side, at the bottom of the keyboard, is named A. The next white key to the right of A is named with the next letter of the alphabet, B. This application of the alphabet in naming white keys continues in order up the keyboard. After G, which is the seventh and last letter of the musical alphabet, A occurs again. This process is repeated through all succeeding white keys, ending with the highest pitch C at the top of the keyboard.

FIGURE 2-3 *Names of the white keys on the piano*

Observe that any C is located to the immediate left of any group of two black keys (Figure 2-4). When studying the keyboard in more detail, we will often use the pitch C as a point of orientation, or as a starting point when playing at the keyboard.

The C nearest the middle of the keyboard is called *middle C*. Middle C on the piano corresponds to middle C on the great staff (Figure 2-5; also see Figures 1-7 and 1-8 of Chapter One).

FIGURE 2-4   *Location of C at left of two black keys*

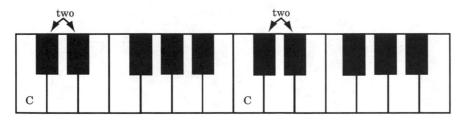
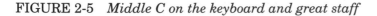

FIGURE 2-5   *Middle C on the keyboard and great staff*

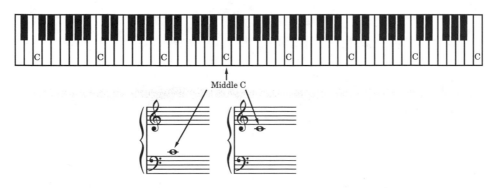
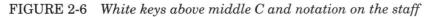

In Figure 2-6, pitches of white keys to the right of (above) middle C are represented as notes in ascending order on lines and spaces of the staff.

In Figure 2-7, pitches of white keys to the left of (below) middle C are represented as notes in descending order on lines and spaces of the staff.

FIGURE 2-6   *White keys above middle C and notation on the staff*

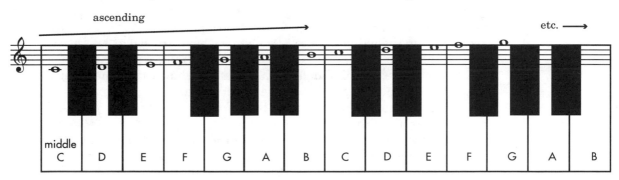

FIGURE 2-7 *White keys below middle C and notation on the staff*

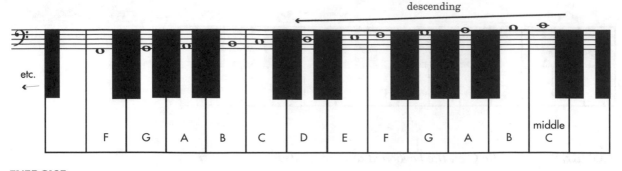

EXERCISE
2-1

We have now named all the *white keys* of the keyboard, with special attention given to the location of C's and, in particular, to the location of middle C. And we have found out how white-key pitches are notated on the staff. *Black keys* are also to be named, but not until we have learned about *intervals* and *accidentals*.

Intervals

An *interval* is the distance between two different pitches, or between two different notes on the staff, or between two different keys on the piano.[1] For the present, we shall study three intervals: the *octave,* the *half step,* and the *whole step.*

The Octave

The word *octave* is derived from the Latin *octo,* meaning "eight." Look at the keyboard illustration, Figure 2-5. Considering any C as 1 and counting consecutively up the white keys to 8, we find we have arrived at another C. 1 and 8 have the same letter name. This interval of eight degrees, from C to C, is called an octave. In similar fashion, it can be shown that the interval from any pitch to the next pitch of the same letter name, either up or down, is an octave.[2] For example, from A up to the next A is an octave, or from A down to the next A is an octave.

The octave is located on the staff in a similar fashion. Call any note 1 and count up to 8 on consecutive lines and spaces and you will arrive at another note with the same letter name. Calling any note 8 and counting down to 1 also produces the interval of the octave.

---

[1]Musical intervals are actually acoustical, but the graphic and spatial aspects of notation and the keyboard are commonly used by musicians in relating to intervallic concepts. Intervals are treated as ratios of frequencies in Appendix A, "Elementary Acoustics."

[2]Pitches with the same letter name but located at different places on the staff can be differentiated by a system known as *octave registers.* See Appendix B.

FIGURE 2-8 *Octaves*

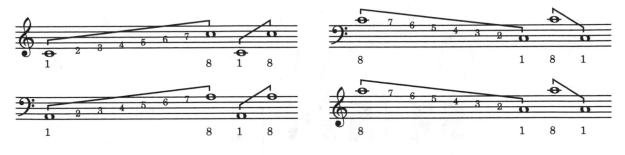

Half Steps and Whole Steps

On the keyboard, a *half step* is the interval from *any key to its adjacent key,* whether that key is white or black. See Figure 2-9. From C, a white key, to the next higher pitch, a black key, is a half step.

From this black key to the adjacent white key above is a half step. From any black key to the adjacent white key is a half step. Notice that there is no black key between E and F or between B and C; therefore, these adjacent white keys are half steps apart.

FIGURE 2-9 *Half steps on the keyboard*

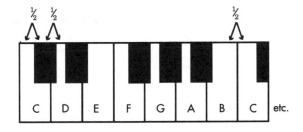

EXERCISES
2-2, 2-3

Two half steps in succession equal *one step,* usually called a *whole step.* See Figure 2-10. C to D is a whole step, because the black key in between produces two half steps. Because of the irregularity of the keyboard, with its black keys in groups of two and three, whole steps on the keyboard are found in three combinations of white and black keys: from one white key to the next white key, between a white and a black key, and between a black and another black key.

FIGURE 2-10   *Whole steps on the keyboard*

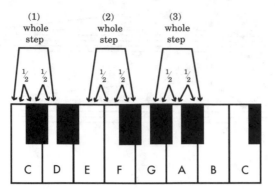

Accidentals

An accidental is a symbol (sign) that alters the pitch of a note. There are five accidentals.

1. The *sharp*, ♯, raises the pitch of a note one half step.
2. The *flat*, ♭, lowers the pitch of a note one half step.
3. The *natural*, ♮, cancels a preceding accidental.
4. The *double sharp*, ×, raises the pitch of a note two half steps, or one whole step.
5. The *double flat*, ♭♭, lowers the pitch of a note two half steps, or one whole step.

*EXERCISE
2-4*

FIGURE 2-11   *Accidentals*

In music writing, the accidental is placed immediately to the left of the note to be altered and precisely on the same line or space of the staff occupied by the note.

When an accidental is to be written in notation, it is, without exception, placed *before* the note, as in Figure 2-11. But when the name of an altered note is spoken, the accidental comes *after* the letter name. Therefore,

is spoken, "C-sharp."

At first, we shall study only sharps and flats. Later, the remaining accidentals will be studied. We are now ready to employ sharps and flats to determine the *names of black keys* of the keyboard.

Names of Black Keys

On the piano keyboard, black keys are named in relationship to the white keys. The black key one half step above C is named *C-sharp*. The black key one half step below D is named *D-flat*. Observe that the same black key is named C♯ and D♭. (*Note:* Beginning with Figure 2-12, many illustrations of the keyboard show without color keys that are ordinarily black. This procedure allows information to be placed in the outlined space representing a black key. In Figure 2-12, "C♯" and "D♭" are "black" keys.)

FIGURE 2-12 *Naming the black key C♯ and D♭.*

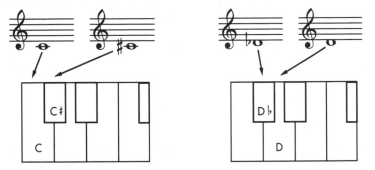

The other black keys are named in a similar manner. For example, the black key one half step above D is D♯; the black (same) key a half step below E is E♭. Figure 2-13 shows names of black and white keys and their representation on the staff.

FIGURE 2-13*a* *The keyboard and treble notes on the staff*

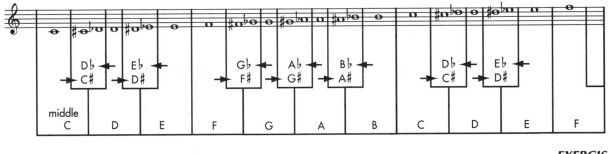

EXERCISE
2-5

FIGURE 2-13*b* *The keyboard and bass notes on the staff*

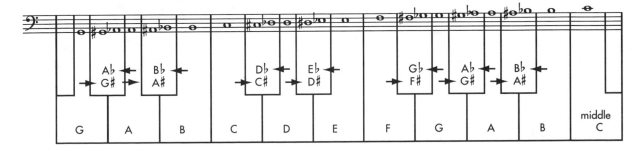

EXERCISES
2-6, 2-7, 2-8

You have noticed that each black key has two names. To describe this and similar situations, we use the term *enharmonic*.

Enharmonic Spellings

An enharmonic spelling occurs when one pitch has different spellings. For example, C♯ and D♭ are enharmonic spellings (see Figure 2-12); they are played on the piano by the same black key. White keys may also have enharmonic spellings, either by the use of ♯ or ♭, or by the use of × or ♭♭. Any pitch or any key on the keyboard may have an enharmonic spelling, as discussed in later chapters.

EXERCISES
2-9, 2-10

Playing, Ear Training, and Singing

The exercises in keyboard playing, ear training, and singing, at the end of this chapter, involve application only of *theoretical concepts* studied in the text. Such exercises in no way substitute for the benefits to be gained from instruction by a private teacher of piano, voice, or other performance.

EXERCISES
2-11, 2-12,
2-13, 2-14

EXERCISE 2-1

Locating C and naming white keys

Write in names of white keys. Locate C first.

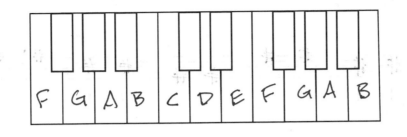

F G A B C D E F G A B

(*Return* to page 20.)

EXERCISE 2-2

Locating half steps above white keys

Indicate with an arrow the key that is one half step above each white key. One example of a half step is illustrated by the arrow, which points from a white key to the black key above. Remember that a half step may also occur from one white key to another white key.

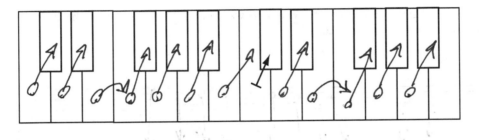

EXERCISE 2-3

Locating half steps below white keys

Indicate with an arrow the key that is one half step below each white key.

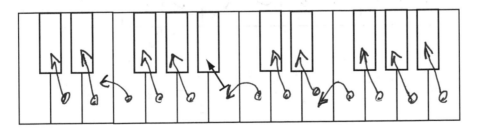

(*Return* to page 21.)

EXERCISE 2-4

Drawing the symbols for sharps and flats

For practice, on the staves below, draw additional sharps and flats, each on the same line or space as the given sharp or flat.

In drawing the symbol for the flat, notice that the length of the vertical line (called *stem*) is approximately equal to the distance of two and one-half spaces of the staff.

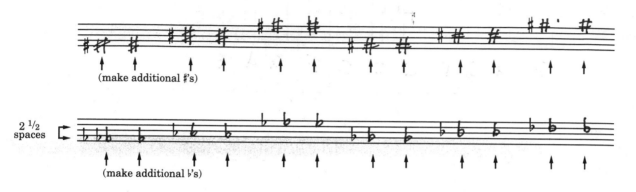

(make additional ♯'s)

2 ½ spaces

(make additional ♭'s)

(*Return* to page 22.)

EXERCISE 2-5

Relating half steps on the staff (treble) to the keyboard

As illustrated, indicate with arrows and write in names of the keys that would play the given notes.

(a) Ascending

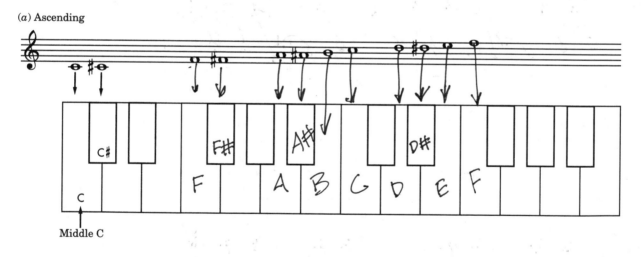

Middle C

26

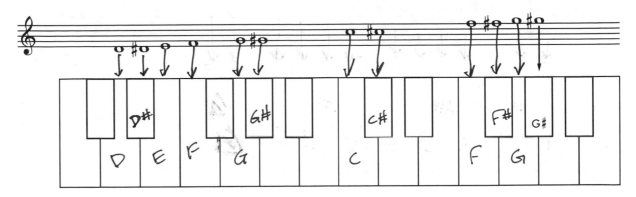

(b) Descending

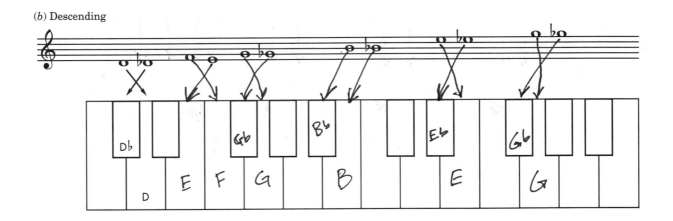

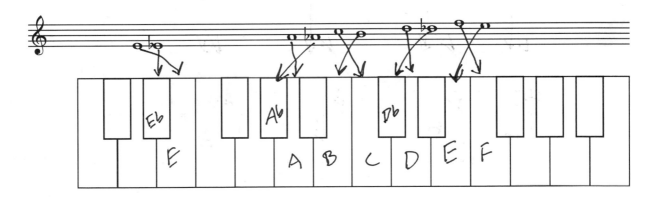

(*Return* to page 23.)

EXERCISE 2-6
Relating half steps on the staff (bass) to the keyboard

As illustrated, indicate with arrows and write in names of the keys that would play the given notes.

(a) Ascending

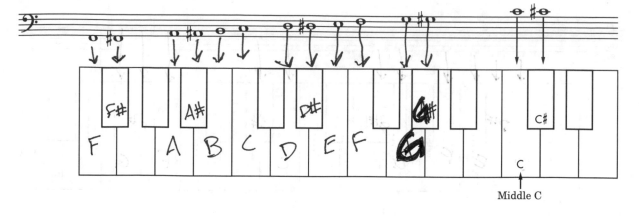

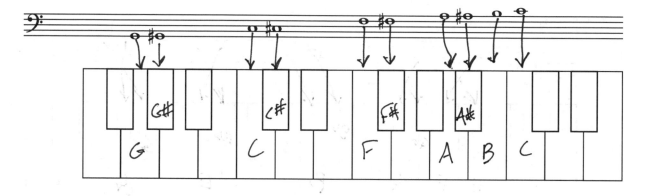

(b) Descending

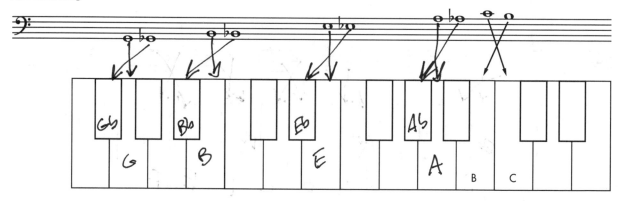

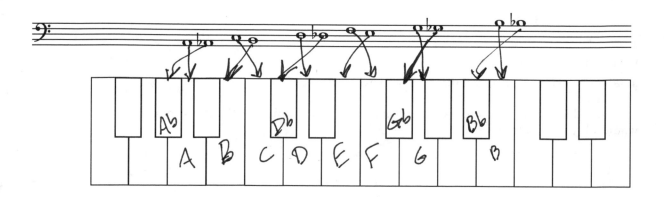

EXERCISE 2-12
Playing half steps

Find the white key for the first note of each pair; then play the half step according to the notation.

EXERCISE 2-13
Playing any white or black key from written notes on the staff

Play each written note on the keyboard. Each accidental refers only to the note immediately following it.

Right hand

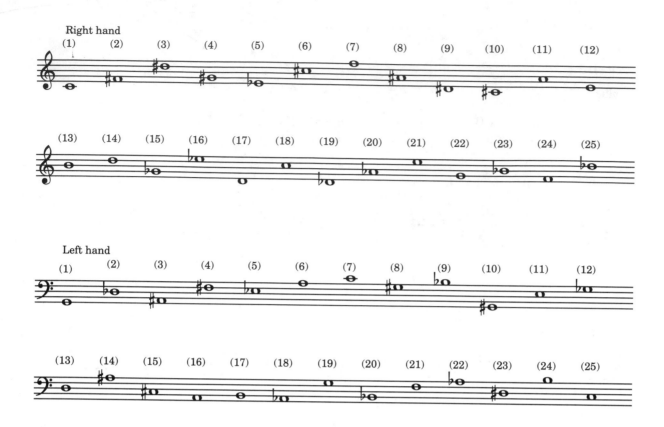

EXERCISE 2-14

Ear training and singing: matching tones

Play each written note individually on the keyboard. After you play a note, sing the same pitch using the neutral syllable *la*. Listen carefully to determine whether the pitch you sing is identical to the one played. This is called *matching the tone*. Women should match the tones of the treble clef pitches; men should match the tones of the bass clef pitches. If at first you find that you are hesitant or unsure in matching tones, continue to practice this exercise to acquire the ability for instant and sure response.

Note to the Instructor: Listen carefully to determine that the matched tones are unisons. If full class participation with both women and men is desired, *a* and *b* can be sung at the same time. In that case, play each pitch in both treble and bass before class response.

(*a*) Women: Sing on *la*

(b) Men: Sing on *la*

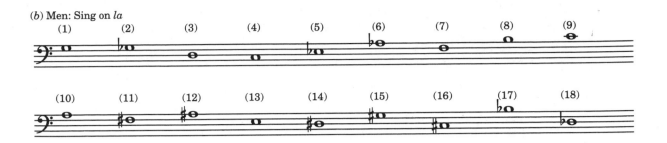

(To continue the study of **Pitch,** *go directly* to **Chapter 4,** page *47.*)

CHAPTER SUMMARY

1. The standard piano keyboard has 88 keys/pitches.

2. Each white and black key is identified by name. White keys are named in order with letters of the musical alphabet.

3. C, located to the left of a group of two black keys, is commonly used as a point for keyboard orientation.

4. *Middle C* is that C nearest the center of the keyboard and corresponds to middle C on the great staff.

5. An *interval* is the distance between two pitches. The two pitches of the interval of the *octave* are eight letter names apart, each pitch having the same letter name. The smallest interval is the *half step,* the distance from any key on the keyboard to its adjacent key, white or black. Two adjacent half steps constitute the interval of a *whole step.*

6. An *accidental* alters the pitch of a note. There are five accidentals: ♯, ♭, ♮, ✕, ♭♭.

7. Black keys are named in relation to white keys; for example, the black key one half step above C is C♯; the black key a half step below D is D♭.

8. When one key (pitch) has two names, such as C♯ and D♭, the names are said to be *enharmonic.*

CHAPTER THREE

Time

The Construction of Notes
Beamed Notes
Note Values and Their Relationship to Each Other
Notation of Rests

Two aspects of time are the *durations* of individual pitches, and the *patterns* created by a succession of various durations. In this chapter, we will consider the first of these.

We have seen that a note on the staff can indicate pitch. That same note can also indicate duration. We have used only the whole note (o) in previous chapters, but this note is just one of several varieties of notes, each indicating a different duration. To learn about these, we begin with the *construction of notes*.

The Construction of Notes

A note is made up of one, two, or three of these elements: (1) the note head, (2) the stem, and (3) the flag.

1. The *note head* is an ellipse, white (open) or black.

FIGURE 3-1   *Note heads*

2. The *stem* is a vertical line connected to a note head. When a single note head is placed on the staff below the third line, the stem points up; when the note head is on or above the third line, the stem points down. Pointing up, the stem is connected to the right side of the note head; pointing down, the stem appears on the left side of the note head. The length of the stem spans three spaces on the staff.

FIGURE 3-2   *Stems*

3. The *flag* is placed at the end of the stem. One to three flags are commonly used; four and five flags are infrequently used. Flags always appear to the right of the stems. Only black notes can have flags.

FIGURE 3-3 *Flags*

EXERCISE
3-1

One flag Two flags Three flags

Beamed Notes

Groups of two or more similar notes requiring flags are written two ways: (1) as separate notes with stems and flags, ♪ ♪ ♪ , or, in place of flags, (2) with the stems of the notes connected by a heavy line called a *beam* or a *ligature,* ♫♫ . One beam serves the same function as one flag; two beams serve as two flags, ♪ ♪ ♪ or ♫♫ , and so forth.

If several notes of different pitch are beamed together, use a stem direction that is correct for a majority of the notes in the group.

FIGURE 3-4 *Beamed notes on the staff*

(a)

EXERCISE
3-2

(b)

Note Values and Their Relationship to Each Other

Notes are named according to mathematical relationships to the number 1. The *whole* note (o) is assigned the value "1." The names of other notes are fractional values of the whole note; for example, two half notes equal one whole note, four quarter notes equal one whole note, and so forth. Figure 3-5 shows the names, symbols, and values of commonly used notes, and Figure 3-6 shows the relationships and the notes used when the whole note "1" is successively halved—1, 1/2, 1/4, and so forth.

FIGURE 3-5 *Note values*[1]

Name	Note		Value
Whole note	o		1
Half note	♩	or ♩	$1/2$
Quarter note	♩	or ♩	$1/4$
Eighth note	♪	or ♪	$1/8$
Sixteenth note	♬	or ♬	$1/16$
Thirty-second note	♬	or ♬	$1/32$

EXERCISE 3-3

FIGURE 3-6 *Note divisions*

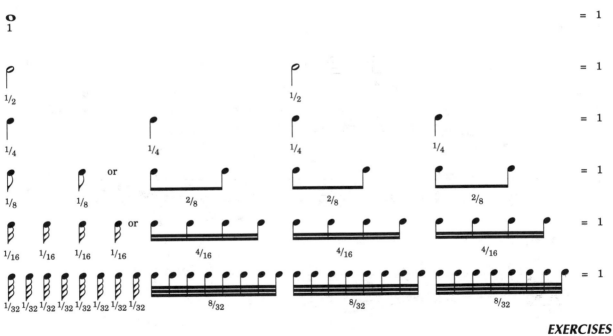

EXERCISES 3-4, 3-5

[1]Infrequently used are the double whole note, ‖o‖ or ⊨ , the sixty-fourth note, ♬ , and the one hundred twenty-eighth note ♬ . For examples of the last two notes, see Beethoven, Sonata for Piano, Op. 27, No.1, last three measures of the third movement.

Notation of Rests

Silence in music is represented by symbols called *rests*. For each note value representing sound, there is a corresponding rest value for silence. Figure 3-7 shows the commonly used rest values and their corresponding note values. The placement of rest values on the staff, treble or bass, is always the same as shown, unlike the varying locations of notes on the staff.

FIGURE 3-7 *Rest values and corresponding note values*[2]

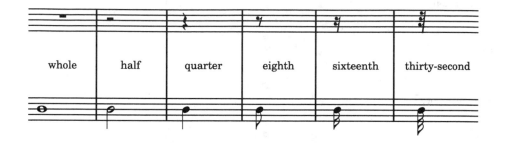

| whole | half | quarter | eighth | sixteenth | thirty-second |

EXERCISES 3-6, 3-7, 3-8

Notes and rests presented above are commonly used in music composition. Many of them are shown in this short excerpt from a Haydn piano sonata (Figure 3-8). The circled numbers are for use in Exercise 3-9.

FIGURE 3-8 *Music excerpt showing many note values*

Haydn, Piano Sonata in E-flat Major, H. XVI:52

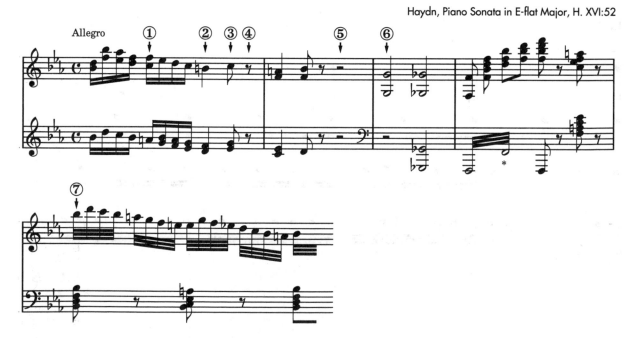

Tremolo, played as sixteen 32nd notes, alternating the notes of the octave F.

EXERCISE 3-9

[2]In many foreign or older editions of music, the symbol Γ is used for the quarter rest. Its use is not recommended because of its resemblance, in reverse, to the eighth rest (Γ = quarter rest; ɣ = eighth rest).

EXERCISE 3-1
Drawing notes on the staff

After each note, copy the given note above each arrow.

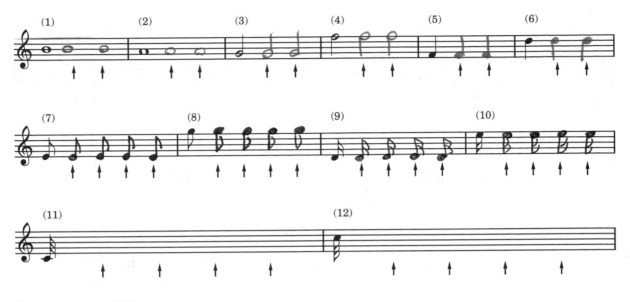

(*Return* to page *38.*)

EXERCISE 3-2
Grouping notes with beams

Connect each group of notes with a single beam. Use correct stem direction.

(*Return* to page *38.*)

EXERCISE 3-3
Writing various note values

Write the designated note values.

(*a*) On the pitch C

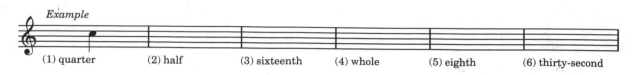

      Example

(1) quarter   (2) half   (3) sixteenth   (4) whole   (5) eighth   (6) thirty-second

(*b*) On the pitch B

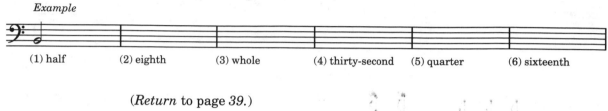

      Example

(1) half   (2) eighth   (3) whole   (4) thirty-second   (5) quarter   (6) sixteenth

(*Return* to page *39*.)

EXERCISE 3-4
Note divisions

Indicate the division of each given note.

EXERCISE 3-5
Relationship of notes

Fill in the blanks, using words only—for example, *two quarter* notes; *eighth* note. Write your answers in the blanks at the right side of the page.

(1) A quarter note equals two
_____ notes.   EIGHTH

(2) An _____ note equals two
sixteenth notes.   EIGHTH

(3) A half note equals two
_____ notes.   QUARTER

(4) A whole note equals two
_____ notes.   HALF

(5) A _____ note equals two
quarter notes.

42

(6) A _____ note equals two eighth notes.

QUARTER

(7) A sixteenth note equals two _____ notes.

THIRTY-SECOND

(8) A _____ note equals two half notes.

WHOLE

(9) An eighth note equals two _____ notes.

SIXTEENTH

(10) A _____ note equals two thirty-second notes.

SIXTEENTH

(*Return* to page 40.)

EXERCISE 3-6

Drawing rests on the staff

After each rest, draw others as indicated. Write the name of the given rest below the staff. When writing rests, observe these features:

1. The whole rest and the half rest are similar in appearance—a black oblong shape ▬. To differentiate, note the following:

   a. The whole note is suspended from the fourth line.

   b. The half rest sits upon the third line.

2. The symbol for the quarter rest, 𝄽, is a bit complex. Start with the three diagonal lines, 𝄽 and add a tilted curve, ⌐, at the bottom: 𝄽 + ⌐ = 𝄽. From lower tip to upper tip, the rest extends from the first space to the fourth space.

3. For the eighth, sixteenth, and thirty-second rests, the stems are slanted and the flags point to the left. The flags are placed as follows:

   a. Eighth rest: The flag is in the third space.

   b. Sixteenth rest: The top flag is in the third space.

   c. Thirty-second rest: The top flag is in the fourth space.

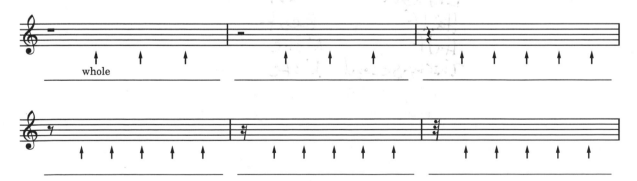

whole

EXERCISE 3-7
Writing various rest values

Write on the staff the rest value designated.

(1) eighth   (2) whole   (3) quarter   (4) half   (5) thirty-second   (6) sixteenth

EXERCISE 3-8
Drawing rests corresponding to notes

For each note value, draw and name the corresponding rest.

whole   HALF   QUARTER

EIGHTH   SIXTEENTH   THIRTY-SECOND

(*Return* to page *40.*)

EXERCISE 3-9
Recognizing note and rest values

In Figure 3-8, seven note and rest values are numbered, ①, ②, and so forth. Identify each of these using two words, such as *quarter note* or *quarter rest*.

(1) Sixteenth   Note
(2) Quarter   Note
(3) Eighth   Note
(4) Eighth   Rest
(5) Half   Rest
(6) Half   Note
(7) Thirty-Second   Note

(To continue the study of **Time,** *go directly* to **Chapter 7,** page 75.)

CHAPTER SUMMARY

1. Duration, the length of time a sound or a silence is held, can be represented on the staff by note or rest values.

2. Note values are differentiated by varying combinations of note head, stem, and flag. Most note values may be found in varying forms according to placement on the staff.

3. *Beams* may replace flags when successive flagged notes are used.

4. Note and rest values are not absolute, but are relative to each other, as indicated by their fractional names.

5. Notes are named according to mathematical relationship to the whole note, (1). Other notes are fractional values of 1, such as the *half* note or the *quarter* note.

CHAPTER FOUR

Pitch (continued)

Chromatic Half Steps
Diatonic Half Steps
Whole Steps

In Chapter Two, you learned about half steps and whole steps to understand the arrangement of white and black keys on the keyboard and how to name the black keys, given the names of the white keys. This chapter will introduce (1) the two varieties of half steps, *diatonic* and *chromatic,* and their spellings, (2) the spelling of whole steps, and (3) the placement of all of these on the staff.

To aid you in this study, a keyboard example similar to Figure 2-13*a* is repeated here as Figure 4-1. The arrows in Figure 2-13*a* have been deleted, since they showed only the chromatic half steps, and added are the enharmonic spellings of E, F, B, and C, making possible the spelling of several half steps and whole steps necessary for use in Chapter Five.

FIGURE 4-1 *The spellings of keys at the keyboard*

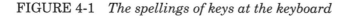

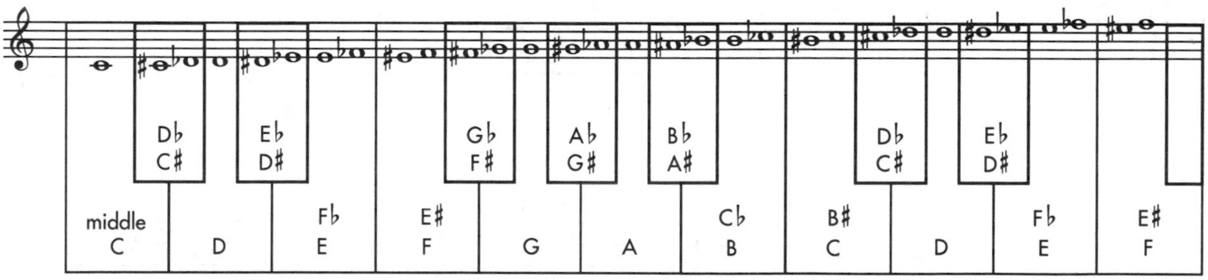

Chromatic Half Steps

Chromatic half steps are those in which the two pitches use the *same letter name.* The half steps you studied in Chapter Two were chromatic half steps, indicated in Figure 2-13 by an arrow pointing from a letter name on one key to a letter name on an adjacent key, such as C–C♯, D–D♭.

Additional chromatic half steps can be created when using these enharmonic equivalents of the spellings of the white-key half steps E–F and B–C:

E = F♭   E♯ = F   B = C♭   B♯ = C

The two letter names of each of these enharmonic pairs represent the same key on the keyboard and the same pitch when sounded. In Figure 4-1, find these chromatic half steps:

1. E–E♯   2. F–F♭   3. B–B♯   4. C–C♭

Diatonic Half Steps

Diatonic half steps are those in which the two pitches use *adjacent letter names*. In Figure 4-1, C–C♯ is a chromatic half step. The C♯ key is also D♭, so a half step spelled C–D♭ is a diatonic half step, since adjacent letter names are used. In the same way, A–A♭ is a chromatic half step, whereas A–G♯ is a diatonic half step (see Figure 4-2*a*).

A diatonic half step from a sharped or a flatted note is created in the same manner. The keyboard shows the diatonic half step above C♯ as C♯–D, and the diatonic half step below D♭ as D♭–C (Figure 4-2*b*).

Are the white-key half steps E–F and B–C chromatic or diatonic? They are diatonic, of course, because they use adjacent letter names. Adding identical accidentals to each note of either pair will also produce a diatonic half step, for example, E♯–F♯ or C♭–B♭ (Figure 4-2*c*). Check these half steps on the keyboard, Figure 4-1, and the reason for the enharmonic spellings of the white-key half steps should be obvious.

FIGURE 4-2   *Chromatic and diatonic half steps*

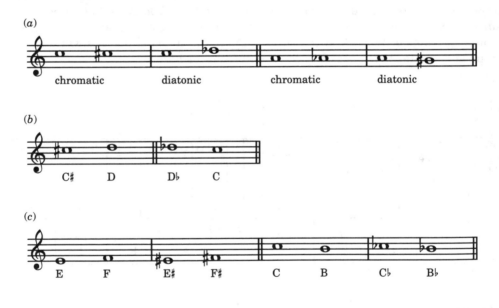

(a)

chromatic   diatonic   chromatic   diatonic

(b)

C♯   D   D♭   C

(c)

E   F   E♯   F♯   C   B   C♭   B♭

EXERCISES
4-1, 4-2, 4-

Whole Steps

Any whole step consists of two half steps, and the notes of the whole step are spelled with *adjacent letter names*. Count the two half steps from the given note and use the appropriate accidental, if any, for the second note. In so doing, you will soon discover that the two adjacent letter names will carry the same accidental (Figure 4-3*a*), except for a whole step *above* E♭, E, B♭, or B, and a whole step *below* C♯, C, F♯, or F (Figure 4-3*b*).[1] In these whole steps, one note carries an accidental and the other does not. These exceptions are necessary because of the two white-key (diatonic) half steps. For example, two descending half steps F–E–E♭ result in the whole step F–E♭.

FIGURE 4-3   *Whole steps*

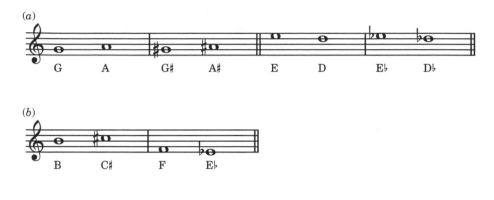

EXERCISE
4-4

[1]Whole steps up from E♯ and B♯, and down from F♭ and C♭, require a double sharp or a double flat and will not be considered here.

EXERCISE 4-1
Identifying chromatic and diatonic half steps

Identify each half step, using "c" for chromatic and "d" for diatonic.

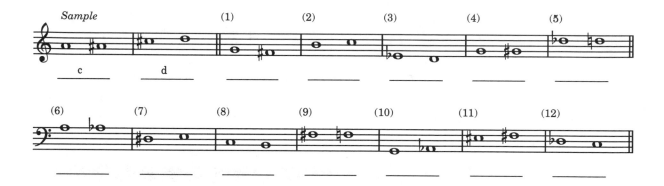

EXERCISE 4-2
Writing half steps

Write first the *chromatic* half step from the given note, then the *diatonic* half step from the same note. When done correctly, the two notes you have written will be enharmonic. Use the keyboard in Figure 4-1 for help if needed.

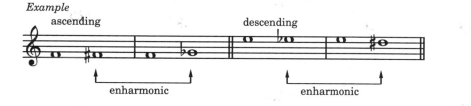

(*a*) Write *ascending* half steps as in the example.

(b) Write *descending* half steps as in the example.

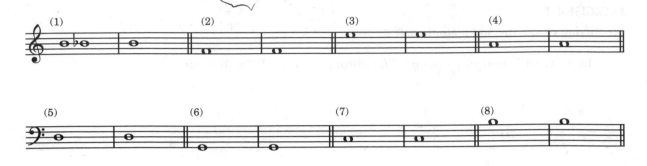

EXERCISE 4-3
Writing diatonic half steps

Write diatonic half steps, ascending (up) or descending (down), as shown in the example. Be sure that each diatonic half step uses *adjacent letter names.*

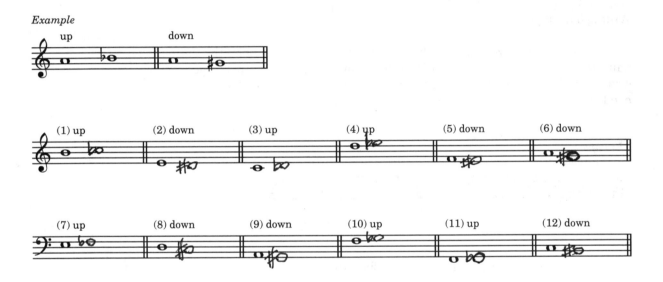

(*Return* to page *48.*)

EXERCISE 4-4
Writing whole steps

Write a whole step in the given direction from the given note. Remember that

1. A whole step uses adjacent letter names.
2. The two letter names use the same accidental, except those *above* E♭, E, B♭, and B, and those *below* C♯, C, F♯, and F.

Use Figure 4-1 for assistance if necessary.

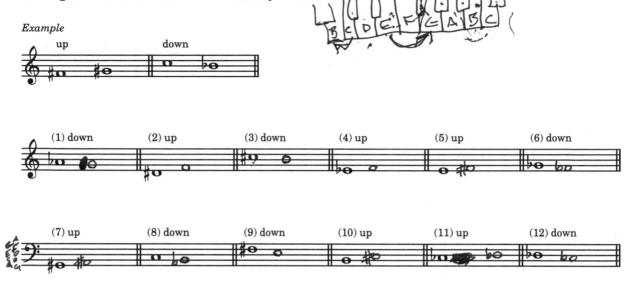

Example

CHAPTER SUMMARY

1. A *chromatic half step* is one in which the two pitches use the same letter name.

2. A *diatonic half step* is one in which each pitch uses a different letter name.

3. A *whole step* consists of two half steps and is spelled using adjacent letter names.

CHAPTER FIVE

Pitch: Major Scales

Scale Characteristics
The C Major Scale
Other Major Scales
Relationship of Major Scales
Spelling Scales

You can readily grasp the concept of a scale through a keyboard illustration. Look back at the keyboard in Figure 4-1 (page 47), where you will see adjacent white keys named with adjacent letter names. Starting with any letter name, if you play or sing eight letter names *successively,* either up or down—for example, A B C D E F G A or A G F E D C B A—you are performing a scale (from the Latin *scala,* "ladder").

Scale Characteristics

The three principal characteristics of a scale are easily demonstrated from Figure 5-1.

FIGURE 5-1   *The scale A B C D E F G A*

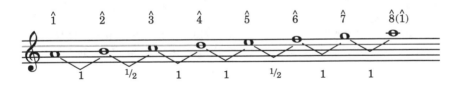

1. The scale consists of eight pitches, called *scale steps* or *scale degrees.* The eight pitches are named by eight successive letter names. Since these encompass the interval of an octave,[1] the first and last pitch names will be the same.

    Above the staff in Figure 5-1, the eight successive letter names and notes are numbered 1̂ through 8̂ (8̂ and 1̂ are interchangeable, since they use the same letter name). The caret, ^, above each number means "scale step"; for example, 5̂ means "fifth scale step" or "fifth scale degree."

[1]Review page 20.

2. The scale ascends or descends through a series of whole steps and half steps, indicated below the staff in Figure 5-1 by "1" (whole step) and "1/2" (half step). Most scales include two half steps. In Figure 5-1, we find

Half steps at $\hat{2}-\hat{3}$ and $\hat{5}-\hat{6}$
Whole steps at $\hat{1}-\hat{2}, \hat{3}-\hat{4}, \hat{4}-\hat{5}, \hat{6}-\hat{7}$, and $\hat{7}-\hat{8}$ ($\hat{1}$)

3. On the staff, the scale is placed on eight successive lines and spaces.

A scale pattern can be described as an orderly, graduated arrangement of ascending or descending pitches. Scales differ from each other based on the relative placement of the half steps and whole steps within the octave. If you play a white-note scale beginning on each of the seven letter names, seven different scales will result, because the location of the half steps E–F and B–C will be different in each.[2] For present purposes, we will consider two scale formations, named *major* and *minor*. We will begin with a particular spelling of the major scale, the *C major scale*.

The C Major Scale

In any spelling of a major scale, diatonic half steps are always found at $\hat{3}-\hat{4}$ and $\hat{7}-\hat{8}$, with whole steps between the remaining scale degrees. The major scale can most easily be demonstrated by the white-key scale starting on C (Figure 5-2).

FIGURE 5-2   *The C major scale*

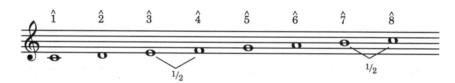

The scale of Figure 5-2 is *major* because the half steps occur at $\hat{3}-\hat{4}$ and $\hat{7}-\hat{8}$, and it is *C* major because it begins and ends on C. Note that in the C major scale, $\hat{3}-\hat{4}$ and $\hat{7}-\hat{8}$ coincide with the white-key half steps E–F and B–C. The major scale starting on C is the only major scale using only the white keys of the keyboard.

Is the scale of Figure 5-1 a major scale? Where are its half steps located? If the half steps are not located at $\hat{3}-\hat{4}$ and $\hat{7}-\hat{8}$, the scale is not major.

Other Major Scales

The characteristic sound of the major scale can be reproduced by beginning on any pitch name or on any key of the piano. When starting on a pitch other than C, however, we must make use of one or more accidentals so that half steps will appear at $\hat{3}-\hat{4}$ and $\hat{7}-\hat{8}$ and whole steps at all other locations.

To write a scale other than C major, first write a white-note scale using the seven letters of the musical alphabet. With G as $\hat{1}$, as in Figure 5-3*a*, half steps are located at $\hat{3}-\hat{4}$ and $\hat{6}-\hat{7}$; the scale is obviously not a major scale because there is no half step at $\hat{7}-\hat{8}$. In Figure 5-3*b*, raising F to F♯ creates at

[2]See Appendix C.

$\hat{7}$–$\hat{8}$ the half step F♯–G while at the same time eliminating the whole step F–G. With the half steps at $\hat{3}$–$\hat{4}$ (B–C) and $\hat{7}$–$\hat{8}$ (F♯–G), the scale is now a G major scale.

FIGURE 5-3 *Addition of sharps to create a major scale*

(a) White-note scale on G

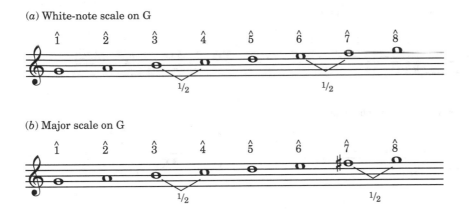

(b) Major scale on G

Flats are required for many major scales. Figure 5-4a shows a white-note scale on F with half steps at $\hat{4}$–$\hat{5}$ and $\hat{7}$–$\hat{8}$. In Figure 5-4b, the flat before B changes the whole step $\hat{3}$–$\hat{4}$ (A–B) to the half step $\hat{3}$–$\hat{4}$ (A–B♭). Note that the half step A♯–B would be incorrect, since G to A♯ ($\hat{2}$–$\hat{3}$), being three half steps, is more than a whole step.

FIGURE 5-4 *Addition of flats to create a major scale*

(a) White-note scale on F

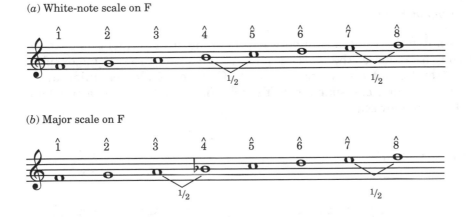

(b) Major scale on F

Major scales may begin on black keys, or on letter names containing an accidental, as in Figure 5-5a and b. The scale is produced as before, with half steps at $\hat{3}$–$\hat{4}$ and $\hat{7}$–$\hat{8}$.

FIGURE 5-5   *Scales with $\hat{1}$ as a sharped or a flatted note*

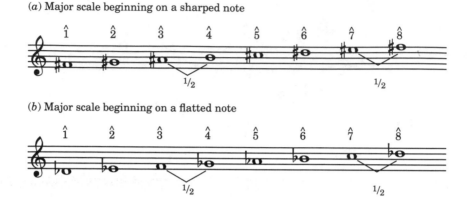

It should make your study of scales easier if you know that no major scale includes both flats and sharps. A scale with flats includes only flats, and a scale with sharps includes only sharps.

Since there are but seven letter names, the maximum number of scales containing sharps will be seven and the maximum number of scales containing flats will also be seven. These together with C major (no sharps or flats) add up to the useful fifteen major scales. Additional scales using the double sharp or the double flat are possible but rarely used, and will not be considered here.

Relationship of Major Scales

There is a definite relationship between the number of accidentals used in a scale and the name of the starting pitch of the scale. From C major, if you start at $\hat{1}$ and count *up* five scale steps to G, a new scale beginning at this point will introduce one sharp more than C (Figure 5-6). This sharp is found as $\hat{7}$ (F♯) of the new scale.

FIGURE 5-6   *Relationship of sharp scales*

Continuing from G, count five scale steps up to D. The scale on D has two sharps, and the new sharp again is $\hat{7}$ (C♯). Now look at Figure 5-8, above the line, where you will see that

1. Following C, G and D mark the beginning of a series in which $\hat{1}$ of each new scale is five scale steps above $\hat{1}$ of the previous scale.
2. Each new scale has one sharp more than the previous scale.

When you count *down* five notes from 8̂ of C major, the new scale on F beginning at this point will introduce one flat. This flat is found on 4̂ (B♭) of the new scale. Continuing as shown in Figure 5-7, you will see that the scale a fifth below F begins on B♭ and the new flat again is 4̂ (E♭).

FIGURE 5-7 *Relationship of flat scales*

In Figure 5-8, below the line, you can see that

1. F and B♭ mark the beginning of a series in which 1̂ of each new scale is five scale steps below 8̂ of the previous scale.
2. Each new scale has one flat more than the previous scale.
3. Each scale containing flats, except F, begins on a flatted note.

FIGURE 5-8 *Table of major scales and number of accidentals*

Scale	C	G	D	A	E	B	F♯	C♯
Accidentals	none	1♯	2♯	3♯	4♯	5♯	6♯	7♯
Scale		F	B♭	E♭	A♭	D♭	G♭	C♭
Accidentals		1♭	2♭	3♭	4♭	5♭	6♭	7♭

EXERCISE 5-1

Spelling Scales

In addition to notating scales on the staff, it is often useful in musical communication to be able to spell or write scales by letter names with appropriate accidentals. In spelling and in speaking, the name of the accidental comes after the letter name, as in this spelling of the B♭ major scale: B♭ C D E♭ F G A B♭.

EXERCISE 5-2

EXERCISE 5-1
Writing major scales on the staff

Write all major scales as indicated on the following staves. The C major scale is given as a model, after which the scale names are presented in the order shown in Figure 5-8. Proceed in this manner:

1. Write each scale ascending and descending, first in the treble clef and then in the bass clef.
2. Use whole notes to represent pitches. Be sure that a pitch name in the treble clef is vertically aligned with the same pitch name in the bass clef.
3. Beginning with $\hat{1}$, write each pair of adjacent notes as a whole step, except for half steps at $\hat{3}$–$\hat{4}$ and $\hat{7}$–$\hat{8}$. Show the location of the half steps.
4. Place each accidental carefully on the line or space before the note to be affected.

Upon completion, these pages containing all fifteen major scales may be valuable for future reference.

(*Instructor:* The student should not use key signatures in this assignment; concentration should be on placement of whole steps and half steps, as required in performance practice. Key signatures are presented in Chapter Eleven, which may follow this chapter if desired.)

C major

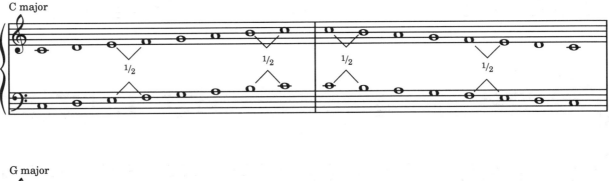

G major

D major

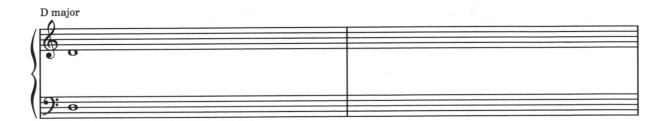

A major

E major

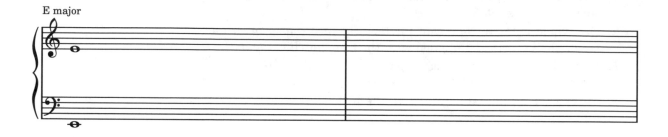

B major

F♯ major

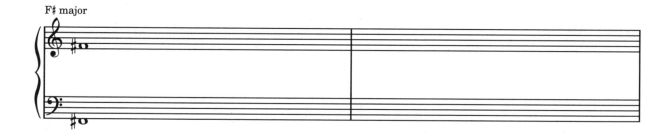

C♯ major

F major

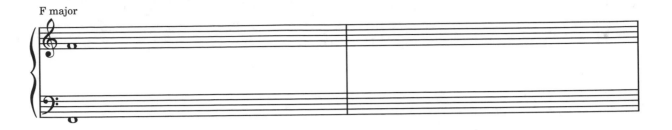

B♭ major

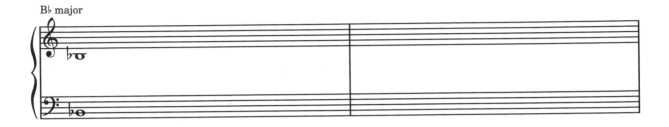

E♭ major

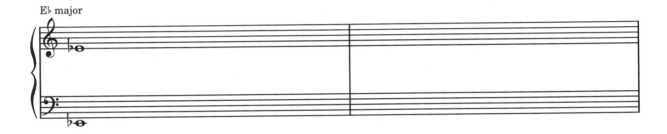

A♭ major

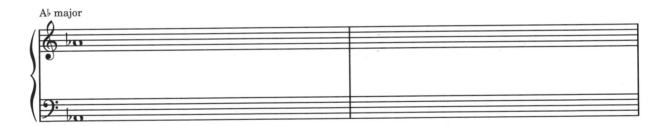

D♭ major

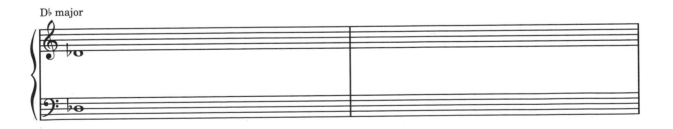

G♭ major

C♭ major

(Return to page 59.)

EXERCISE 5-2

Spelling major scales

Write major scales using letter names with accidentals where needed. Show half steps.

Example: D (Spell the D major scale.)

Answer: D   E   F♯ ⌄ G   A   B   C♯ ⌄ D
                        ½   ½

(1) G

(2) F

(3) A

(4) E♭

(5) E

(6) A♭

For additional practice, spell these scales:

B, D♭, F♯, G♭, C♯, C♭

CHAPTER SUMMARY

1. A scale is an orderly graduated arrangement of ascending or descending pitches.

2. There are many different scales. The two most used in our music are *major* and *minor*. These scales are spelled with successive letter names or notated on consecutive lines and spaces of the staff.

3. The major scale is characterized by the location of half steps between $\hat{3}$ and $\hat{4}$ and between $\hat{7}$ and $\hat{8}$. All other intervals are whole steps. Whether ascending or descending, the major scale is the same.

4. The major scale can be written/played beginning on fifteen different pitch locations. C contains no accidentals. Scales starting on other pitches require one or more accidentals. Seven scales require sharps and seven scales require flats.

5. Scales are related to each other. The new scale on the fifth scale step up from $\hat{1}$ of a given scale will have one additional sharp. The new scale on the fifth scale step down from $\hat{1}$ will have one additional flat.

CHAPTER SIX

Pitch: Major Scales (continued)

Names of the Scale Degrees

When you wrote scales on the staff in Chapter Five, you identified the eight notes of the scale simply by the numbers $\hat{1}$ $\hat{2}$ $\hat{3}$ $\hat{4}$ $\hat{5}$ $\hat{6}$ $\hat{7}$ $\hat{8}$ ($\hat{1}$) and referred to each as "first scale step," "second scale step," and so forth. Each of the scale degrees also has a specific name. Here, with a discussion of each, are the *names of the scale degrees.*

Names of the Scale Degrees

The name of the first scale degree is *tonic* (Greek, *tonikos*[1]). It is the main tone, the tone that gives the scale its identity. In the *C* major scale, *C* is the tonic tone.

Since the tonic is the most important tone, all other degrees are signified by their relationships to it.

Second only to the tonic in importance is the fifth scale tone, which is called *dominant*. It dominates or is dominant to all the scale tones except tonic. The dominant is the fifth degree above tonic. In the C major scale, G is the dominant tone.

[1] *Tonikos,* "stretching," referring to the fact that a string must be stretched to produce a tone. Greek, *tonos,* Latin, *tonus,* "tone."

The scale tone five steps below the tonic and ranking next in importance to the dominant is called *subdominant*. The prefix *sub-* indicates a tone under or below the tonic.

Notice that whereas the dominant is five steps above the tonic, the subdominant is five steps below the tonic. In the C major scale, F is the subdominant tone, the fourth scale degree.

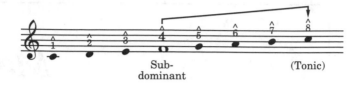

The third scale tone, which is midway between the tonic and the dominant, is called *mediant*. In the C major scale, E is the mediant tone.

The sixth scale tone, which is the middle or median tone between the tonic and the subdominant, is called *submediant*. Notice that whereas the mediant is three steps above the tonic, the submediant is three steps below the tonic. In the C major scale, A is the submediant tone.

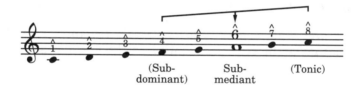

The seventh tone in the major scale, because of its strong tendency to lead upward to the tonic, is called *leading tone*.[2] In the C major scale, B is the leading tone.

The second scale tone, the scale degree immediately above tonic, is called *supertonic*. Notice that whereas the leading tone is the tone just below tonic, the supertonic is the tone just above tonic. In the C major scale, D is the supertonic tone.

---

[2]Occasionally, you may see $\hat{7}$ in major scales referred to as *subtonic* (step below tonic). To avoid confusion, the term "subtonic" is better reserved for use in minor scales, where "leading tone" and "subtonic" refer to different pitches.

In ascending order, the names of the scale tones are shown in Figure 6-1.

FIGURE 6-1 *Names of the scale tones*

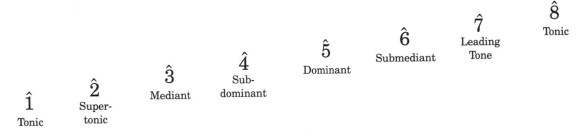

In Figure 6-2, names of the scale tones in ascending and consecutive order are shown for C major.

FIGURE 6-2 *Names of the scale tones, C major*

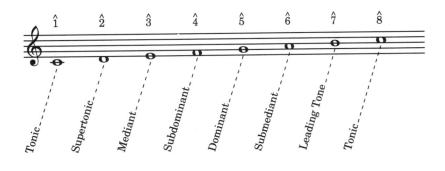

Scale-tone names are applied in similar manner for all major scales.

CHAPTER SEVEN

Time (continued)

Beats
Tempo
Grouping of Beats
Bar Lines and Measure

In Chapter Three, we studied notation of durations and the mathematical relationships of notes and rests. Now we will learn how durations of time are measured through beats (pulsations), and how these measurements are put on paper so they can be interpreted by a performer.

Other than mechanical and electronic chronometers, several time-measuring devices or sensations are common to the human experience. The heart normally beats with a regular pulsation, marking off regular units of time. When you walk, each step usually takes the same amount of time as the preceding and following steps, unless you consciously change your rate of speed. These two physical sensations, among many others, mark off units of time of equal length. For purposes of measuring equal lengths of time in music, these regularly recurring pulsations are called *beats*.

Beats

Beats are regularly recurring physical pulsations that divide time into units of equal length. In your ordinary experiences in music, you have already felt this sensation and responded by regular tapping of your fingers or your feet, or you have danced or marched in conformity with the beats of the music. We will begin our study of time by experiencing again the sensation of beats. The instructor will play several melodies. Your reaction is simply to tap naturally with the right hand. The melodies you will hear are shown in Figure 7-1. The vertical lines below the staff represent the taps or beats.

FIGURE 7-1 *Tapping beats*

(e)　M.M. ♩ = 120　　　　　　　　　　　　　　　　　　　　　　　　　　　"Jingle Bells"

(f)　M.M. ♩ = 100　　　　　　　　　　　　　　　　　　　　　　　　　　　"Auld Lang Syne"

You may have noticed that you tapped at a different rate of speed for different melodies. This phenomenon is explained by the term *tempo*.

Tempo

Tempo (pl. tempos, or tempi) is the rate of speed of the beats. The faster the succession of beats, the faster is the tempo; the slower the succession of beats, the slower is the tempo. In a fast tempo, the beats measure relatively short durations of time; in a slow tempo, the beats measure relatively long durations of time. The varying durations of the beat depend on the kind of music and the intent of the composer.

The length of the beat can be precisely measured by a mechanical device known as a metronome, which produces a regular, recurring ticking sound. The metronome can be regulated to produce the ticking sound from very fast successions to very slow successions. It is calibrated so that when set on "60" it produces one tick per second; at "120," two ticks per second, and so on. Composers often indicate tempo by placing the abbreviation M.M.[1] plus the desired number at the beginning of a piece (for example, M.M. 60).

While listening to music, you feel certain beats more strongly than others. There are heavy beats and light beats; the combinations of heavy and light beats in succession produce *grouping of beats*.

Grouping of Beats

Beats tend to group themselves into regular, recurring patterns. Three patterns are commonly found in music: a heavy beat followed by a light beat (duple); a heavy beat followed by two light beats (triple); and a heavy beat followed by three lighter beats, with the third beat slightly stronger than the second and fourth (quadruple). See Figure 7-2. As the instructor plays, you

---

[1]M.M. stands for Mälzel's metronome. Johann Mälzel improved the instrument invented by Dietrich Winkel, ca. 1812. Beethoven was the first important composer to use metronome markings.

will experience these groupings as shown in Figure 7-3. As in Figure 7-2, the vertical lines below the staff represent beats. A taller line represents a heavy beat, a shorter line a light beat. When listening to each melody, tap the beats as before with the right hand, but make a stronger tap at the place of each tall vertical line and a weaker tap at each short vertical line in accordance with the sensation of heavy and light beats in the music.

FIGURE 7-2 *Beat patterns*

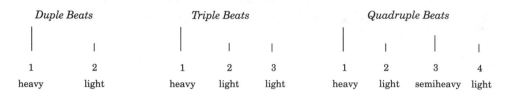

FIGURE 7-3 *Grouping of beats*

It is sometimes difficult in listening to distinguish between groupings of two and groupings of four because the semiheavy beat on "3" in quadruple can easily be mistaken for the heavy beat "1" in a group of two beats. For a comparison see Figure 7-4.

FIGURE 7-4   *Comparison of duple and quadruple groups of beats*

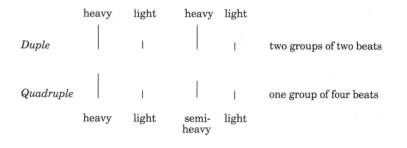

In addition to identifying the grouping of beats by *hearing* relative pulsations in the music, you can *see* (in the music examples throughout this chapter) a simple device that also indicates grouping of beats. This visual aid is the *bar line,* with resulting *measure.*

Bar Lines and Measure

A *bar line* is a single vertical line extending from the top to the bottom line of the staff. It serves to separate one group of beats from the next.

A *measure* ("meas." in Figure 7-5) is the distance from one bar line to the next. Each measure is heard as a group of beats.

A *double bar line* consists of two parallel bar lines, the second often of double thickness. It marks the end of a composition or the end of a section within a composition.

"Measure" is included in the further study of Time in Chapter Nine. Other uses of bar lines are included in Appendix B.

FIGURE 7-5   *Bar lines and measure*

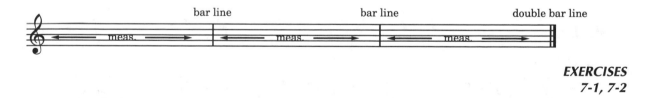

*EXERCISES
7-1, 7-2*

Instructor: In the next exercises and throughout this book, the designation "(Instructor)" following an exercise number indicates need for a qualified person to conduct the drills.

EXERCISE 7-1 (Instructor)
Aural identification of beat groupings (with tapping)

Listen to a melody played by the instructor. On the second hearing, tap the beats, making a heavy tap where you hear the heavy beat in the music. Determine whether the beats are in groups of two, three, or four, and be prepared to identify the grouping for the piece as "duple," "triple," or "quadruple." For this exercise, use music found after Exercise 7-2.

EXERCISE 7-2 (Instructor)
Aural identification of beat groupings (without tapping)

Listen to a melody played by the instructor. On the second hearing, try to recognize the beats without tapping. Identify the grouping of beats as before.

Melodies for Exercises 7-1 and 7-2

Instructor: As you play these melodies, a moderate emphasis on each first beat will facilitate the aural identification of beat groupings, especially in differentiating between duple and quadruple time.

(1)   M.M. 80

Bayly, "Long, Long Ago"

(2)   M.M. 108

Denmark

(3)   M.M. 92

France

(4)   M.M. 112

"The Blue Bell of Scotland"

Verdi, *Il Trovatore*, "Ai nostri monti"

(5)   M.M. ♪ = 120

Lambert, "When Johnny Comes Marching Home"

(6)   M.M. 104

If additional melodies are desired, they can be found in abundance in various books written primarily for instruction in sight singing. The tempo for playing a melody should be chosen carefully. Too rapid a tempo may give the aural impression of fewer beats per measure, whereas too slow a tempo may seem to indicate more beats per measure.

The melodies listed on page 82 include suitable tempo (M.M.) markings and can be found in *Music for Sight Singing*, fourth edition, by Robert W. Ottman ©1996 by Prentice-Hall, Inc.

(1)	102	M.M. ♩ = 108	(7)	259	M.M. ♩ = 116
(2)	113	M.M. ♩ = 116	(8)	376	M.M. ♩. = 63
(3)	164	M.M. ♩. = 76	(9)	389	M.M. ♩. = 80
(4)	233	M.M. ♩ = 100	(10)	394	M.M. ♩ = 120
(5)	251	M.M. ♩ = 138	(11)	402	M.M. ♩ = 142
(6)	252	M.M. ♩ = 108	(12)	405	M.M. ♩ = 104

CHAPTER SUMMARY

1. The *beat,* a temporal measuring device in music, indicates a regular succession of lengths of time.

2. *Tempo* is the rate of speed of the beats. The faster the succession of beats, the faster the tempo; the slower the succession of beats, the slower the tempo.

3. *Bar lines* mark off groups of beats.

4. A *measure* is the distance between two bar lines. Each measure usually encompasses two, three, or four beats.

CHAPTER EIGHT

Time (continued)

Divisions of Beats
Simple Beat
Compound Beat
Meter

In Chapter Seven, you were asked to listen to a number of musical examples. One characteristic common to all the melodies was the sensation of a regular, recurring beat. Readily noticeable, however, was the fact that in different melodies the beats grouped themselves in different combinations of two, three, or four. Now we will consider another characteristic quality of the beat, the sensation of *divisions of beats*.

Divisions of Beats

There are two varieties of the beat, each identified by the way the beat duration can be divided. You can demonstrate this when listening to a melody by making either two or three taps with the left hand to each tap in the right hand. Whether you tap two or three in the left hand will be sensed from the sound of the melody itself, as will be shown in the following discussion of *simple* and *compound beats*.

Simple Beat

A beat that can be divided into two parts is called a *simple beat*. Listen to the melody in Figure 8-1. On the second hearing, tap the beats in the right hand as shown in step 1. On the third hearing, tap twice with the left hand for each tap in the right hand as shown in step 2.

In Figure 8-1, the taps in the right hand determine the duration of each beat. The taps in the left hand divide each of these durations into two equal parts. This division is called *simple division of the beat*.

FIGURE 8-1 *Tapping simple division*

Compound Beat

A beat that can be divided into three parts is called a *compound beat*. Listen to the melody in Figure 8-2. On the second hearing, tap the beats in the right hand as shown in step 1. On the third hearing, tap three times with the left hand for each tap in the right hand as shown in step 2. The left hand is *dividing the beat* into three parts; this division is called *compound division of the beat.*

FIGURE 8-2 *Tapping compound division*

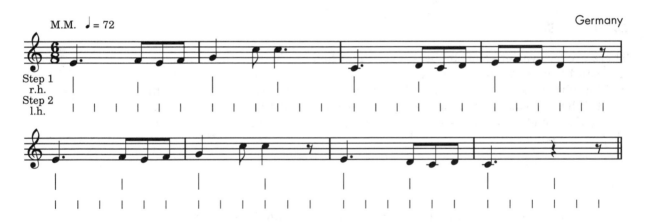

In Chapter Seven, we recognized groupings of beats in patterns of two, three, or four; in this chapter, we have examined the two varieties of beats. We have now found three different groupings of beats and two different divisions for each beat, making a total of six possible combinations for groupings of beats and their divisions. The terminology for identifying these various combinations comes under the general term *meter.*

Meter

In music, *meter* is the systematic grouping of beats and their divisions in regularly recurring patterns of pulsations. Meter is described as being *duple, triple,* or *quadruple* according to the grouping of beats, and *simple* or *compound* according to the division of each beat. Therefore, the six possible meter designations are these:

FIGURE 8-3   *Meter designations*[1]

1. duple simple   4. duple compound
2. triple simple   5. triple compound
3. quadruple simple   6. quadruple compound

The sensations for these six meter designations can be manifested by tapping: The right hand taps the particular grouping of beats while the left hand taps the particular division of each beat. Figure 8-4 shows diagrams for tapping the various combinations.

FIGURE 8-4   *Diagrams for tapping meter*

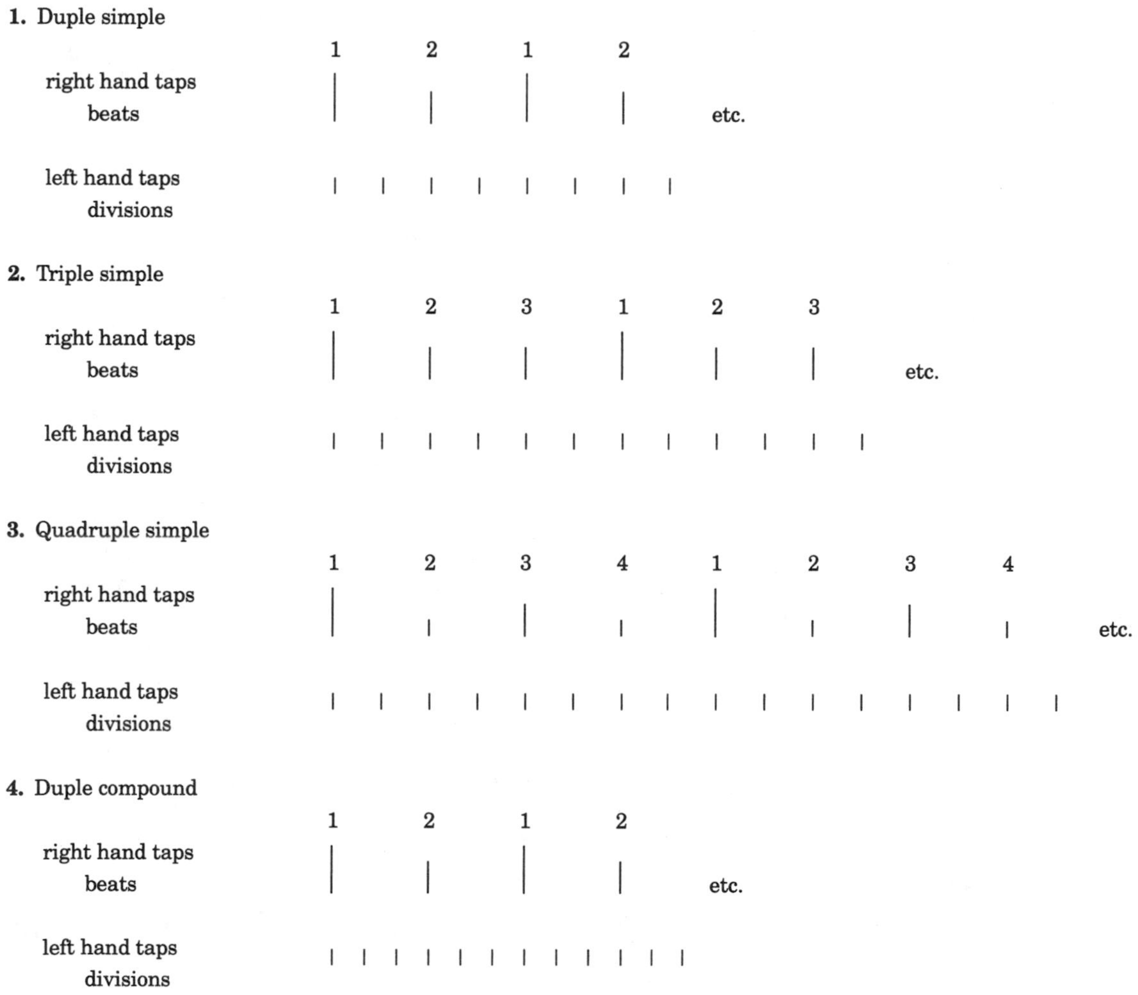

1. Duple simple

```
                    1       2       1       2
right hand taps
  beats             |       |       |       |        etc.

left hand taps      |  |  |  |  |  |  |  |
  divisions
```

2. Triple simple

```
                    1       2       3       1       2       3
right hand taps
  beats             |       |       |       |       |       |      etc.

left hand taps      |  |  |  |  |  |  |  |  |  |  |  |
  divisions
```

3. Quadruple simple

```
                    1       2       3       4       1       2       3       4
right hand taps
  beats             |       |       |       |       |       |       |       |      etc.

left hand taps      |  |  |  |  |  |  |  |  |  |  |  |  |  |  |  |
  divisions
```

4. Duple compound

```
                    1       2       1       2
right hand taps
  beats             |       |       |       |        etc.

left hand taps      |  |  |  |  |  |  |  |  |  |  |  |
  divisions
```

[1]Some theorists prefer to reverse these designations—simple duple, compound triple, and so on.

5. Triple compound

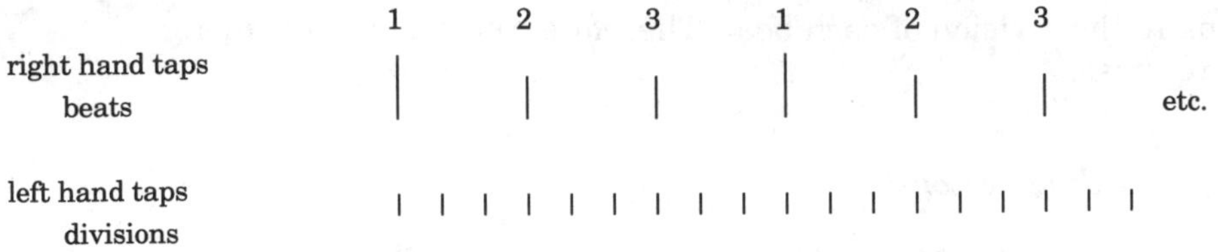

	1	2	3	1	2	3	

right hand taps
beats

| | | | | | | | etc. |

left hand taps
divisions

| | | | | | | | | | | | | | | | | | |

6. Quadruple compound

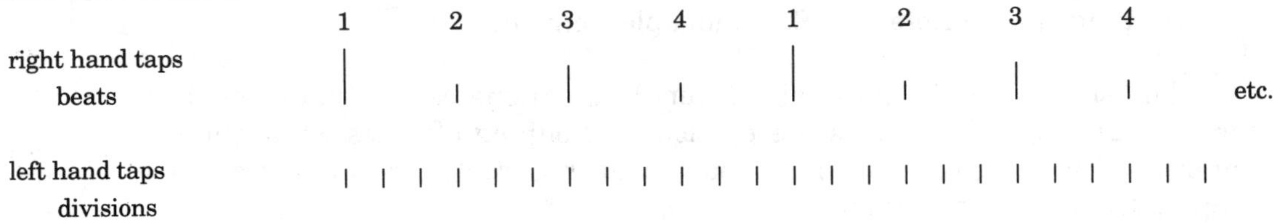

	1	2	3	4	1	2	3	4	

right hand taps
beats

| | | | | | | | | | etc. |

left hand taps
divisions

| | | | | | | | | | | | | | | | | | | | | | | | |

How these meters are expressed as time signatures is included in Chapter Nine.

EXERCISE 8-1 (Instructor)

Tapping simple meters without music

The instructor will announce a meter designation as duple simple, or triple simple, or quadruple simple. The student taps the beats and background as shown in Figure 8-4. If you use the metronome, the tempo for the beats should be neither slower than M.M. 52 nor faster than M.M. 116.

EXERCISE 8-2 (Instructor)

Tapping simple meters with music

Listen to a melody played by the instructor. On the second hearing, tap the groupings of beats with the right hand. On the third playing, add the background of two with the left hand. Be prepared to identify the meter by one of the three simple meter designations.

(5)   M.M.   ♩ = 100

(6)   M.M.   ♩ = 108

Brahms, Hungarian Dance No. 5

EXERCISE 8-3 (Instructor)

Tapping compound meters without music

The instructor will announce a meter designation as duple compound, or triple compound, or quadruple compound. The student taps the beats and divisions as shown in Figure 8-4. If you use the metronome, the tempo for the beats should be neither slower than M.M. 46 nor faster than M.M. 96.

EXERCISE 8-4 (Instructor)

Tapping compound meters with music

Listen to a melody played by the instructor. On the second hearing, tap the groupings of beats with the right hand. On the third playing, add the division of three with the left hand. Be prepared to identify the meter as either duple compound or triple compound. (Quadruple compound time is not frequently used in music composition, since one quadruple unit usually sounds like two duple units. For that reason, no quadruple compound meter is included in this exercise.)

Barnby, "Sweet and Low"

(1)   M.M.   ♩. = 54

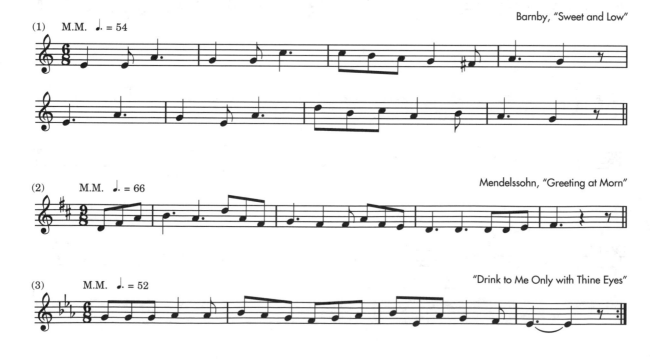

Mendelssohn, "Greeting at Morn"

(2)   M.M.   ♩. = 66

"Drink to Me Only with Thine Eyes"

(3)   M.M.   ♩. = 52

Silcher, "Die Lorelei"

(4)   M.M. ♩. = 64

"Down in the Valley"

(5)   M.M. ♩. = 66

EXERCISE 8-5 (Instructor)
Tapping simple or compound meters with music

Listen to a melody played by the instructor. It may be in either a simple or a compound meter as selected by the instructor. On the second hearing, tap both the groupings of beats and the divisions, and identify as before. (There will be no quadruple compound meter included in this exercise.)

Offenbach, Barcarolle

(1)   M.M. ♩. = 48

Beethoven, Concerto in D for violin

(2)   M.M. ♩ = 96

Foster, "Beautiful Dreamer"

(3)   M.M. ♩. = 60

MacDowell, "To a Wild Rose"

(4)   M.M. ♩ = 50

(5) M.M. ♩ = 76

For optional additional drill, continue Exercise 8-5 using the following melodies from *Music for Sight Singing*.

(1)	88	M.M. ♩ = 92	(9)	275	M.M. ♪ = 100
(2)	101	M.M. ♩ = 108	(10)	338	M.M. ♩ = 86
(3)	112	M.M. ♩ = 116	(11)	350	M.M. ♩ = 60
(4)	199	M.M. ♩. = 92	(12)	355	M.M. ♩. = 69
(5)	201	M.M. ♩. = 84	(13)	364	M.M. ♩. = 80
(6)	213	M.M. ♩ = 100	(14)	376	M.M. ♩. = 69
(7)	244	M.M. ♩ = 112	(15)	379	M.M. ♩ = 112
(8)	262	M.M. ♩ = 92	(16)	396	M.M. ♩ = 80

CHAPTER SUMMARY

1. Beats are of two varieties, identified by how the beat is divided. A beat divisible into two parts is a *simple beat,* and a beat divisible into three parts is a *compound beat.*

2. *Meter* is the systematic grouping of beats and their divisions in regularly recurring patterns of pulsations.

3. *Duple, triple,* and *quadruple* meter refer to groupings of two, three, and four beats, respectively.

4. *Simple meter* refers to a grouping whose beats are divisible by two. *Compound meter* refers to a grouping whose beats are divisible by three.

5. Combining the concepts of beat groupings and beat divisions results in six types of time signatures:

duple simple	duple compound
triple simple	triple compound
quadruple simple	quadruple compound

CHAPTER NINE

Time (continued)

Notation of the Simple Beat
Meter (Time) Signatures
Simple Meter Signatures
Notation of the Compound Beat
Compound Meter Signatures

We have found that beats in music can be grouped in twos, threes, and fours, and that each of these beats can be divided into two or three equal parts. Through listening and tapping, we have experienced these sensations, and we have depicted them on paper with the diagrams of six meter designations (Figure 8-4). Although we can differentiate these six patterns when listening, only when a specific note value is assigned to a beat can any one of these metrical patterns be represented on paper as *notation*.

Notation of the Simple Beat

A simple beat divides into two equal parts. Therefore, a note assigned to represent a simple beat must have a value divisible by two. The value most often used by composers to represent the simple beat is a quarter note.

FIGURE 9-1 *Note values assigned to represent the simple beat*

The quarter note may represent the beat:

♩ = $1/4$ value

♫ = simple division

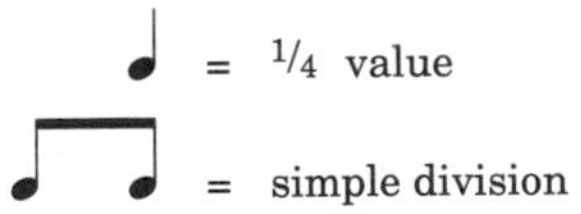

The eighth note may represent the beat:

♪ = $1/8$ value

♬ = simple division

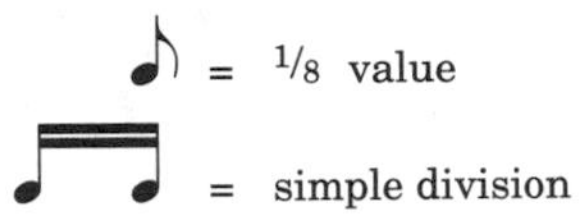

The half note may represent the beat:

𝅗𝅥 = $1/2$ value

♩ ♩ = simple division

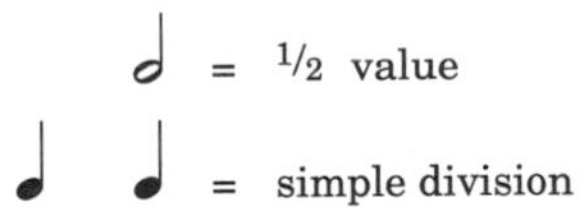

When we know the number of beats in a group and the assigned value of a beat, we can derive a *meter signature,* commonly called a *time signature.*

Meter (Time) Signatures

A meter signature is a compact symbol that tells us the metrical pattern and the notation in which the music is written. These features of meter signatures are illustrated in Figure 9-2 and are observable in any melodies from previous chapters.

1. The meter signature appears as a pair of numbers aligned vertically, such as $\frac{2}{4}$ or $\frac{3}{8}$. It resembles an arithmetical fraction but without the horizontal line between the numerator and the denominator.
2. The numerator of the signature is placed above the third line of the staff, and the denominator is placed below the third line.
3. The signature follows the clef sign. It also follows any grouping of accidentals (called *key signature,* described in Chapter Eleven).
4. The signature appears only at the beginning of the composition, unless a change of meter takes place later.

Meter signatures for simple time are interpreted somewhat differently from meter signatures for compound time. We will begin with *simple meter signatures.*

Simple Meter Signatures

Figure 9-2 shows how the meter signatures in simple time are interpreted.

1. The numerator indicates which of the simple metrical patterns is used in each measure. The 2 of a $\frac{2}{4}$ signature, for example, indicates duple simple meter.
2. The denominator indicates the note value that represents the beat. The 4 of a $\frac{2}{4}$ signature indicates that a quarter note represents one beat.

FIGURE 9-2 *The functions of a $\frac{2}{4}$ signature*

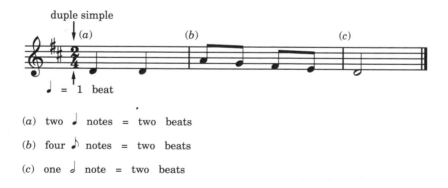

(a) two ♩ notes = two beats

(b) four ♪ notes = two beats

(c) one ♩ note = two beats

Figure 9-3 shows all the commonly used simple meter signatures. You can see that when the *numerator* is

2, the meter is always duple simple.
3, the meter is always triple simple.
4, the meter is always quadruple simple.

You can also see that when the *denominator* is

4, the quarter note (♩) always represents one beat.
8, the eighth note (♪) always represents one beat.
2, the half note (𝅗𝅥) always represents one beat.

Figure 9-4 shows the meaning of these same meter signatures by illustrating the notation of their metrical patterns. In parentheses, you will see alternative signatures, used occasionally since about 1920 by a few composers. The denominators in these signatures show a note value instead of a number—for example ♩ instead of 4. Meter signatures in this form are actually much easier to read and to understand, especially in the case of compound meters.

FIGURE 9-3 *Derivation of simple meter (time) signatures*

Beat Value	Beat Grouping (per measure)				Meter (Time) Signature	Meter Name
♩ 1/8	one 1/8	+	two 1/8	=	**2/8**	
♩ 1/4	one 1/4	+	two 1/4	=	**2/4**	DUPLE SIMPLE
♩ 1/2	one 1/2	+	two 1/2	=	**2/2** or ₵ *	
♩ 1/8	one 1/8	+ two 1/8 +	three 1/8	=	**3/8**	
♩ 1/4	one 1/4	+ two 1/4 +	three 1/4	=	**3/4**	TRIPLE SIMPLE
♩ 1/2	one 1/2	+ two 1/2 +	three 1/2	=	**3/2**	
♩ 1/8	one 1/8 + two 1/8 + three 1/8 + four 1/8			=	**4/8**	
♩ 1/4	one 1/4 + two 1/4 + three 1/4 + four 1/4			=	**4/4** or C **	QUADRUPLE SIMPLE
♩ 1/2	one 1/2 + two 1/2 + three 1/2 + four 1/2			=	**4/2**	

* Called *cut time*; ₵ is a symbol substituting for 2/2.
** Called *common time*; C is a symbol substituting for 4/4.

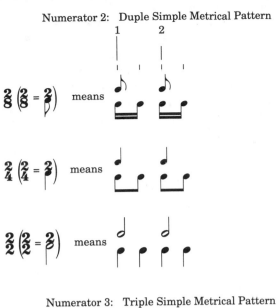

Numerator 2: Duple Simple Metrical Pattern

FIGURE 9-4 *Meaning of simple meter signatures*

two beats per measure, the eighth note represents the beat; each beat divides into two sixteenth notes

two beats per measure, the quarter note represents the beat; each beat divides into two eighth notes

two beats per measure, the half note represents the beat; each beat divides into two quarter notes

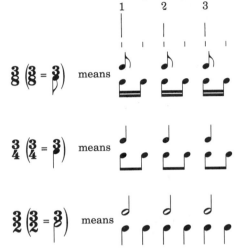

Numerator 3: Triple Simple Metrical Pattern

three beats per measure, the eighth note represents the beat; each beat divides into two sixteenth notes

three beats per measure, the quarter note represents the beat; each beat divides into two eighth notes

three beats per measure, the half note represents the beat; each beat divides into two quarter notes

Numerator 4: Quadruple Simple Metrical Pattern

four beats per measure, the eighth note represents the beat; each beat divides into two sixteenth notes

four beats per measure, the quarter note represents the beat; each beat divides into two eighth notes

four beats per measure, the half note represents the beat; each beat divides into two quarter notes

EXERCISES
9-1, 9-2

Notation of the Compound Beat

A compound beat divides into three equal parts. Therefore, a note representing a compound beat must have a value divisible by three. Such a value requires a *dotted note*. A dot placed after a note (♩.) increases the duration by one half of the value of the note. The value most often used by composers to represent the compound beat is the dotted quarter note.

FIGURE 9-5   *Note values assigned to represent the compound beat*

The dotted quarter note may represent the compound beat:

beat

♩. = ♩ + ♪   therefore ♩. = $3/8$ value

$1/4$ + $1/8$ = compound division

($2/8$ + $1/8$ = $3/8$)

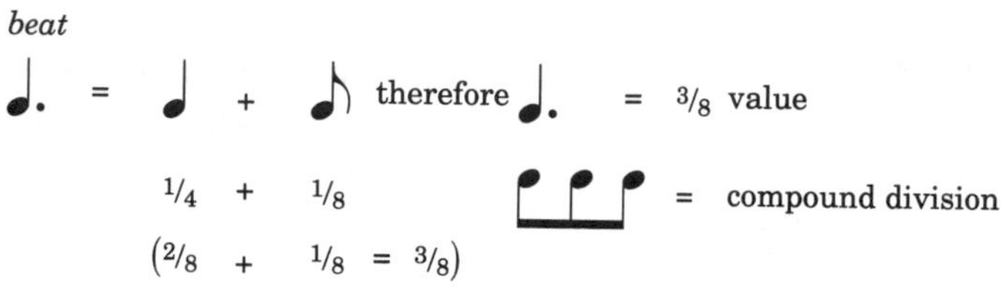

The dotted eighth note also may be used to represent the compound beat:

beat

♪. = ♪ + ♬   therefore ♪. = $3/16$ value

$1/8$ + $1/16$ = compound division

($2/16$ + $1/16$ = $3/16$)

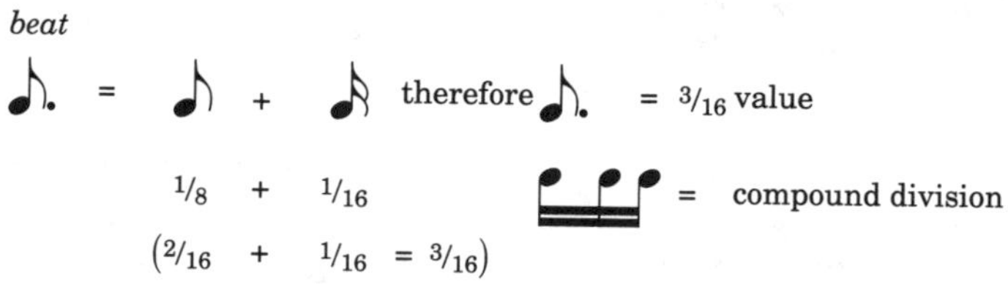

The dotted half note may be used to represent the compound beat:

beat

♩. = ♩ + ♩   therefore ♩. = $3/4$ value

$1/2$ + $1/4$ = compound division

($2/4$ + $1/4$ = $3/4$)

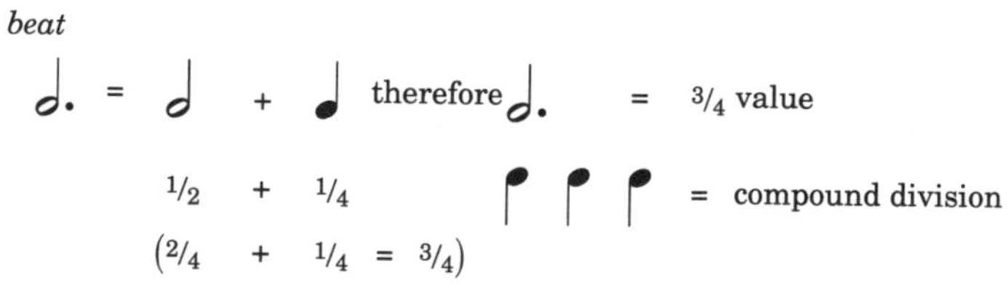

Notice that a dotted quarter can be represented mathematically only by the fraction $3/8$; the dotted eighth only by the fraction $3/16$; and the dotted half note only by the fraction $3/4$.

From the number of beats in a group and the assigned value of a beat, we can derive the *compound meter signatures*.

Compound Meter Signatures

The compound meter signature is derived from the beat value and the beat grouping as shown in Figure 9-6.

FIGURE 9-6 *Derivation of compound meter signatures*

Beat Value	Beat Grouping (per measure)		Meter (Time) Signature	Meter Name
	one two			
$\frac{3}{16}$	$\frac{3}{16}$ + $\frac{3}{16}$ =		$\mathbf{\frac{6}{16}}$	
	one two			DUPLE COMPOUND
$\frac{3}{8}$	$\frac{3}{8}$ + $\frac{3}{8}$ =		$\mathbf{\frac{6}{8}}$	
	one two			
$\frac{3}{4}$	$\frac{3}{4}$ + $\frac{3}{4}$ =		$\mathbf{\frac{6}{4}}$	
	one two three			
$\frac{3}{16}$	$\frac{3}{16}$ + $\frac{3}{16}$ + $\frac{3}{16}$ =		$\mathbf{\frac{9}{16}}$	
	one two three			TRIPLE COMPOUND
$\frac{3}{8}$	$\frac{3}{8}$ + $\frac{3}{8}$ + $\frac{3}{8}$ =		$\mathbf{\frac{9}{8}}$	
	one two three			
$\frac{3}{4}$	$\frac{3}{4}$ + $\frac{3}{4}$ + $\frac{3}{4}$ =		$\mathbf{\frac{9}{4}}$	
	one two three four			
$\frac{3}{16}$	$\frac{3}{16}$ + $\frac{3}{16}$ + $\frac{3}{16}$ + $\frac{3}{16}$ =		$\mathbf{\frac{12}{16}}$	
	one two three four			QUADRUPLE COMPOUND
$\frac{3}{8}$	$\frac{3}{8}$ + $\frac{3}{8}$ + $\frac{3}{8}$ + $\frac{3}{8}$ =		$\mathbf{\frac{12}{8}}$	
	one two three four			
$\frac{3}{4}$	$\frac{3}{4}$ + $\frac{3}{4}$ + $\frac{3}{4}$ + $\frac{3}{4}$ =		$\mathbf{\frac{12}{4}}$	

Observe in Figure 9-6 that all meter signatures with the numerator of 6 indicate duple compound meter; all with the numerator of 9 indicate triple compound meter; and all with the numerator 12 indicate quadruple compound meter. Unlike the simple meter signature, where the numerator is identical with the number of beats in a group, in a compound meter signature the numerator is identical with the number of divisions of the beats. This variance is necessary because for the denominator there is no whole number that can represent a note divisible into three parts. For example, the beat note ♩. can be represented numerically only by the fraction ³⁄₈ (Figure 9-5). A signature of 2 over ³⁄₈ is, of course, impractical. Therefore, the denominator shows a number representing a *divided beat,* requiring the numerator to show the number of *divided beats per measure.* Literally, ⁶⁄₈ means six divided beats per measure, each divided beat represented by an eighth note. But to the ear, ⁶⁄₈ sounds like two ♩. beats per measure, each with a division of ♪ ♪ ♪.

Now we can clearly see how the alternative meter signatures shown in parentheses in Figure 9-7 describe the nature of the meter more clearly than do the traditional compound signatures. For example, ²⁄♪. (instead of ⁶⁄₈) means simply two beats per measure and a dotted eighth note receives one beat. The logic for the use of such signatures has not yet overcome the traditions of the past.

FIGURE 9-7 *Meaning of compound meter signatures*

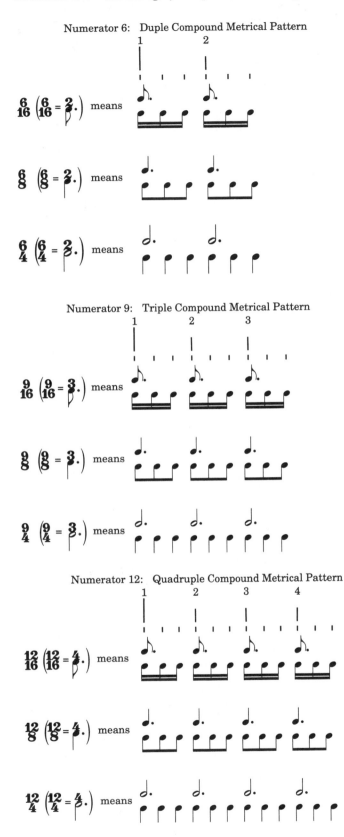

Numerator 6:   Duple Compound Metrical Pattern

$\frac{6}{16}$ $\left(\frac{6}{16} = \frac{2}{\text{♪}.}\right)$ means — two beats per measure, the dotted eighth note represents the beat; each beat divides into three sixteenth notes

$\frac{6}{8}$ $\left(\frac{6}{8} = \frac{2}{\text{♩}.}\right)$ means — two beats per measure, the dotted quarter note represents the beat; each beat divides into three eighth notes

$\frac{6}{4}$ $\left(\frac{6}{4} = \frac{2}{\text{♩}.}\right)$ means — two beats per measure, the dotted half note represents the beat; each beat divides into three quarter notes

Numerator 9:   Triple Compound Metrical Pattern

$\frac{9}{16}$ $\left(\frac{9}{16} = \frac{3}{\text{♪}.}\right)$ means — three beats per measure, the dotted eighth note represents the beat; each beat divides into three sixteenth notes

$\frac{9}{8}$ $\left(\frac{9}{8} = \frac{3}{\text{♩}.}\right)$ means — three beats per measure, the dotted quarter note represents the beat; each beat divides into three eighth notes

$\frac{9}{4}$ $\left(\frac{9}{4} = \frac{3}{\text{♩}.}\right)$ means — three beats per measure, the dotted half note represents the beat; each beat divides into three quarter notes

Numerator 12:   Quadruple Compound Metrical Pattern

$\frac{12}{16}$ $\left(\frac{12}{16} = \frac{4}{\text{♪}.}\right)$ means — four beats per measure, the dotted eighth note represents the beat; each beat divides into three sixteenth notes

$\frac{12}{8}$ $\left(\frac{12}{8} = \frac{4}{\text{♩}.}\right)$ means — four beats per measure, the dotted quarter note represents the beat; each beat divides into three eighth notes

$\frac{12}{4}$ $\left(\frac{12}{4} = \frac{4}{\text{♩}.}\right)$ means — four beats per measure, the dotted half note represents the beat; each beat divides into three quarter notes

EXERCISES
9-3, 9-4

EXERCISE 9-1

Identifying the metrical grouping in simple time

Place a meter signature before the given notation and name the meter in the blanks provided.

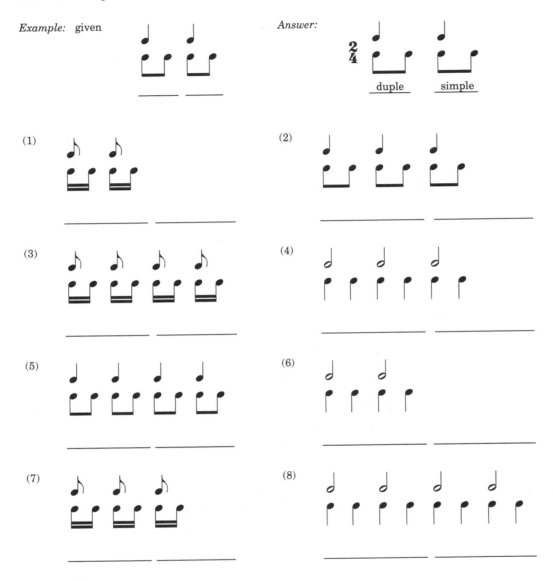

EXERCISE 9-2

Supplying metrical patterns for given simple time signatures

After the given time signature, write the metrical pattern using correct notation and name the meter.

(a) $\frac{3}{4}$

(b) $\frac{2}{8}$

_____   _____

_____   _____

(c) $\frac{4}{4}$

(d) $\frac{2}{2}$

_____   _____

_____   _____

(e) $\frac{4}{2}$

(f) $\frac{3}{8}$

_____   _____

_____   _____

(g) $\frac{4}{8}$

(h) $\frac{3}{2}$

_____   _____

_____   _____

(*Return* to page 95.)

EXERCISE 9-3
Identifying the metrical grouping in compound time

Place a meter signature before the given notation and name the meter in the blanks provided, as done in Exercise 9-1.

(1)

_____   _____

(2)

_____   _____

(3)

_____   _____

(4)

_____   _____

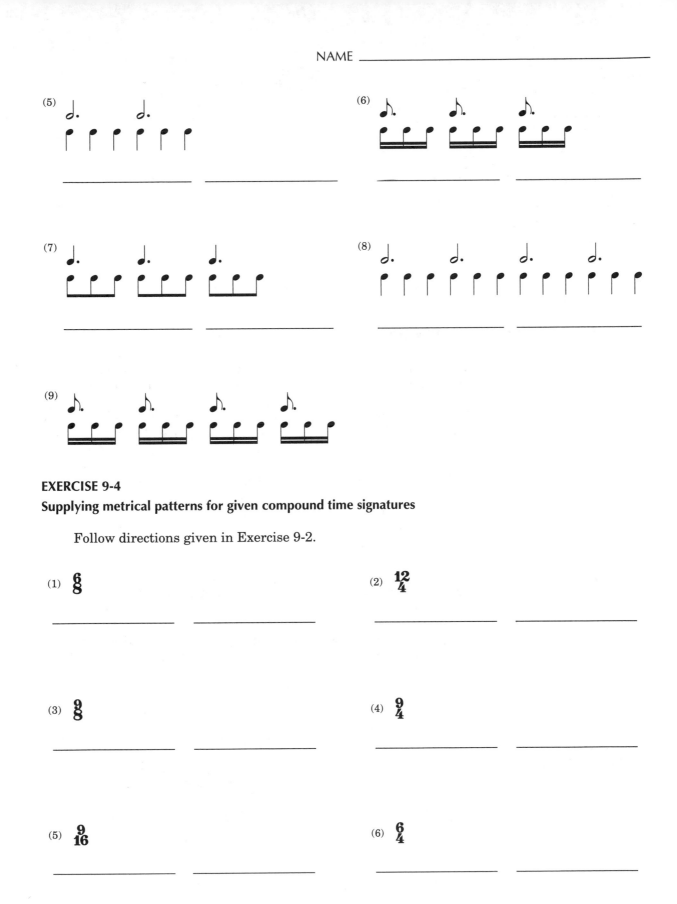

EXERCISE 9-4

Supplying metrical patterns for given compound time signatures

Follow directions given in Exercise 9-2.

(1) $\frac{6}{8}$

(2) $\frac{12}{4}$

_____   _____

_____   _____

(3) $\frac{9}{8}$

(4) $\frac{9}{4}$

_____   _____

_____   _____

(5) $\frac{9}{16}$

(6) $\frac{6}{4}$

_____   _____

_____   _____

(7) $\frac{12}{8}$ (8) $\frac{6}{16}$

_____ _____   _____ _____

(9) $\frac{12}{16}$

_____ _____

(To continue the study of **Time,** *go directly* to **Chapter 12,** page *129.*)

CHAPTER SUMMARY

1. A *time signature* is a device placed at the beginning of a piece of music to indicate the number of beats in a measure and the notation to be used.

2. *Simple time signatures* are those which use simple time values (notes divisible into two parts) as the beat, and can be recognized by numerators of 2, 3, and 4.

3. Unlike those in simple time, the numerators of time signatures in compound time are 6, 9, and 12, indicating the number of beat divisions in a measure. Since three beat divisions equal one beat, 6 indicates two beats in a measure—duple compound time—9 indicates triple compound time, and 12 indicates quadruple compound time.

4. Unlike that in simple time, the denominator in compound time indicates the note value receiving a beat division, three of which equal one beat.

5. As an example, in $\frac{6}{8}$ the 6 indicates duple compound time (two beats per measure, each divisible by three), and 8 indicates the beat division to be an eighth note, three of which equal the beat note, a dotted quarter note. Therefore, in $\frac{6}{8}$, there are two beats per measure, each a dotted quarter note.

CHAPTER TEN

Pitch: Major Scales (continued)

Playing Major Scales at the Keyboard
Singing Major Scales

Playing scales at the keyboard may be studied for one or both of these reasons: (1) to aid in learning the sound and the construction of a scale, in which case the fingering of the scale is left to oneself; and (2) to develop skill in performance, in which the fingering is a vital concern ordinarily supervised by a piano teacher. Scale fingerings are shown in Appendix D. Within the purview of this book, we shall study only the first approach.

Keep in mind the order of whole steps and half steps that produces the major scale. Though this may not seem particularly important at the piano, where the keys play fixed pitches, it becomes essential in singing or in playing such instruments as the violin or the trombone, where the performer is responsible for fixing the pitches and the intonation. Development of the ability to produce or to differentiate whole steps and half steps is an important result of *playing scales at the keyboard.*

Playing Scales at the Keyboard

The C Major Scale. Playing the white key C and the next seven white keys above it produces a C major scale. Playing only white keys from this given pitch C automatically places the half steps in their correct scale locations, between $\hat{3}$ and $\hat{4}$ and between $\hat{7}$ and $\hat{8}$, as shown in Figure 10-1.

FIGURE 10-1 *Playing the C major scale*

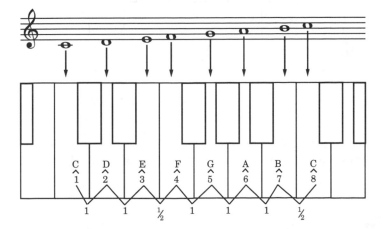

To Play Major Scales Other than C

1. Use the same pattern of whole steps and half steps as in the C major scale.

2. Play a black key when the note name includes an accidental (except for one or two instances in the scales of F♯, C♯, G♭, and C♭, which are described later).

3. Begin the scale on a black key when the tonic note includes an accidental (except in the scale of C♭ major). See the E♭ scale in Figure 10-2.

4. Expect various combinations of black and white keys to produce whole steps. In Figure 10-2,

E♭ to F	is black to white
F to G	is white to white
A♭ to B♭	is black to black

FIGURE 10-2 *Playing the E♭ major scale*

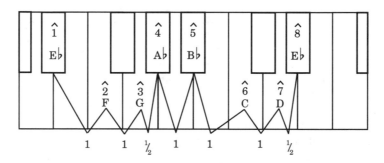

The scales of F♯, C♯, G♭, and C♭ will make use of these enharmonic white-key spellings:

F♯ major requires the enharmonic white key E♯ (see Figure 10-3).

C♯ major requires the enharmonic white keys B♯ and E♯.

G♭ major requires the enharmonic white key C♭.

C♭ major starts on the enharmonic white key C♭ and also requires the enharmonic white key F♭.

FIGURE 10-3 *Playing the F♯ major scale*

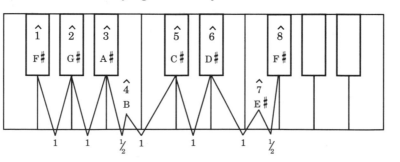

**EXERCISES
10-1, 10-2, 10-3**

Singing Major Scales

Singing is ordinarily the vocal performance of a musical setting of a literary text, usually poetry, called a song. However, in a course of study in music theory and in the preparation and training of a musician, the student will often be required to sing, not songs with words having artistic expression, but exercises with vocal sounds having theoretical significance. Singing major scales is such an exercise. The vocal sounds can be expressed in three ways:

1. *By numbers*. Figure 10-4 shows application for the C major scale.

FIGURE 10-4   *Singing the scale by numbers, C major*

Sing: 1   2   3   4   5   6   7   8   8   7   6   5   4   3   2   1

2. *By letter names*. Figure 10-5 shows application for the D major scale. When a letter name includes an accidental, sing on two repeated pitches—for example, "f-sharp."

FIGURE 10-5   *Singing the scale by letter names, D major*

Sing: d   e   f♯   g   a   b   c♯   d   d   c♯   b   a   g   f♯   e   d

3. *By syllables*. Singing with syllables is known as solmization. Two important systems of solmization are known as *tonic sol-fa* and *solfeggio*.[1] Figure 10-6 shows a solmization of the C major scale.

FIGURE 10-6   *Singing the scale by syllables, C major*

Sing: do   re   mi   fa   sol   la   ti   do   do   ti   la   sol   fa   mi   re   do

The syllables are pronounced

do—*doe*
re—*ray*
mi—*me*
fa—*fah*
sol—*soh*
la—*lah*
ti—*tee*

EXERCISE 10-4

---

[1]In the tonic sol-fa system, the syllables are movable; that is, "do" is always the tonic note of the scale. In solfeggio, the syllables are fixed: C, for example, is always "do" regardless of its location in the scale. This text will make use only of tonic sol-fa.

Accounts of the invention of a system of solmization by Guido d'Arezzo (A.D. 980–1050) and its development into modern syllable systems may be found in music history books, encyclopedias, or dictionaries.

EXERCISE 10-1

Playing major scales on the keyboard

Using the example as a guide, (1) indicate by arrows and by numbers $\hat{1}$–$\hat{8}$ the keys on the keyboard required to produce the sound of the scale, (2) indicate whole steps and half steps, (3) then play the scale ascending for one octave.

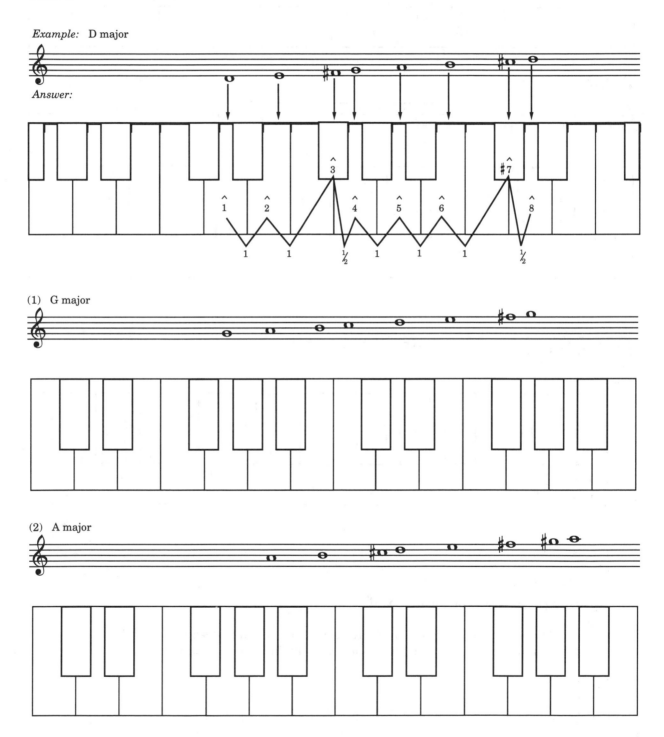

Example: D major

Answer:

(1) G major

(2) A major

(3) F major

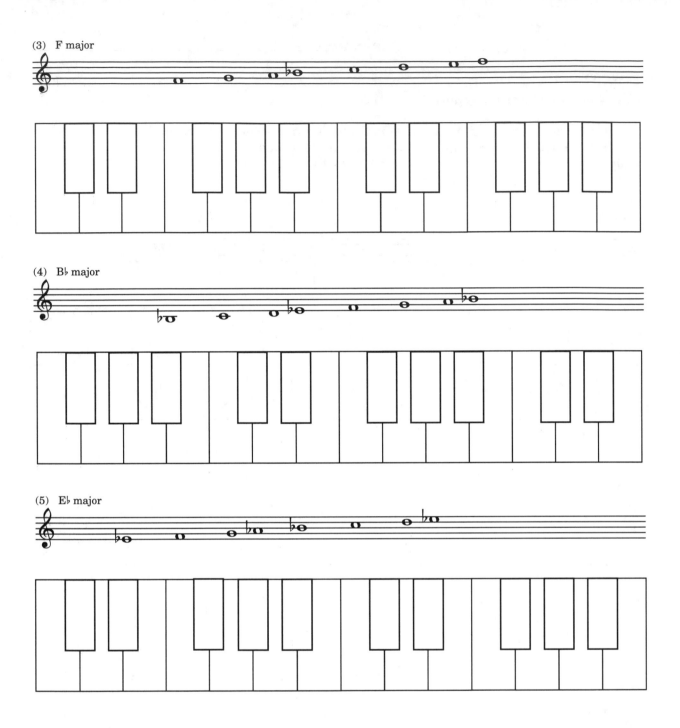

(4) B♭ major

(5) E♭ major

EXERCISE 10-2

Playing major scales on the keyboard

This exercise is similar to Exercise 10-1, although it does not show the staff. Number the keys, indicate whole steps and half steps, then play.

(1) E major

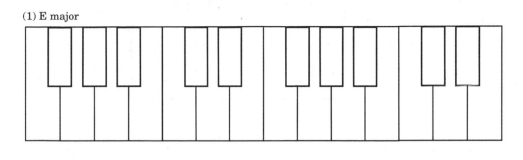

(2) B major

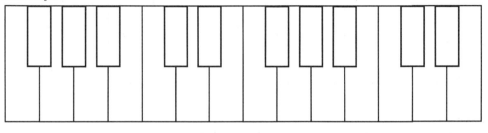

(3) F♯ major

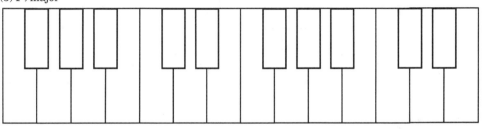

(4) C♯ major

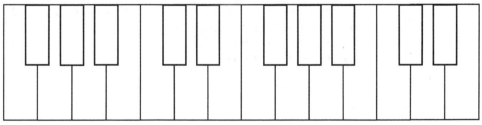

(5) A♭ major

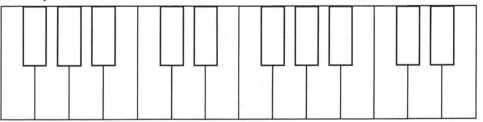

(6) D♭ major

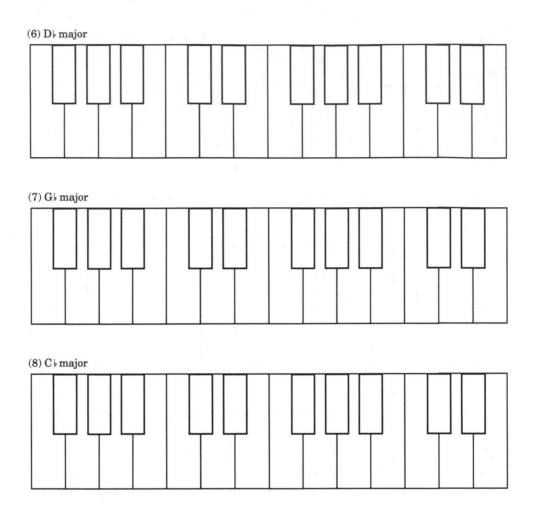

(7) G♭ major

(8) C♭ major

EXERCISE 10-3

Playing all major scales at the keyboard

Play any of the fifteen major scales. Spell each scale as you play it. Be sure that each interval is the correct whole step or half step. Play *both* ascending and descending for one octave. You may refer to the scales you wrote in Exercise 5-1. Practice until you can play without looking at the music.

(*Return* to page *106*.)

EXERCISE 10-4

Singing major scales

Choose any pitch that can be used as the tonic tone of a major scale. Sing the scale in three ways: (1) by numbers, (2) by letter names, and (3) by syllables, as shown in Figures 10-4 through 10-6. Sing each of the fifteen major scales in this manner. You may sing these from the scales you wrote in Exercise 5-1. If necessary, play the scale as you sing until you feel able to sing without the piano. Use the piano at any time to check your accuracy.

CHAPTER ELEVEN

Pitch: Major Key Signatures

Key
Key Signature
Key Signatures on the Staff
Circle of Fifths

The major scale, with its characteristic locations of half steps and whole steps, constitutes a musical pattern having its own unique aural quality. We have found that the major scale pattern can be written with fifteen locations (letter names) as tonic, with each location other than that of C requiring a varying number of sharps or flats to maintain the correct half-step and whole-step relationships. Since each of these fifteen scales has the same characteristic sound, there are not really fifteen different scales; there is simply *one* major scale structure, whose tonic tone can be located at any one of fifteen pitch spellings.

Much of the music commonly performed today is based upon two scale patterns: the major scale, already studied, and the minor scale, to be studied in Chapter Fourteen. Music is said to be in *major* when the pitches used can be arranged in alphabetical order with a resulting major scale pattern. In Figure 11-1, the first line of the melody already assumes the pattern of a D major descending scale.[1]

FIGURE 11-1   *D major scale*

In the folk song in Figure 11-2, we find the same tones in a different order, but still resulting in the same D major scale.

---

[1]Figures 11-1 and 11-2 include all members of the major scale. Many melodies do not include all scale tones, but enough are present to make the scale easily discernible—for example, the melody "Auld Lang Syne" (see page 10).

FIGURE 11-2 *Folk song, D major scale*

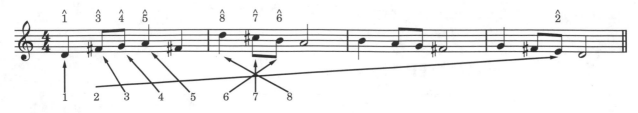

Both of these tunes are said to be in *major* because they are based on the construction of the major scale.

It is possible to begin "Joy to the World" on a different note, with a resulting change in scale spelling.

FIGURE 11-3 *"Joy to the World," B♭ major scale*

We also can write the folk song in Figure 11-2 based on any other major scale. In Figure 11-4, the scale is built on a tonic of F♯.

FIGURE 11-4 *Folk song, F♯ major scale*

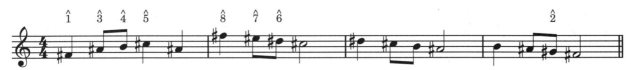

It is easy to see that each of these tunes could be written using any of the fifteen major scale locations. We could identify a piece of music by saying it uses a certain scale, but instead, we say the music is in a certain *key*.

Key

The term *key* refers to the letter name of the tonic (first degree) of that scale upon which the composition is based. The letter name of the tonic is also called *keynote*. Figures 11-1 and 11-2 are therefore in the *key* of D major, because each uses a major scale with the tonic, or keynote, of D. In similar manner, we would identify "Joy to the World" in Figure 11-3 as being in the key of B♭ major, and the folk song in Figure 11-4 as being in the key of F♯ major.

Music could be written with the correct accidentals placed before each note where needed, as in the preceding figures, but this is obviously cumbersome and makes the music appear unduly complicated. To facilitate the notation of accidentals, we use a device called *key signature*.

To the Instructor: Many students find that a thorough knowledge of the circle of fifths contributes significantly to the rapid identification and writing of key signatures. For that reason, it is suggested that you assign Exercises 11-3 through 11-6 before Exercises 11-1 and 11-2.

EXERCISE 11-1

Identifying the name of a major key when the key signature is given

For each key signature, (1) write the name of the major key below the staff, and (2) write the tonic note of the key on the staff, using a whole note.

Reminder: The last sharp of the signature is $\hat{7}$ of a major scale.

The last flat of the signature is $\hat{4}$ of a major scale.

Example:

The last sharp is D♯; therefore, E is $\hat{1}$.

Answer: → E major

TREBLE

BASS

EXERCISE 11-2
Writing major key signatures

Write the correct number of sharps or flats on the correct lines and spaces of the great staff for each given major key.

Example: given   A major

Answer:

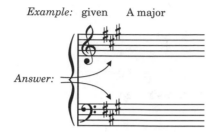

(1) G major   (2) E♭ major   (3) C♯ major   (4) G♭ major

(5) F major   (6) F♯ major   (7) D major   (8) C♭ major

(9) E major   (10) D♭ major   (11) B major   (12) B♭ major   (13) A♭ major

(*Return* to page *118*.)

EXERCISE 11-3
Writing the numbers of accidentals for keys on the circle of fifths

On the circle of fifths below, the key names are given. Beside each key name, write the correct number of sharps or flats. The answer for G major is given.

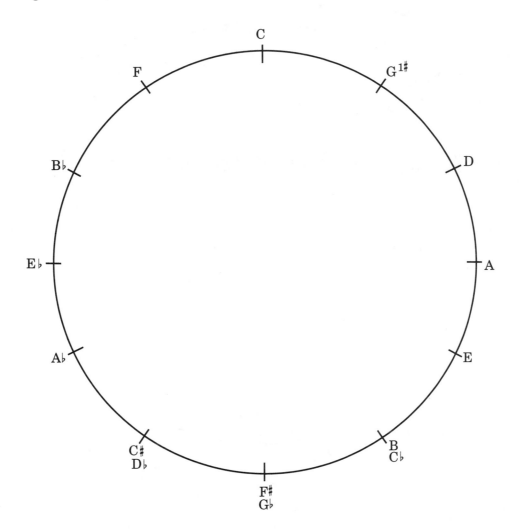

EXERCISE 11-4

Writing names of keys on the circle of fifths

On the following circle, the numbers of accidentals for key signatures are given. Beside each, write the name of the major key. The answer for one flat is given.

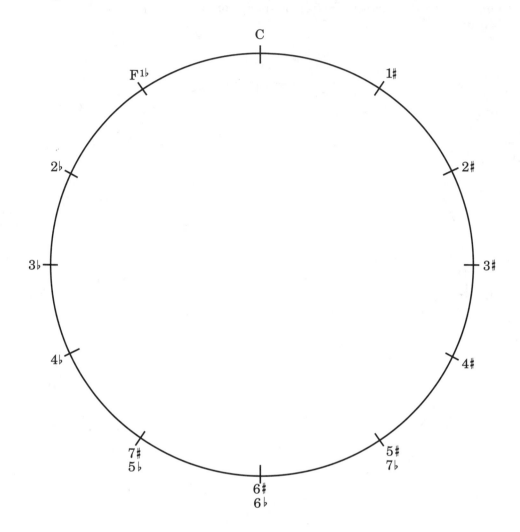

EXERCISE 11-5

Constructing the circle of fifths for major keys

1. On the following circle, mark twelve points like the face of a clock. This provides places for all fifteen keys, including three enharmonic keys.
2. At 12 o'clock place C (no sharps or flats).
3. Proceeding clockwise, at 1 o'clock place the letter name of the key a fifth above C, which is G (1 sharp); continue clockwise in fifths and add sharps, ending with the key of C♯ (7 sharps).
4. Proceeding counterclockwise, at 11 o'clock place the letter name of the key a fifth below C, which is F (1 flat); continue counterclockwise in fifths and add flats, ending with the key of C♭ (7 flats).

With practice, you should be able to demonstrate the circle (from memory) on paper or at the board in *one minute*. Compare your results with Figure 11-13.

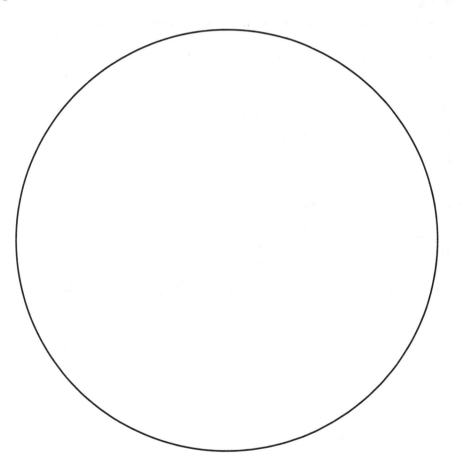

EXERCISE 11-6

Identifying major key names from the number of accidentals

In each blank space, write the correct major key name according to the number of sharps or flats given.

(1) 2♯   __D__   (8) 7♯ _____

(2) 4♭ _____   (9) 6♭ _____

(3) 3♭ _____   (10) 5♭ _____

(4) 5♯ _____   (11) 4♯ _____

(5) 1♯ _____   (12) 1♭ _____

(6) 7♭ _____   (13) 6♯ _____

(7) 3♯ _____   (14) 2♭ _____

EXERCISE 11-7

Naming the number of sharps or flats when the major key is given

In each blank space, write the correct number of sharps or flats for the given major key.

(1) B   __2♭__   (8) G♭ _____

(2) D♭ _____   (9) E _____

(3) A _____   (10) F♯ _____

(4) G _____   (11) F _____

(5) C♯ _____   (12) C♭ _____

(6) E♭ _____   (13) B _____

(7) D _____   (14) A♭ _____

(To continue the study of **Pitch,** *go directly* to **Chapter 14,** page *159.*)

CHAPTER SUMMARY

1. Major melodies are based on major scales.

2. *Key* refers to the tonic of that scale upon which a composition is based. The first note of a scale, the tonic, and the *keynote* are the same.

3. Accidentals used in the scale of a composition are grouped together to form the *key signature*.

4. There are fifteen major keys, just as there are fifteen major scales.

5. The *circle of fifths* enables us to organize knowledge of keys, including relationships of keys, number of accidentals required for each key signature, and enharmonic keys.

6. The order for major keys is (beginning with C, no sharps or flats):

	G	D	A	E	B	F♯	C♯
	1♯	2♯	3♯	4♯	5♯	6♯	7♯
C							
	F	B♭	E♭	A♭	D♭	G♭	C♭
	1♭	2♭	3♭	4♭	5♭	6♭	7♭

CHAPTER TWELVE

Time (continued)

Conductor's Beats
Rhythm
Anacrusis
Rhythmic Reading

The knowledge gained thus far concerning pitch and time provides the background for building skills in reading music. There are two stages of development in reading: In one, the performer looks at a given note and reacts in some mechanical manner, such as depressing a key on the piano or placing a finger on a violin string; in the other, the performer looks at a given note and knows before playing how it will sound. The ultimate goal through both stages is competency in reading music of varying complexities, from the single melodic line to the two staves of notation necessary for piano music, or even a score with a page full of staves representing all the instruments of a concert band or a symphony orchestra.

An effective approach to the desired skills of music reading is through practicing the technique of singing a melody at sight (sight singing). Singing is preferable to performance at an instrument because in singing, it is impossible to fall back on any mechanical device (such as a key) to help locate a correct pitch. In sight singing, two kinds of reading are required: reading time and reading pitch. We will begin with time, learning to read the durations of different note values. Most students have found that their study is made easier if they can actually feel the metrical grouping as they perform. This can be experienced in a dramatic way by use of *conductor's beats*.

Conductor's Beats

Conductor's beats are patterns of hand gestures used to indicate groupings of beats.[1] Although the motions or diagrams of the beats may vary among conductors, certain basic movements are so standardized that they are accepted by musicians throughout the world.

---

[1]Herman Scherchen (*Handbook of Conducting*, Oxford University Press, London, 1933) considers that there are three distinct purposes in conducting: (1) to present the metric course of the music; (2) to indicate its expressive, structural features; and (3) to actually guide the musicians—preventing faulty performance and correcting fluctuations or inequalities. In this present course of study, the student will be concerned only with the first purpose, to present the metric course of the music.

The following right-hand diagrams for conductor's beats are recommended because all beats occur approximately on the same horizontal plane. For the student seated in a classroom, this horizontal plane might be at desktop level; if the student is standing, the horizontal plane is about waist high.

FIGURE 12-1   *Conductor's beats*[2]

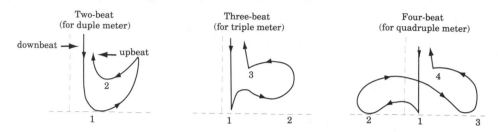

EXERCISES
12-1, 12-2

The numbers indicate the place in the conductor's beat where each beat begins, just as tapping marks the beginning of each beat as practiced in Chapter Seven. The first beat in all diagrams is called the *downbeat* and always coincides with the first beat of a measure. In any of these patterns, the last beat is described by an upward motion of the hand and is called an *upbeat*.

The two-beat can be used for duple simple meter signatures (numerator of 2) or duple compound signatures (numerator of 6). In the same way, the three-beat can be used for meter signatures with numerators of 3 or 9, and the four-beat for meter signatures with numerators of 4 or 12.

FIGURE 12-2   *Meter signatures and accompanying conductor's beats*

	Meter Signatures						Accompanying Conductor's Beats
	Simple			Compound			
DUPLE	$\frac{2}{8}$	$\frac{2}{4}$	$\frac{2}{2}$ (¢)	$\frac{6}{16}$	$\frac{6}{8}$	$\frac{6}{4}$	TWO-BEAT
TRIPLE	$\frac{3}{8}$	$\frac{3}{4}$	$\frac{3}{2}$	$\frac{9}{16}$	$\frac{9}{8}$	$\frac{9}{4}$	THREE-BEAT
QUADRUPLE	$\frac{4}{8}$	$\frac{4}{4}$ (c)	$\frac{4}{2}$	$\frac{12}{16}$	$\frac{12}{8}$	$\frac{12}{4}$	FOUR-BEAT

EXERCISE
12-3

Use of the conductor's beats alone does not differentiate simple and compound meter. The difference can be demonstrated by tapping with the left hand while conducting with the right hand. Two taps with the left hand for each of the beats in the right hand will describe simple meters; three taps with the left hand for each of the beats in the right hand will describe compound meters.

---

[2]In addition to two, three, and four, there are other beat-patterns for one, five, six, and so forth. The student can expect to study these other beat-diagrams in later theory or conducting courses.

Using the conductor's beat and tapping with the left hand simultaneously is basically the same procedure shown in Chapter Eight in the diagrams in Figure 8-4 and practiced in the exercises. The only difference is in the right hand, where the conductor's beat is substituted for the beat-tap.

EXERCISES
12-4, 12-5,
12-6, 12-7,
12-8

In our exercises in listening to melodies, you have also noticed that the pitches are of various durations, some the same as the beat, some the same as the division, and still others of lengths different from the beat or the division. This feature of musical composition is called *rhythm*.

Rhythm

Rhythm is the occurrence of various time durations within the meter.

FIGURE 12-3   *Rhythm and meter*

Brahms, Wiegenlied, Op. 49, No. 4

Rhythm, the occurrence of various note values, is revealed in the melody.

Meter is the regularly recurring pulsation of beats.

Observe that the melody in Figure 12-3 does not start on the first beat of a measure; it begins with an *anacrusis*.

Anacrusis

The anacrusis is that part of the music occurring before the downbeat of the first complete measure. It may be described as an incomplete measure before the first full measure, and it may consist of one, two, or several notes. When the anacrusis occurs on the last beat or fraction of the last beat before the first complete measure, it is often called the "upbeat" or "pickup."

The anacrusis is usually written as an incomplete measure, in which case, its value and the note values found in the final measure are equal to one full measure. In Figure 12-3, the value of the anacrusis, ♪♪, added to the value of the final measure, ♩♩, is equal to a full measure of ¾ meter.

EXERCISE
12-9

Having now defined meter and rhythm, and having recognized the factor of anacrusis, we will combine these in a practical application known as *Rhythmic Reading*.

Rhythmic Reading

Rhythmic Reading, or rhythmic recitation, is a process in music by which note durations only, not pitches, are expressed in vocal sounds. Rhythmic reading is based on these principles:

1. Any note occurring on a beat is recited by the number of that beat.

Recite: 4   1   2   3   4   1   2   3

2. Any note, not recited by number, occurring on a fraction of a beat is recited by the syllable *ta* (tah).³

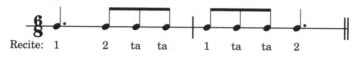

Recite: 1   2   3 ta   1   2 ta   3

also,

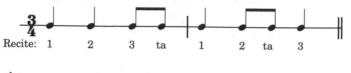

Recite: 1   2 ta ta   1 ta ta   2

3. The syllable that originates with a note is held for the duration until the next appropriate syllable is articulated.⁴

Recite: 1 ——— ta   1 ——————— 2

also,

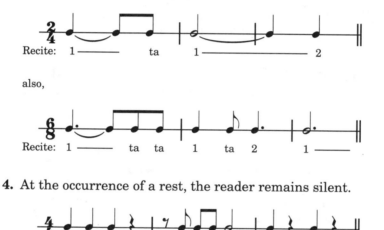

Recite: 1 —— ta ta   1 ta 2   1 ——

4. At the occurrence of a rest, the reader remains silent.

Recite: 1 2 3   ta 2 ta 3 ——— 3

EXERCISES
12-10, 12-11,
12-12, 12-13,
12-14

---

³A variety of rhythmic syllables for beat division is used by different theorists and teachers; for example, is a system widely used for younger students. Rhythmic reading of more complex music favors the use of a syllable beginning with the articulate sound of a consonant, such as *ta,* in place of the broad sound of *and.*

⁴The *tie* is a curved line that connects two notes of the same pitch. The second note is not articulated and the result is a sustained, unbroken sound equal to the duration of both notes.

EXERCISE 12-1
Drawing diagrams of conductor's beats

Draw right-hand diagrams and number the beats.

(a) Two-beat

(b) Three-beat

(c) Four-beat

EXERCISE 12-2
Practicing conductor's beats

Practice the two-, three-, and four-beats. Practice sometimes in front of a mirror. Have other students criticize your beats. Observe especially the clarity of your execution of the diagrams.

(*Return* to page *130.*)

EXERCISE 12-3
Selecting the conductor's beat according to the meter signature

What conductor's beat would be used to accompany the following meter signatures?

Example: *Answer:*

$\frac{2}{8}$ two-beat

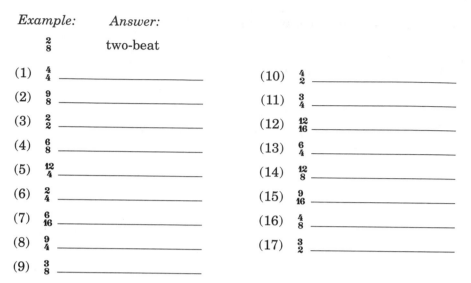

(1) $\frac{4}{4}$ _____

(2) $\frac{9}{8}$ _____

(3) $\frac{2}{2}$ _____

(4) $\frac{6}{8}$ _____

(5) $\frac{12}{4}$ _____

(6) $\frac{2}{4}$ _____

(7) $\frac{6}{16}$ _____

(8) $\frac{9}{4}$ _____

(9) $\frac{3}{8}$ _____

(10) $\frac{4}{2}$ _____

(11) $\frac{3}{4}$ _____

(12) $\frac{12}{16}$ _____

(13) $\frac{6}{4}$ _____

(14) $\frac{12}{8}$ _____

(15) $\frac{9}{16}$ _____

(16) $\frac{4}{8}$ _____

(17) $\frac{3}{2}$ _____

(*Return* to page *130.*)

EXERCISE 12-4
Conducting and tapping simple meters (without music)

While conducting two (duple), three (triple), or four (quadruple), tap the simple division of the beat (division of two) with the other hand. The student can practice alone and outside of class. Ordinarily, this exercise requires repetitious practice before the student feels at ease.

EXERCISE 12-5 (Instructor)
Conducting and tapping simple meters

The instructor will designate a melody from Exercise 8-2. Observe the meter signature, make the appropriate conductor's beat, and tap the simple background in the left hand. As you continue conducting, the instructor will play the given melody. Observe that not all melodies start on the downbeat: Some may start on other beats of the measure, or on the second division of the beat.

EXERCISE 12-6
Conducting and tapping compound meters (without music)

While conducting two, three, or four, tap the compound division of the beat (division of three) with the other hand. The student can practice alone and outside of class.

EXERCISE 12-7 (Instructor)

Conducting and tapping compound meters

The instructor will designate a melody from Exercise 8-4. Observe the meter signature, make the appropriate conductor's beat, and tap the compound division in the left hand. Observe that the melody may begin on any beat, or on a division of a beat (if on a division of a beat, usually the third division). As you continue conducting, the instructor will play the melody.

EXERCISE 12-8 (Instructor)

Conducting and tapping simple or compound meters

Listen to a melody played by the instructor. Listen for meter (beat grouping and division) and location of downbeat. Conduct with the right hand and tap the division with the left hand. Use the music supplied for Exercise 8-5. For additional material, use the following melodies from *Music for Sight Singing*. Observe the recommended metronome indications.

(1)	88	M.M. ♩ =	92	(9)	272	M.M. ♪. =	100
(2)	101	M.M. ♩ =	108	(10)	283	M.M. ♩. =	112
(3)	112	M.M. ♩ =	116	(11)	336	M.M. ♩ =	86
(4)	191	M.M. ♩. =	69	(12)	347	M.M. ♩. =	60
(5)	201	M.M. ♩. =	92	(13)	348	M.M. ♩. =	69
(6)	202	M.M. ♩. =	84	(14)	389	M.M. ♩. =	80
(7)	239	M.M. ♩ =	100	(15)	395	M.M. ♩ =	112
(8)	262	M.M. ♩ =	92	(16)	409	M.M. ♩ =	80

(*Return* to page *131*.)

EXERCISE 12-9

Anacrusis

In the last measure of each example, place one note that will make a complete measure when added to the anacrusis.

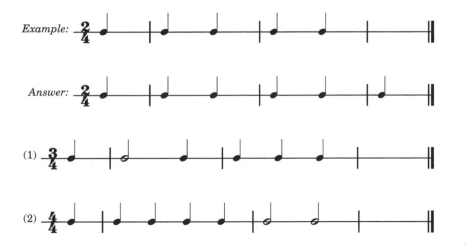

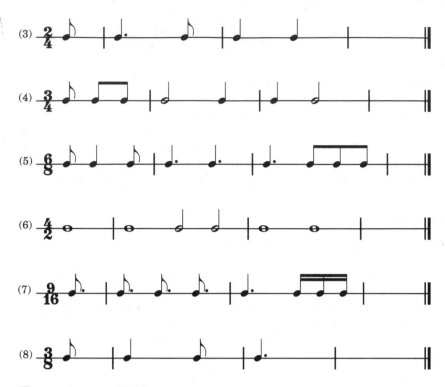

(3)
(4)
(5)
(6)
(7)
(8)

(*Return* to page *131*.)

EXERCISE 12-10
Writing rhythmic syllables

Below each note write the rhythmic syllable.

Example:

1   1   2   1 ta 2 ta 1

(1)

(2)

(3)

EXERCISE 12-11

Rhythmic reading (with the syllables written out)

While conducting and tapping the meter, read aloud the rhythmic syllables for each of the examples in Exercise 12-10.

EXERCISE 12-12

Rhythmic reading, simple meter

While conducting and tapping the meter, read with rhythmic syllables the rhythm of the melodies found in Exercise 8-2. For additional practice, read the rhythm patterns and the rhythm of melodies from *Music for Sight Singing*, Chapters 1 and 2.

EXERCISE 12-13

Rhythmic reading, compound meter

While conducting and tapping the meter, read the rhythm of the melodies found in Exercise 8-4. For additional practice, read the rhythm patterns and the rhythm of melodies from *Music for Sight Singing*, Chapter 3.

EXERCISE 12-14

Rhythmic reading, simple and compound meters

While conducting and tapping the meter, read the rhythm of the melodies found in Exercise 8-5. For additional practice, read melodies from *Music for Sight Singing*, Chapter 4, Sections 1 and 2, and Chapter 5, Sections 1–5.

CHAPTER SUMMARY

1. *Rhythm* is the occurrence of various time durations within the meter.

2. *Conductor's beats* are hand movements indicating duple, simple, or quadruple time. In each, the first beat of the measure is indicated by a downward movement *(downbeat)* and the last beat by an upward movement *(upbeat)*. Although intended for directing performing groups, they are valuable in aiding the development of rhythmic reading and sight singing.

3. *Anacrusis* is that part of a measure occurring before the first downbeat.

CHAPTER THIRTEEN

Time
(continued)

Beams in Notation
Rests in Notation
Rhythmic Transcription
Rhythmic Dictation

The practice of rhythmic reading in Chapter Twelve supports the next step in the study of time: development of the ability to perceive the rhythm of a melody upon hearing it and to write it on paper as notation. This process is called *rhythmic dictation*. This is, in a sense, the reverse process of rhythmic reading. In rhythmic reading, notation becomes sound; in dictation, sound becomes notation. To write correctly the rhythm you hear, you must understand certain principles of the use of *beams* and *rests* in notation.

Beams in Notation

Beams have been described as heavy lines that connect the stems of notes. Beams make music easier to read by eliminating a long series of flagged notes and by clarifying the location of the beats in a measure. Figure 13-1 shows a measure of $\frac{9}{8}$ meter containing nine eighth notes written in three ways. In Figure 13-1*a*, the notation is correct, but in Figure 13-1*b*, the notation is easier to read because the beams clarify the location of each of the three beats in triple compound meter. Incorrect beaming, as seen in Figure 13-1*c*, makes the same rhythmic pattern more difficult to read because the beginnings of beamed groups do not coincide with the second and third beats of triple compound meter.

A beam once begun does not ordinarily extend into the next beat unit.[1] If additional notes are to be beamed, a new beam will start at the new beat, as shown in Figure 13-2. The following examples show various correct and incorrect applications of this principle. The bracket (⌞‾‾‾⌟) indicates the duration of a beat.

---

[1]Exceptions will be found in actual music, but always with good cause. You should adhere to the basic principles for writing beams and rests presented in this chapter until, in later study, you become experienced in the intricacies of music editing.

FIGURE 13-1   *Use of beams*

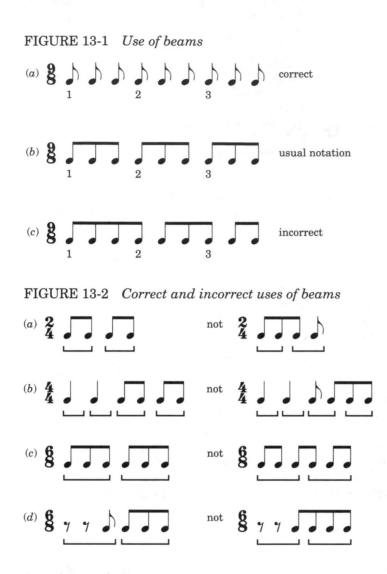

FIGURE 13-2   *Correct and incorrect uses of beams*

*EXERCISES
13-1, 13-2*

Rests in Notation

1. *Dotted rests.* Rests, like notes, may be dotted. The dot increases the value of the rest by one-half— 𝄾· = 𝄾 𝄿, 𝄼· = 𝄼 𝄾, 𝄻· = 𝄻 𝄼 .

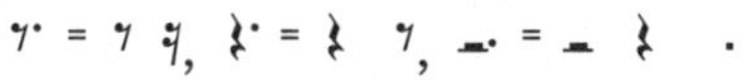

2. *The whole rest.* Whenever an entire measure is to be silent, a whole rest is written, whatever the meter signature in use at the time.

FIGURE 13-3   *Use of the whole rest*

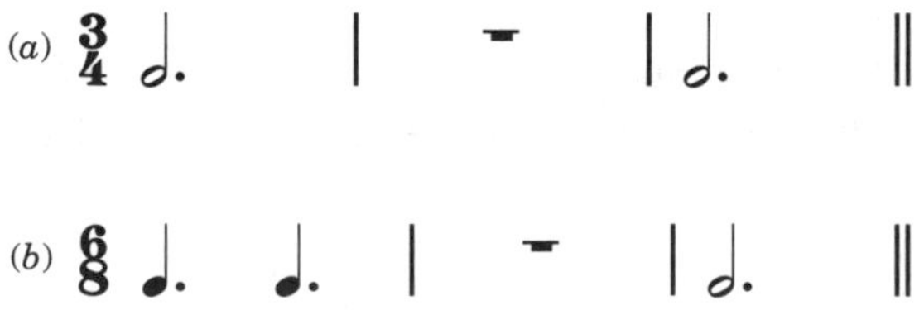

3. *Separate or combined rests*
   a. When a period of silence lasts more than one beat, individual (separate) rests may be used for each beat; or, when the silence begins on a

strong beat, rests may be combined and shown as a single rest. For example,

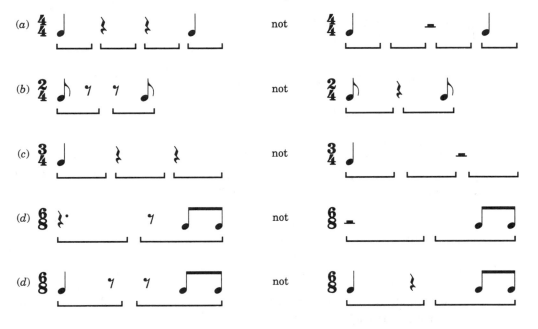

b. If a combining of rests would make the location of the beats of a measure unclear, separate rests should be used. In Figure 13-4, each example in the right-hand column contains a rest that obscures the location of one of the beats of the measure.

FIGURE 13-4 *Correct and incorrect uses of rests*

c. In compound meter, separate rests are ordinarily used for the second and third divisions of the beat; for example,

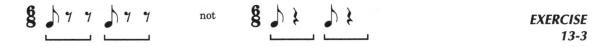

EXERCISE 13-3

Although composers write much music in the familiar $\frac{2}{4}$, $\frac{3}{4}$, $\frac{4}{4}$, and $\frac{6}{8}$ time signatures, they frequently employ a variety of other signatures. You can develop the ability to work confidently in a wide range of time signatures through exercises in *rhythmic transcription*.

Rhythmic Transcription

Rhythmic transcription is the rewriting of a piece using a meter signature with the same numerator but a different denominator. This will produce a notation that looks different from the original but sounds identical when performed. For example, when you hear a rhythmic pattern in quadruple simple time, there is no way of knowing what the notation will be until you know the note value of the beat. A pattern in quadruple simple meter can be written using a half note, a quarter note, or an eighth note as the beat unit. Although the notation looks different, one will sound like the others, assuming all have the same tempo indication. In Figure 13-5, each rhythmic pattern will sound the same as the others (when the tempo for the beat unit is the same); only the notation is different.

FIGURE 13-5 *Rhythmic transcription*

EXERCISE
13-4

We are now ready to listen to a melody and write its rhythmic pattern on paper.

Rhythmic Dictation

To develop most efficiently the skill of rhythmic dictation, follow these steps in *listening to a melody* and *writing the rhythm.*

Listening to a Melody. When the instructor is ready to play a melody for rhythmic dictation, observe this procedure:

Step 1. The meter signature will be announced. Using the appropriate conductor's beat and tapping the divisions, follow the instructor's lead in establishing the meter. Students continue to conduct and tap throughout steps 2, 3, and 4.

Step 2. As the instructor plays, listen to the melody and commit it to memory.

Step 3. Sing back the melody, using the neutral syllable *la.*[2]

Step 4. Sing the melody again, this time using rhythmic syllables, *or* recite without pitch using rhythmic syllables. For Figure 13.7a, these syllables would be "one two three-ta four-ta / one two three."

Writing the Rhythm. For the first exercises in rhythmic dictation, diagrams are supplied to help you in writing the notation. Each diagram consists of three lines:

1. *The top line* shows the beat durations of each measure (the same as the right-hand conductor's beat).
2. *The bottom line* shows the beat divisions of each measure (the same as the left-hand division).
3. On *the middle line* you are to write the rhythm.

---

[2]Identifying the rhythmic location of the first note is necessary in achieving an individual or unified class response when the melody is sung back. In a common procedure, the instructor counts the beats aloud as the students synchronize conducting and tapping, and, when they are prepared, speaks "ready, sing" on the two beats immediately preceding the first note of music.

FIGURE 13-6 *Rhythmic dictation: meter diagram*

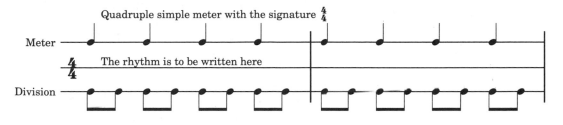

Figure 13-7a shows a rhythmic dictation problem as played by the instructor. The solution, *(b),* is the rhythmic pattern placed on the middle line of the diagram.

FIGURE 13-7 *Example of rhythmic dictation*

(a) Problem played by the instructor:

(b) Solution written on the middle line:

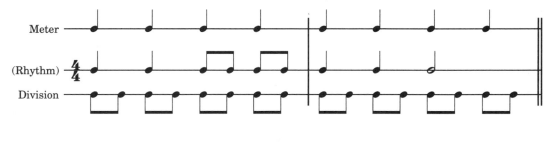

EXERCISES
13-5, 13-6

EXERCISE 13-1
Improving notation by use of beams

Rewrite each rhythmic pattern by using beams where feasible.

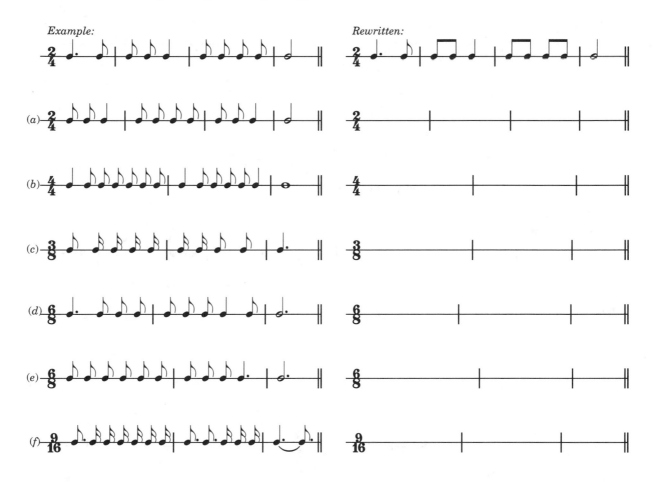

EXERCISE 13-2
Correcting examples showing incorrect use of beams

Rewrite each exercise with correct beaming.

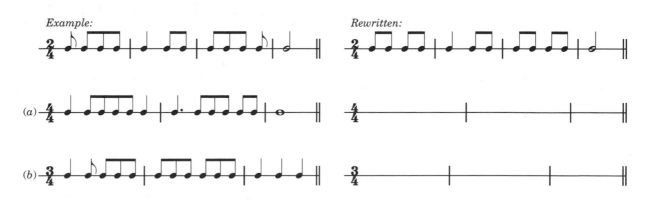

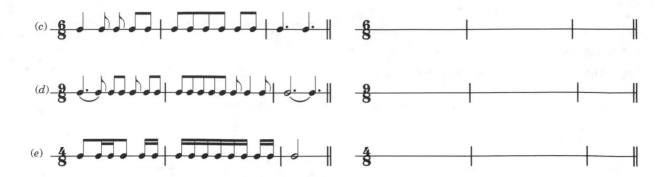

(*Return* to page *140.*)

EXERCISE 13-3
Correcting examples showing incorrect use of rests

Rewrite each exercise with correct rests.

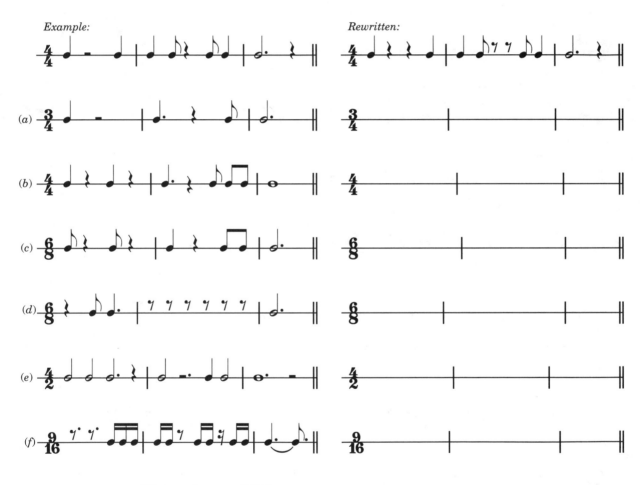

(*Return* to page *141.*)

EXERCISE 13-4
Rhythmic transcription

Rewrite each given rhythm *(a)* using the meter signatures indicated in *(b)* and *(c)*.

1. *(a)* (music notation in 2/8)

   (b) (music notation in 2/4)

   (c) (music notation in 2/2)

2. *(a)* (music notation in 3/2)

   (b) (music notation in 3/4)

   (c) (music notation in 3/8)

3. *(a)* (music notation in 4/4)

   (b) (music notation in 4/8)

   (c) (music notation in 4/2)

4. *(a)* (music notation in 6/4)

   (b) (music notation in 6/8)

   (c) (music notation in 6/16)

5. *(a)* (music notation in 9/8)

   (b) (music notation in 9/16)

   (c) (music notation in 9/4)

6. (a) $\mathbf{^{12}_{16}}$ ♪. | ♪. ♪. ♪. ♫♫ | ♩.‿ ♪. ♪ ♪ | ♩.‿ ♪. ‖

(b) $\mathbf{^{12}_{8}}$ | | | ‖

(c) $\mathbf{^{12}_{4}}$ | | | ‖

(*Return* to page *142.*)

EXERCISE 13-5 (Instructor)
Rhythmic dictation, simple meter

Follow basic directions given on pages 142–143. Observe headings below that list contents of exercises and/or changes in methods of writing. The instructor will play from correspondingly numbered melodies on pages 151–153. Upon completion of an exercise, the student may turn to these pages to check the answer.

Group A. Duple simple meter; ♩ = 1 beat; begin on the downbeat; use diagram.

Write answers when only the center line is given.

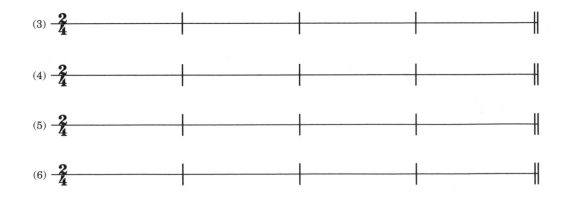

Group B. Triple simple meter: ♩ = 1 beat; begin on the downbeat; use diagram.

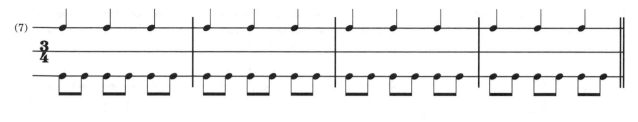

Write answers when only the center line is given.

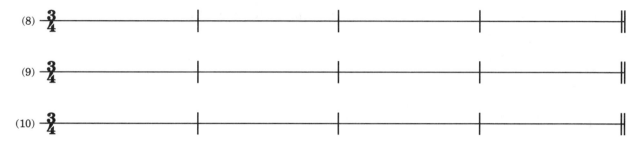

Group C. Quadruple simple meter; ♩ = 1 beat; begin on the downbeat; use diagram.

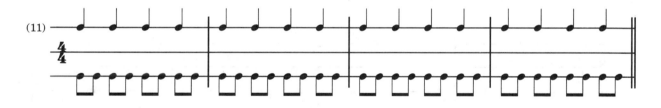

Write answers when only the center line is given.

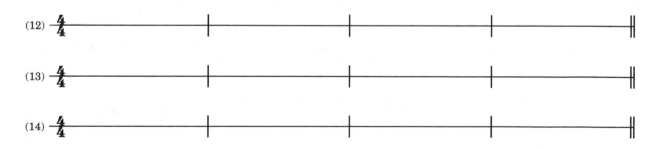

Group D. Simple meter; ♩ = 1 beat; begin on the upbeat; use diagram.

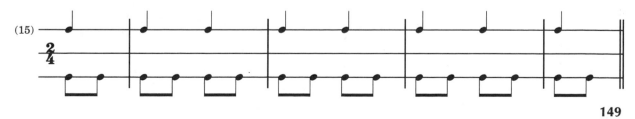

Write answers when only the center line is given.

Group E. Simple time; ♩ or ♪ = 1 beat; use diagram.

150

Write answers when only the center line is given.

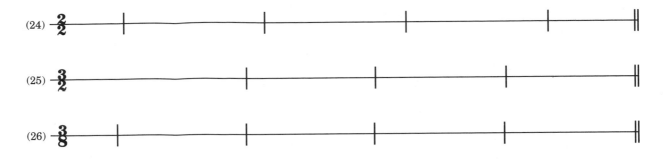

Group F. Melodies 27–36. Various simple meter signatures. Write your answers without benefit of lines, using any convenient piece of paper.

Instructor: Here are optional additional sources for dictation in simple meters.

1. Use any dictation material in Exercise 13-5, supplying a different but appropriate denominator in the meter signature. For example, using melody 1, announce the meter as ⅔ and play as written. The student's response should be

2. Use melodies from *Music for Sight Singing,* Chapters 1 and 2.

Dictation material for Exercise 13-5 (Instructor)

The symbol ' found in each of these exercises indicates a convenient place to divide the exercise into two sections, should the entire exercise prove to be overly long.

(5)

(6)

Group B

(7)

(8)

(9)

(10)

Group C

(11)

(12)

(13)

(14)

Group D

(15)

(16)

(17)

(18)

(19)

(20)

Group E

(21)

(22)

(23)

(24)

152

(25)   (26)

Group F
(27)   (28)

(29)   (30)

(31)   (32)

(33)   (34)

(35)   (36)

EXERCISE 13-6 (Instructor)

Rhythmic dictation, compound meter

Follow basic directions given on pages 142–143. Observe headings below that list contents of exercises and/or changes in methods of writing. The instructor will play from correspondingly numbered melodies on pages 156–158. Upon completion of an exercise, the student may turn to these pages to check the answer.

The instructor may divide any example into two two-measure sections if shorter exercises are desired.

Group A. Duple compound meter; ♩. = 1 beat; begin on the downbeat; use diagram.

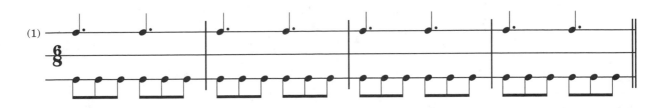

Write answers when only the center line is given.

Group B. Triple compound meter; ♩. = 1 beat; begin on the downbeat; use diagram.

Write answer when only the center line is given.

Group C. Quadruple compound meter; ♩. = 1 beat; begin on the downbeat; use diagram.

Write answer when only the center line is given.

(9)

Group D. Compound meter; ♩. = 1 beat; begin on the upbeat; use diagram. In compound meter, the upbeat may be a ♩. or a smaller note value. In the last measure, be sure that the note values consider the anacrusis.

(10)

(11)

(12)

Write answers when only the center line is given.

(13)

(14)

(15)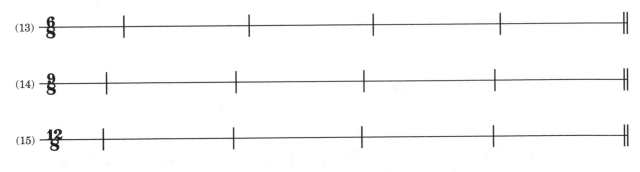

Group E. Compound meter; 𝅗𝅥. or ♪. = 1 beat; use diagram.

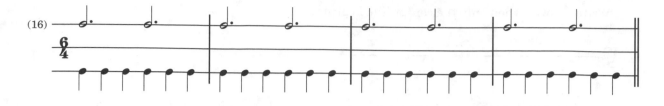

(17) The upbeat occurs on a beat division. The notation in the final measure will consequently be less than a full measure though a full measure of diagram is supplied.

    Group F. Melodies 18–24. Various compound meter signatures. Write your answer without benefit of diagrams or lines, using any convenient piece of paper.

    Instructor: Here are optional additional sources for dictation in compound meters.

    1. Use any dictation material in Exercise 13-6, supplying a different but appropriate denominator in the meter signature. For example, using melody 1, announce the meter as $\frac{6}{16}$ and play as written. The student's response should be

    2. Use melodies from *Music for Sight Singing,* Chapter 3 and Section 2 of Chapter 4.

Dictation material for Exercise 13-6

CHAPTER SUMMARY

1. *Beams* are used not only to replace flags in notation but also to clarify the location of beats in a measure—for example, $\frac{6}{8}$ ♪♪♪♪♪♪ and not ♪♪♪♪♪♪ .

2. *Dotted rests* are possible, but use of a rest sign instead of the dot is more common—for example, ⅞ ⅞ instead of ⅞. .

3. *Rests* should be written so as not to obscure the location of the beat—for example, $\frac{4}{4}$ ♩ ‡ ‡ ♩, not ♩ ▬ ♩.

CHAPTER FOURTEEN

Pitch:
Minor Scales

Accidentals, continued
Minor Scales: Natural (Pure), Harmonic, and Melodic Forms
Use of Minor Scales

We observed in Chapter Eleven that much of the music commonly performed today is based on two scale patterns, major and minor. We have learned that the sound of a scale is determined by the location of half steps and whole steps in the scale. Therefore, we can expect that the minor scale, which sounds different from the major scale, will have a different arrangement of half steps and whole steps. That is true, but there are actually three forms of the minor scale.

Writing certain minor scales requires use of accidentals in addition to sharps and flats. Therefore, we will first study the remaining accidentals: the *double sharp,* the *double flat,*[1] and the *natural sign* (listed on page 22).

Accidentals, continued:
Double Sharp, Double Flat, and Natural Sign

The *double sharp,* ✗, raises the pitch of a note two half steps or one whole step.

FIGURE 14-1   *The double sharp*

| ½ step | 1 step | | ½ step | 1 step |
| above f | above f | | above c | above c |

You can see that a note carrying a double sharp will always be enharmonic with another pitch name. In Figure 14-1, F✗ is enharmonic with the pitch G; C✗ is enharmonic with D.

The *double flat,* ♭♭, lowers the pitch of a note two half steps or one whole step.

---

[1]Though not found in major or minor scale spelling, the double flat is included here to complete the study of accidentals.

FIGURE 14-2 *The double flat*

| ½ step below d | 1 step below d | | ½ step below c | 1 step below c |

Dbb is enharmonic with C; Cbb is enharmonic with Bb.

The *natural sign,* ♮, cancels a previously used accidental or the accidental in the key signature.

FIGURE 14-3 *The natural sign*

Considerations in Using Accidentals

1. Any accidental placed before a note affects the pitch on that line or space only.

2. The effect of an accidental lasts only until the next bar line.

3. An accidental may be used optionally as a reminder. The preceding illustration is repeated here with the reminder in measure 2. The ♯ before C does not imply double sharp.

4. When it is necessary for a note to carry a double sharp or a double flat, the symbol ✗ or bb is always used, even if there is already a sharp or a flat in the signature.

5. When it is necessary to place a sharp or a double sharp before a note already carrying a flat, or to place a flat or a double flat before a note already carrying a sharp, the natural sign has traditionally preceded the new accidental, but in current practice it is not necessary.

Now that we are informed in the use of accidentals, we are ready to proceed to the study of the minor scale and its three forms, *natural (pure)*, *harmonic*, and *melodic*.

The Natural (Pure) Form of the Minor Scale

The *natural (pure)* form of the minor scale consists of a series of eight tones with the following succession of intervals between tones: whole step, half step, whole step, whole step, half step, whole step, whole step.

FIGURE 14-4   *Structure of the natural (pure) minor scale*

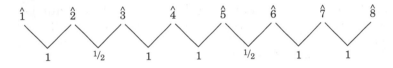

You can see that the natural minor scale consists of whole steps except between the second and third degrees and the fifth and sixth degrees, where the intervals are half steps. On a keyboard, notice that the natural minor scale starting on A involves only white keys because the half steps $\hat{2}$–$\hat{3}$ and $\hat{5}$–$\hat{6}$ coincide with the white keys B–C and E–F.

FIGURE 14-5   *The A minor scale, natural form*

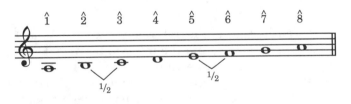

All natural minor scales starting on pitches other than A require one or more accidentals to maintain the characteristic half-step and whole-step pattern of the scale structure shown in Figure 14-4. For example, the natural minor scale of E requires one sharp.

FIGURE 14-6   *The E minor scale, natural form*

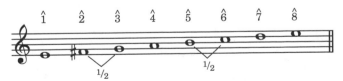

As with major scales, there are seven natural minor scales containing sharps and seven containing flats, which, including A minor (no sharps or flats) make up the fifteen natural minor scales.

FIGURE 14-7 *Table of minor scales and numbers of accidentals for the natural form*

Scale	A	E	B	F♯	C♯	G♯	D♯	A♯
Accidentals	none	1♯	2♯	3♯	4♯	5♯	6♯	7♯

Scale		D	G	C	F	B♭	E♭	A♭
Accidentals		1♭	2♭	3♭	4♭	5♭	6♭	7♭

Figure 14-7 also shows relationship by fifths between minor scales, as we saw earlier in major scales. The circle of fifths for minor scales will be studied in Chapter Sixteen.

Harmonic Form of the Minor Scale

The *harmonic* form of the minor scale is derived from the natural form by raising its seventh scale degree one half step. In the scale-degree numbers above the staff in Figures 14-8 and 14-9, ♯$\hat{7}$ means that the seventh scale degree is raised one half step in relation to the natural minor scale. In Figure 14-8, ♯$\hat{7}$ is G♯, raised one half step from G.

FIGURE 14-8 *The A minor scale, harmonic form*

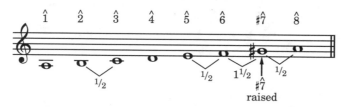

Notice that with the seventh raised, the interval between $\hat{6}$ and ♯$\hat{7}$ becomes a step-and-a-half (three half steps), and the interval between ♯$\hat{7}$ and $\hat{8}$ becomes a half step. Any natural minor scale can be changed to the harmonic form by raising the seventh scale degree. For example, the E natural minor scale shown in Figure 14-6 becomes the harmonic form when the seventh, D, is raised by the sharp.

FIGURE 14-9 *The E minor scale, harmonic form*

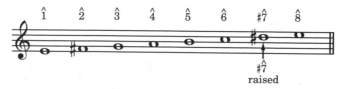

Melodic Form of the Minor Scale

The *melodic* form of the minor scale is derived from the natural form. Unlike all other major and minor scales, its ascending and descending forms are different. The ascending form of the melodic minor scale is the natural form but with *raised sixth and raised seventh degrees*. The descending form is the same as the natural form; the *seventh and sixth degrees are lowered* from their ascending form. The descending seventh and sixth scale degrees are often called "lowered," even though they are natural scale steps. Actually, they are lowered only in relation to the ascending form of the melodic minor scale.

The symbol ♯6̂ means that the sixth scale degree is raised one half step in relation to the natural minor scale. In Figure 14-10, ♯6̂ is F♯, raised one half step from F.

FIGURE 14-10   *The A minor scale, melodic form*

Any natural minor scale can be changed to the melodic form by (1) raising the sixth and seventh degrees in the ascending scale structure and (2) lowering the sixth and seventh scale degrees to their natural form in the descending scale structure. For example, the E natural minor scale shown in Figure 14-6 becomes the ascending melodic form shown in Figure 14-11 when the sixth scale degree, C, and the seventh degree, D, are raised by sharps. In descending, the seventh and the sixth are lowered by natural signs; the descending scale is identical to the natural form.

FIGURE 14-11   *The E minor scale, melodic form*

Figure 14-12 shows a comparison of the three forms of the minor scale.

FIGURE 14-12   *A minor: Natural, harmonic, and melodic forms*

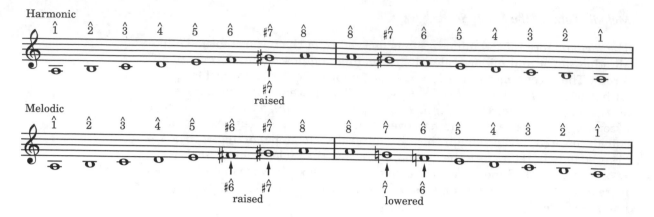

When 7 of a natural minor scale is already a sharped note, ♯7 indicates the use of a double sharp. In Figure 14-13a, ♯7̂ is F𝄪, raised from the F♯ of the natural minor scale. In the same way, when 6̂ and 7̂ of the natural minor scale are flatted, ♯6̂ and ♯7̂ indicate the use of the natural sign. In Figure 14-13b, ♯6̂ and ♯7̂ are G♮ and A♮, raised from G♭ and A♭ of the natural minor scale.

FIGURE 14-13   *Less-frequent use of accidentals with ♯6̂ and ♯7̂*

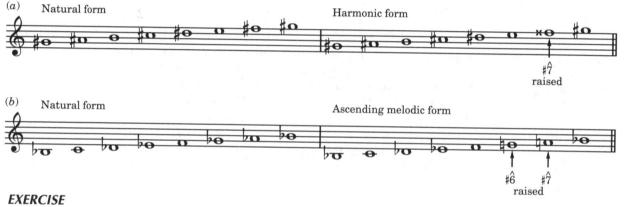

EXERCISE
14-1

As we discovered previously in working with major scales, it is useful to be able to spell (write) scales by letter names using appropriate accidentals. Remember that the name of the accidental comes after the letter. As a rule, the natural sign is optional in spelling.

FIGURE 14-14   *Spelling the B minor scale, three forms*

Natural:	B	C♯	D	E	F♯	G	A	B
Harmonic:	B	C♯	D	E	F♯	G	A♯	B
Melodic							
ascending:	B	C♯	D	E	F♯	G♯	A♯	B
descending:	B	A(♮)	G(♮)	F♯	E	D	C♯	B

EXERCISE
14-2

Use of Minor Scales

When an ascending melody displays raised sixth and seventh scale steps in a minor scale, it is obvious that these notes are from the melodic form. When descending, the melody usually displays lowered seventh and sixth scale steps.

In measure 3 of Figure 14-15, had the F♯ been F♮, the distance from it to the leading tone (F♮–G♯) would be more than a whole step. This interval of three half steps (a step-and-a-half[2]) has been found objectionable by most composers and performers, except in certain circumstances. Raising the sixth scale step eliminates this awkward interval while still retaining a leading tone.

FIGURE 14-15   *Use of the melodic form of the minor scale*

Bach, "Herr, straf mich nicht in deinem Zorn"

Confusion about scale formation, whether melodic or harmonic, often exists when the lowered sixth scale step and the raised seventh (or vice versa) are separated by intervening tones; this is the way in which these two tones are most frequently found.

FIGURE 14-16   *Characteristic tones in the minor scale*

Schubert, *Erstarrung*

Use of F♮ and G♯ from the A minor scale would seem to indicate the harmonic form of the scale. Yet each of these tones is used as being in the melodic form of the scale: The seventh scale step, G♯, is raised because it ascends; the sixth scale step, F♮, is lowered because it descends.

The melodic minor, as its name implies, is especially suited for melody writing because it explains situations involving the sixth and seventh scale steps. Therefore, most melodies in minor can be described as exhibiting characteristics of the melodic minor scale, unless obvious characteristics of the other forms are displayed.[3]

Melodies that display adjacent lowered sixth and raised seventh scale steps as in the harmonic minor scale are not rare, but are less commonly found.

---

[2]Called *augmented second;* included in the study of intervals, Chapter Nineteen.

[3]Intervallic leaps from the sixth and seventh scale steps may also be found in melodic writing. Explanation of these and other melodic considerations must be deferred until study of theory more advanced than is presented in this text.

FIGURE 14-17 *Use of harmonic form of the minor scale*

D minor, harmonic: D E F G A B♭ C♯ D

Melodies using the natural form of the scale are actually making use of the Aeolian mode, one of the *medieval modes,* a system of six early scale forms.[4] These were in general use up to the seventeenth century in composed music; they are frequently found in folk music of the Western world, both from that era and from later centuries; and in the present century, they have found favor in all styles of composition, including jazz and popular music. The folk song in Figure 14-18 uses the Aeolian mode, or natural form of the minor scale.

FIGURE 14-18 *Use of natural form of the minor scale*

D minor, natural: D E F G A B♭ C D

EXERCISE
14-3

[4]The medieval modes are described in Appendix C. Many examples of all modes in both composed and folk music can be found in *Music for Sight Singing*, fourth edition, Chapter 19.

EXERCISE 14-1

Writing minor scales on the staff

Write all fifteen minor scales, each in the three forms, as shown in the model in A minor at (1). Indicate location of half steps in the natural minor; indicate additional accidentals as needed in the harmonic and melodic forms. Observe that the scales are presented in the order of fifths, as shown in Figure 14-7.

Upon completion, these pages containing all fifteen minor scales, each in three forms, may be valuable for future reference.

(*Instructor:* The student should not use key signatures in this assignment. Minor key signatures will be studied in Chapter Sixteen.)

(1) A natural minor

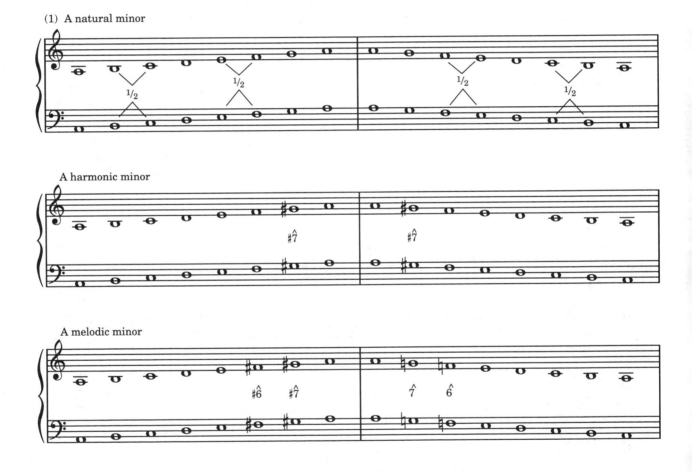

A harmonic minor

A melodic minor

(2) E natural minor

E harmonic minor

E melodic minor

(3) B natural minor

B harmonic minor

B melodic minor

(4) F# natural minor

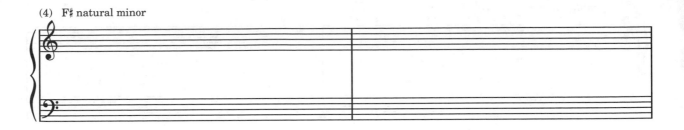

F# harmonic minor

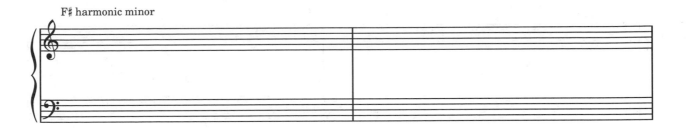

F# melodic minor

(5) C# natural minor

C# harmonic minor

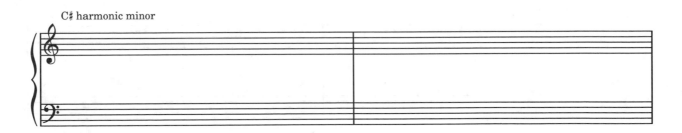

C# melodic minor

(6) G♯ natural minor

G♯ harmonic minor

G♯ melodic minor

(7) D♯ natural minor

D♯ harmonic minor

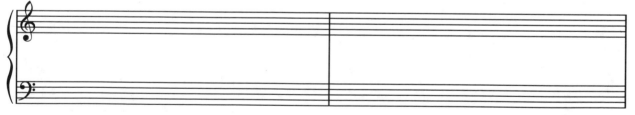

D♯ melodic minor

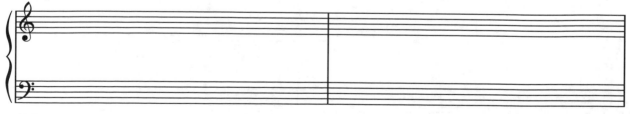

(8) A♯ natural minor

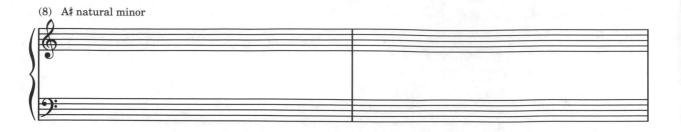

A♯ harmonic minor

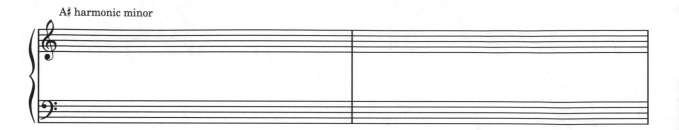

A♯ melodic minor

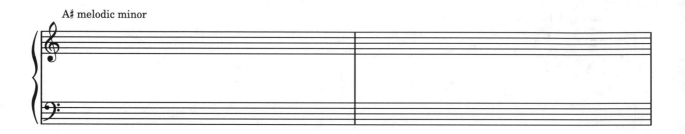

(9) D natural minor

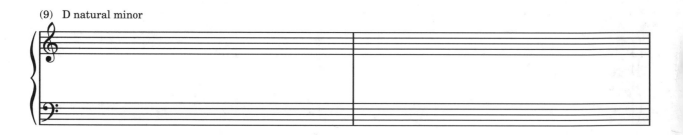

D harmonic minor

D melodic minor

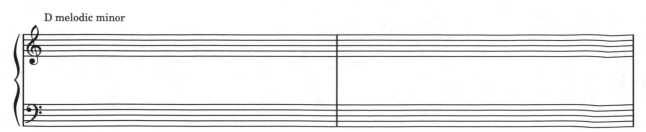

(10) G natural minor

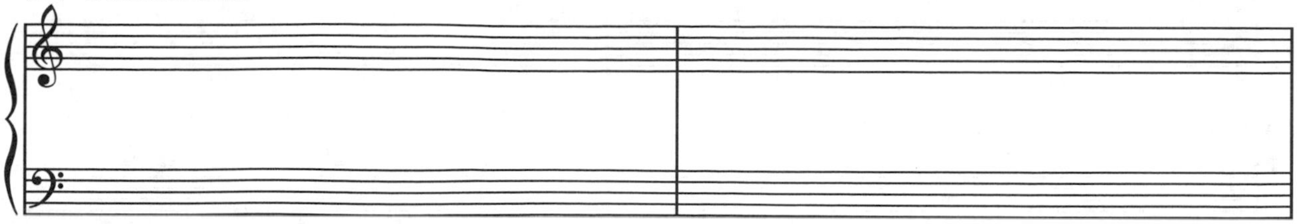

G harmonic minor

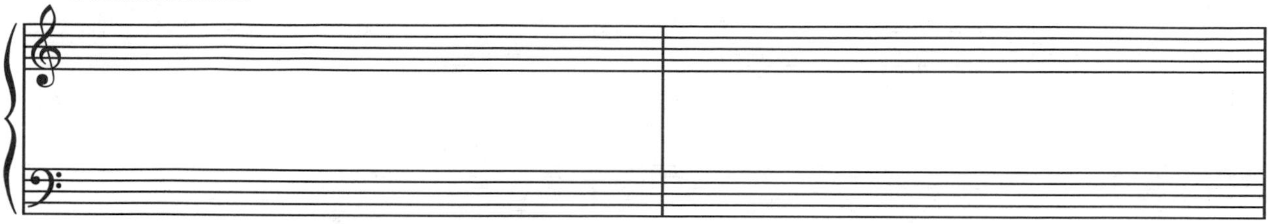

G melodic minor

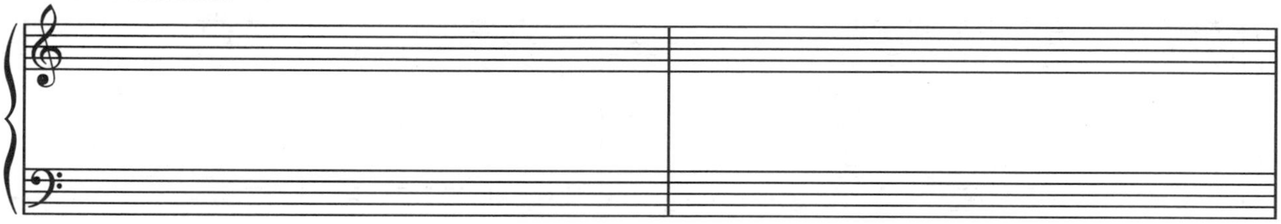

(11) C natural minor

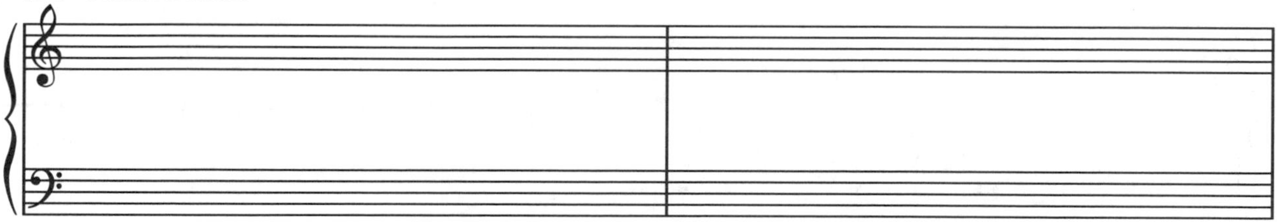

C harmonic minor

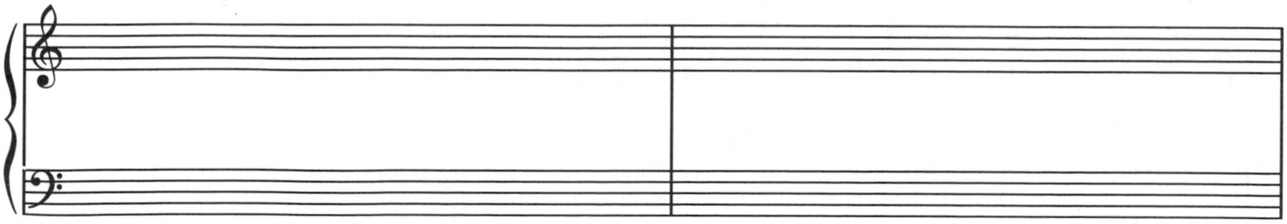

C melodic minor

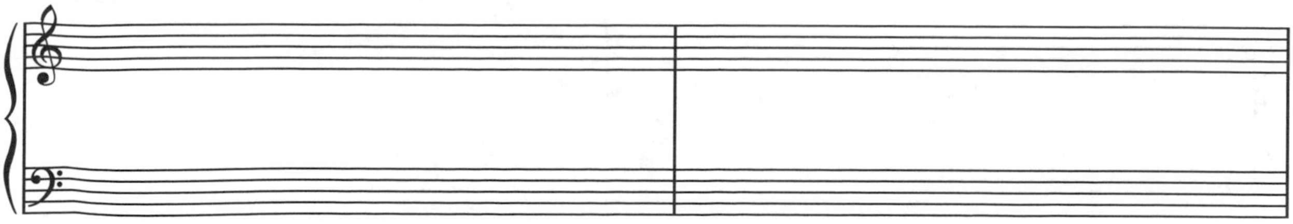

(12) F natural minor

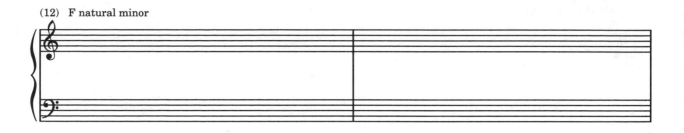

F harmonic minor

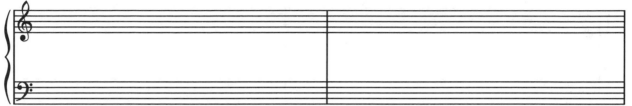

F melodic minor

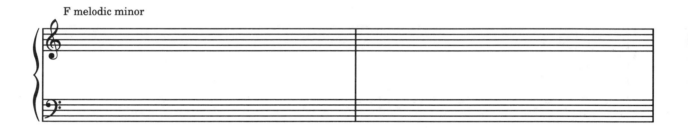

(13) B♭ natural minor

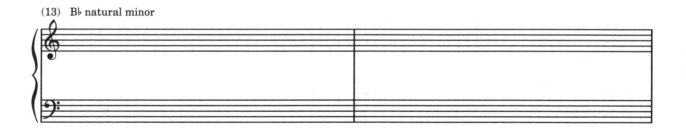

B♭ harmonic minor

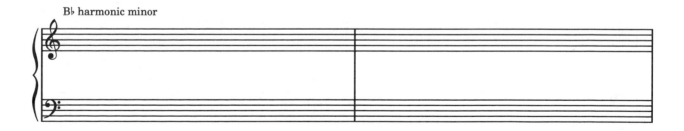

B♭ melodic minor

(14) E♭ natural minor

E♭ harmonic minor

E♭ melodic minor

(15) A♭ natural minor

A♭ harmonic minor

A♭ melodic minor

(*Return* to page *164.*)

EXERCISE 14-2

Spelling minor scales

Write minor scales using letter names with accidentals where needed. Indicate half steps in the natural minor and the additional accidentals needed in the harmonic and melodic forms.

Example: C minor (spell the three forms of the C minor scale)

Answer: Natural

C   D   E♭   F   G   A♭   B♭   C

        1/2   1/2

Harmonic

C   D   E♭   F   G   A♭   B♮   C

                                    $\sharp\hat{7}$

Melodic

(ascending)   (descending)

C   D   E♭   F   G   A♮   B♮   C | C   B♭   A♭   G   F   E♭   D   C

                                $\sharp\hat{6}$ $\sharp\hat{7}$ $\hat{7}$ $\hat{6}$

(1)   A minor

Natural

Harmonic

Melodic

(2)   E minor

Natural

Harmonic

Melodic

(3)   D minor

Natural

Harmonic

Melodic

(4)   G minor

Natural

Harmonic

Melodic

(5)   F# minor

Natural

Harmonic

Melodic

(6) F minor

Natural

Harmonic

Melodic

(7) C♯ minor

Natural

Harmonic

Melodic

For additional practice, spell the three forms of these scales: B♭ minor, G♯ minor, E♭ minor, D♯ minor, A♭ minor, and A♯ minor.

(*Return* to page *165*.)

EXERCISE 14-3

Identifying the forms of the minor scale

Each of the following melodies uses a particular form of the minor scale. The first scale tone (tonic) is given and shown on the staff (●). In the blank space, identify the scale as natural, harmonic, or melodic.

Example: Beethoven, Quartet, Op. 59, No. 3

A minor,_____ harmonic _____ form

(1)   Brahms, Ballade, Op. 118, No. 3

G minor,_____ form

(2) England

D minor, _____ form

(3) Bach, Lute Suite, BWV 996

E minor, _____ form

(4) "God Rest Ye Merry, Gentlemen"

C minor, _____ form

(5) Paganini, Caprice, Op. 1, No. 6

G minor, _____ form

CHAPTER SUMMARY

1. Accidentals used in writing minor scales are ♯, ♭, ♮, and ✕.

2. The *natural (pure) form* of the minor scale has half steps between $\hat{2}$ and $\hat{3}$ and between $\hat{5}$ and $\hat{6}$. All other intervals are whole steps. Whether ascending or descending, the pitches are the same.

3. The minor scale can be written/played beginning on fifteen different pitch locations. The natural form of A minor contains no accidentals. Scales starting on other pitches require one or more accidentals.

4. The *harmonic form* of the minor scale is like the natural form but with $\hat{7}$ *raised one half step.* This scale is characterized by the interval of a step and a half between $\hat{6}$ and ♯$\hat{7}$.

5. The *melodic form* of the minor scale, unlike all other major and minor scales, has different ascending and descending pitches. The ascending scale is the natural form but with *raised $\hat{6}$* and *raised $\hat{7}$*. The descending scale is the same as the natural form—that is, $\hat{7}$ and $\hat{6}$ are lowered from their ascending form.

CHAPTER FIFTEEN

Pitch: Minor Scales (continued)

Names of Scale Degrees in Minor
Playing Minor Scales at the Keyboard
Singing Minor Scales

Scale degrees in minor use the same names as scale degrees in major (Chapter Six), but because of the alteration of $\hat{6}$ and $\hat{7}$, additional terminology is required for *names of scale degrees in minor*.

Names of Scale Degrees in Minor

The term *leading tone* in minor refers to the tone one half step below the tonic, just as in major. Therefore, in minor, the leading tone is the raised seventh scale degree. When the seventh degree is not raised, it is known as the *subtonic*.

FIGURE 15-1   *The leading tone and the subtonic in the minor scale*

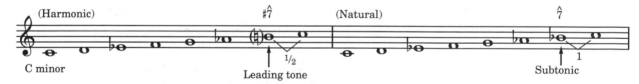

Submediant in minor refers to the natural sixth scale step. When the sixth scale step is raised, it is called *raised submediant*.

FIGURE 15-2   *The submediant and the raised submediant in the minor scale*

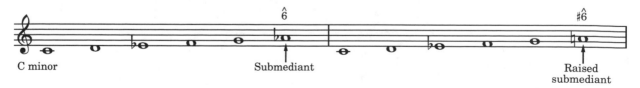

The ascending and descending melodic minor scale displays all possible scale-degree names.

FIGURE 15-3   *Names of the scale degrees in melodic minor*

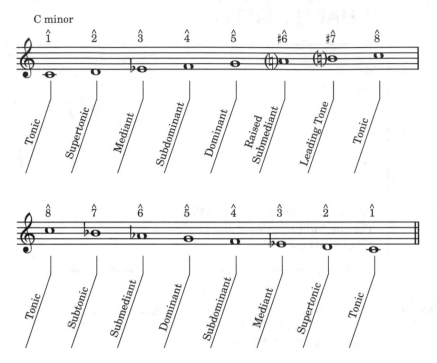

EXERCISES
15-1, 15-2

The minor scales are played following the same procedure, outlined in Chapter Ten for playing major scales.

Playing Minor Scales at the Keyboard[1]

The A Minor Scale

Playing the white key A and the next seven white keys above it produces an A minor scale (natural form). Playing only white keys from this given pitch A automatically places the half steps in their correct scale locations, between $\hat{2}$ and $\hat{3}$ and between $\hat{5}$ and $\hat{6}$, as shown in Figure 15-4.

FIGURE 15-4   *Playing the A minor scale, natural form*

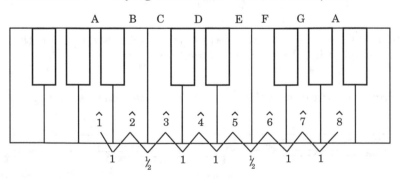

[1]See Appendix D for fingering of minor scales.

To play the harmonic form of the A minor scale, raise the seventh scale step G to G♯.

FIGURE 15-5   *Playing the A minor scale, harmonic form*

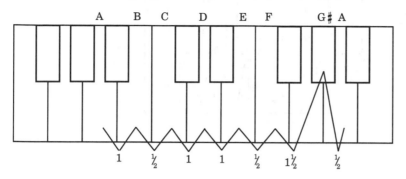

To play the melodic form of the A minor scale, raise the sixth scale step F to F♯ and the seventh scale step G to G♯ when ascending.

FIGURE 15-6   *Playing the A minor scale, melodic form*

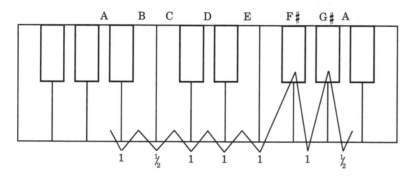

When descending, play the natural form of the scale as shown in Figure 15-4.

All Other Minor Scales Except Those on G♯, D♯, and A♯

To play any minor scale, keep in mind the familiar pattern for the natural form, with half steps between 2̂–3̂ and 5̂–6̂. Determine the succession of keys on the keyboard needed to produce the natural form, then alter as necessary for the harmonic and melodic forms. Figure 15-7 shows the keys needed to play the three forms of the B♭ minor scale.

FIGURE 15-7 *Playing the B♭ minor scale*

Natural form

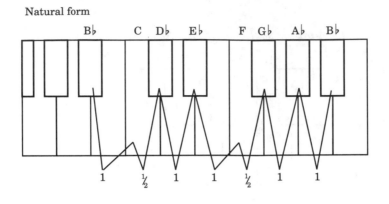

Harmonic form

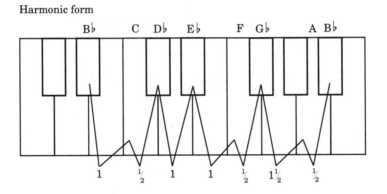

Melodic form

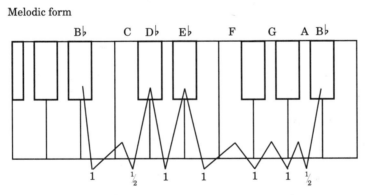

To play this scale descending, use the natural form.

Minor Scales on G♯, D♯, and A♯

Minor scales on G♯, D♯, and A♯ require the use of double sharps. These specific double sharps are used:

G♯ minor	♯$\hat{7}$	F✗
D♯ minor	♯$\hat{7}$	C✗
A♯ minor	♯$\hat{6}$	F✗
	♯$\hat{7}$	G✗

Here is how these doubly sharped notes appear on the keyboard:

FIGURE 15-8   *Locating C✗, F✗, and G✗ on the keyboard*

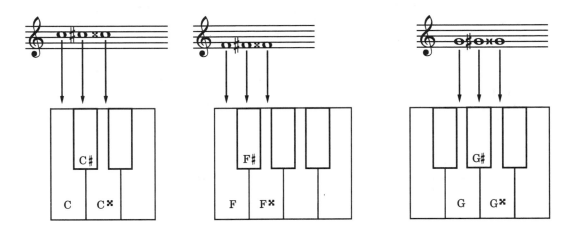

In the G♯ minor scale, shown in Figure 15-9, the x is used to raise the seventh scale degree (F♯) one half step to F×.

FIGURE 15-9 *Playing the G♯ minor scale*

Natural form

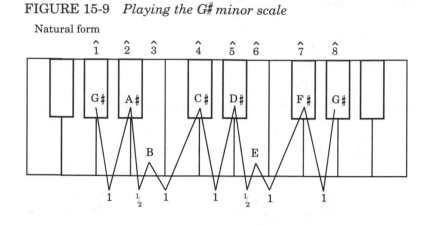

Harmonic form

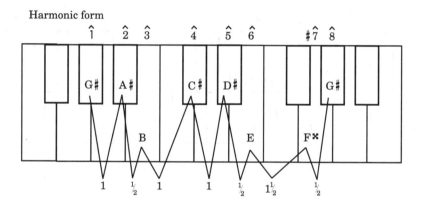

Melodic form

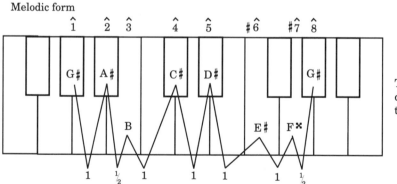

To play this scale descending, use the natural form.

In addition to the foregoing procedures, you will find that your previous experience in playing major scales will be helpful in playing minor scales, because of the similarities between a given major scale and the minor scale using the same tonic note.[2]

[2]Most, but not all, major and minor scales share a common tonic. Exceptions are major scales D♭, G♭, C♭, and minor scales G♯, D♯, and A♯.

Major scale →	lower its third scale step	=	minor scale, melodic form ascending
Major scale →	lower its third and sixth scale steps	=	minor scale, harmonic form
Major scale →	lower its third, sixth, and seventh scale steps	=	minor scale, natural form

FIGURE 15-10   *Comparing major and minor scales*

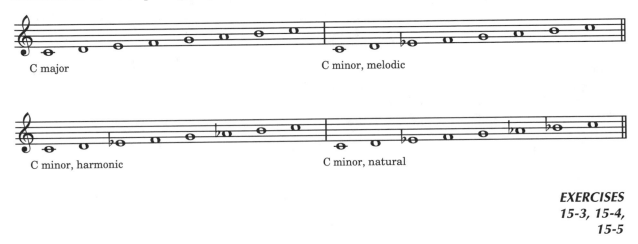

C major   C minor, melodic

C minor, harmonic   C minor, natural

EXERCISES 15-3, 15-4, 15-5

Singing Minor Scales

Minor scales can be sung using the three methods practiced in singing major scales: by numbers, by letter names, and by syllables. In public schools, the syllable most widely used for singing the tonic in a minor scale is *la*.[3] Figure 15-11 shows application of the three methods for singing all forms of minor scales.

FIGURE 15-11   *Singing the three forms of the minor scale on numbers, letter names, and syllables, in C minor*

Natural

Sing Numbers :	1	2	3	4	5	6	7	8	8	7	6	5	4	3	2	1
Letters :	c	d	e♭	f	g	a♭	b♭	c	c	b♭	a♭	g	f	e♭	d	c
Syllables :	la	ti	do	re	mi	fa	sol	la	la	sol	fa	mi	re	do	ti	la

[3]The relationship of syllables in major and minor will be shown in Chapter Seventeen.

Harmonic

Sing Numbers :	1	2	3	4	5	6	7	8	8	7	6	5	4	3	2	1
Letters :	c	d	e♭	f	g	a♭	b	c	c	b	a♭	g	f	e♭	d	c
Syllables :	la	ti	do	re	mi	fa	si	la	la	si	fa	mi	re	do	ti	la

sol raised is *si* (see)[4]

Melodic

Sing Numbers :	1	2	3	4	5	6	7	8	8	7	6	5	4	3	2	1
Letters :	c	d	e♭	f	g	a	b	c	c	b♭	a♭	g	f	e♭	d	c
Syllables :	la	ti	do	re	mi	fi	si	la	la	sol	fa	mi	re	do	ti	la

fa raised is *fi* (fee)[4]

EXERCISE 15-6

[4]For chromatic syllables, see Appendix C.

EXERCISE 15-1

Naming scale degrees in minor

Supply names of the scale degrees for the scales given below.

(1) E minor, natural form

(2) E minor, harmonic form

(3) E minor, melodic form

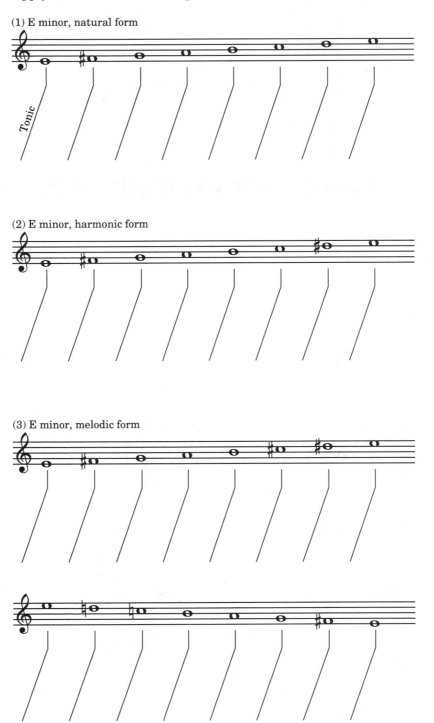

(4) F♯ minor, melodic form (only)

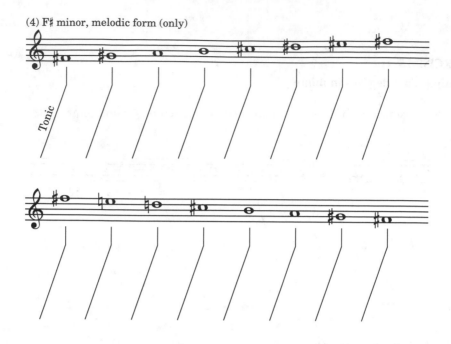

EXERCISE 15-2
Identifying scale degrees in minor

Give the pitch name for each scale degree listed; the tonic is identified.

(1) Tonic   A
     Leading tone   G♯
     Dominant   E
     Supertonic   _____
     Subtonic   _____
     Submediant   _____
     Subdominant   _____
     Mediant   _____
     Raised submediant _____

(3) Tonic   B
     Mediant   _____
     Subtonic   _____
     Submediant   _____
     Leading tone   _____
     Supertonic   _____
     Raised submediant _____
     Dominant   _____
     Subdominant   _____

(2) Tonic   D
     Subdominant   _____
     Subtonic   _____
     Mediant   _____
     Raised submediant _____
     Submediant   _____
     Supertonic   _____
     Dominant   _____
     Leading tone   _____

(4) Tonic   G
     Submediant   _____
     Supertonic   _____
     Subtonic   _____
     Leading tone   _____
     Subdominant   _____
     Mediant   _____
     Raised submediant _____
     Dominant   _____

(*Return* to page *180.*)

EXERCISE 15-3

Playing minor scales at the keyboard

Using the example as a guide, (1) indicate by arrows and by numbers 1–8 the keys on the keyboard required to produce the sound of the scale; (2) indicate whole steps and half steps; and (3) play the scale (for the melodic form, play ascending and descending).

Example: B♭ minor

Natural form

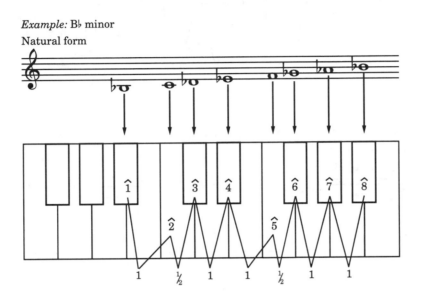

Harmonic form

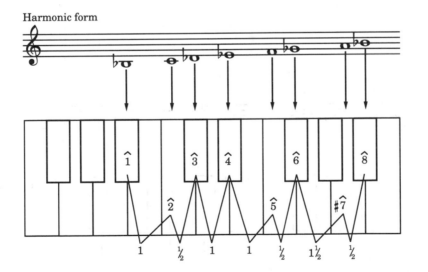

Melodic form (When descending, use natural form)

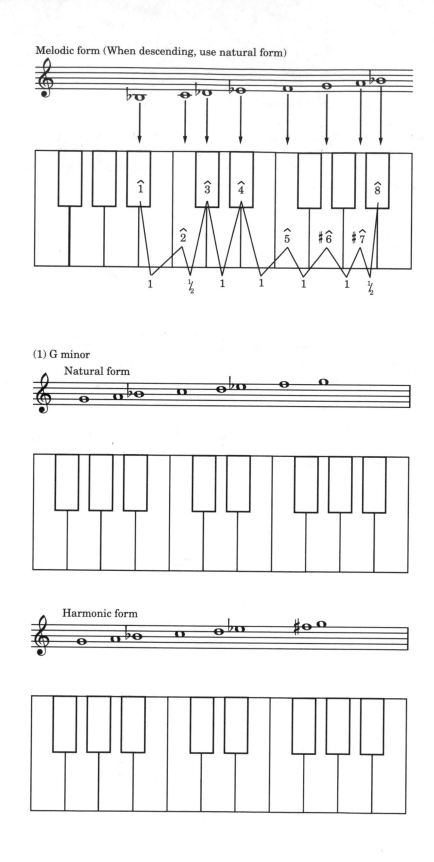

(1) G minor

Natural form

Harmonic form

Melodic form, ascending

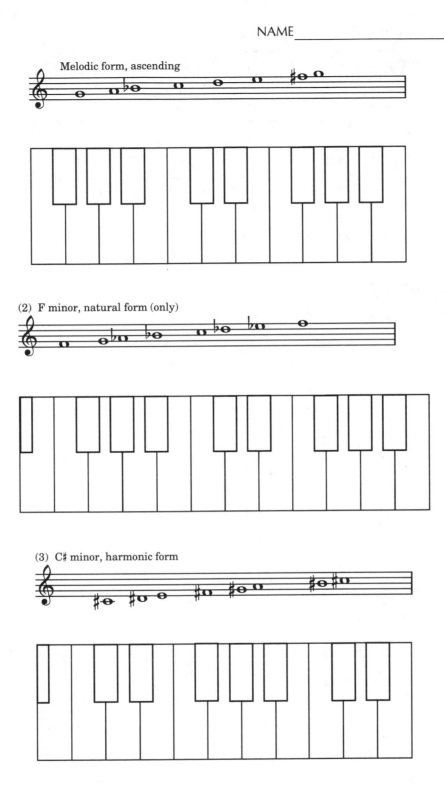

(2) F minor, natural form (only)

(3) C♯ minor, harmonic form

(4) D# minor, melodic form, ascending

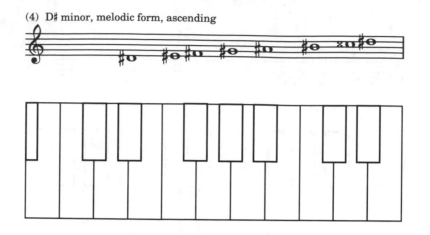

EXERCISE 15-4

Playing minor scales at the keyboard

This exercise is similar to Exercise 15-3, but without the staff. Number the keys, indicate whole steps and half steps, and then play.

(1) E minor, natural form

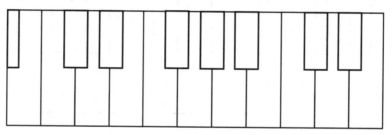

(2) D minor, harmonic form

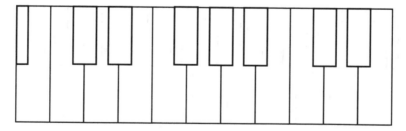

NAME

(3) C minor, melodic form, ascending

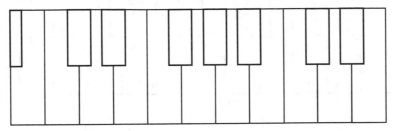

(4) F♯ minor, natural form

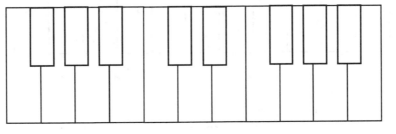

(5) B minor, harmonic form

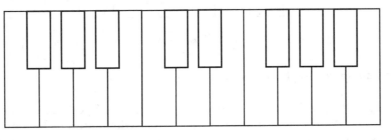

(6) G♯ minor, melodic form, ascending

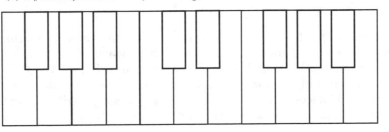

(7) E♭ minor, natural form

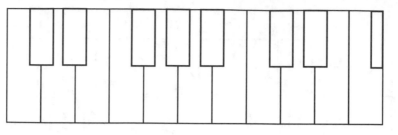

(8) A♯ minor, harmonic form

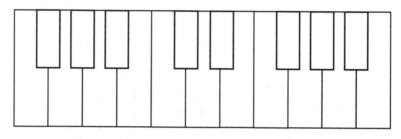

(9) A♭ minor, melodic form, ascending

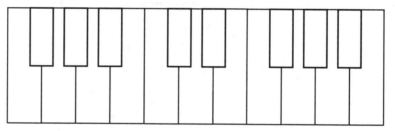

EXERCISE 15-5

Playing all minor scales at the keyboard

Play any form of any of the fifteen minor scales. Spell each scale as you play it. Be sure that each interval is the correct whole step or half step. Play the scale ascending and descending for one octave. You may refer to the scales you wrote in Exercise 14-1. Practice until you can play without looking at the music.

(*Return* to page *185.*)

EXERCISE 15-6

Singing minor scales

Choose any pitch name that can be used as the tonic of a minor scale. Sing the three forms of the scale in each of three ways: (1) with numbers, (2) with letter names, and (3) with syllables, as shown in Figure 15-16. Sing each of the fifteen scales in this manner. You may sing from the scales you wrote in Exercise 14-1. If necessary, play the scale as you sing until you feel able to sing without the piano. Use the piano at any time to check your accuracy.

CHAPTER SIXTEEN

Pitch: Minor Key Signatures

Derivation of Key Signatures in Minor
Minor Key Signatures on the Staff
Circle of Fifths for Minor Keys

Most of what you learned about major key signatures in Chapter Eleven will apply equally to the study of minor key signatures. Differences between the two exist only because minor key signatures are derived from minor scale spellings.

Derivation of Key Signatures in Minor

The key signature in minor uses the accidentals found in the natural (pure) form of the minor scale. When the accidentals in a given scale are extracted and grouped together, they form a minor key signature. Including A minor (no sharps or flats), there are fifteen minor key signatures.

It is easy to see in Figure 16-1 that minor keys are related to each other by perfect fifth, just as major keys are. As each new sharp is added, the new key name is a perfect fifth higher; for example, from E minor (one sharp) to B minor (two sharps) is up a perfect fifth. In the same way, as each new flat is added, the new key name is a perfect fifth lower; for example, from D minor (one flat) to G minor (two flats) is down a perfect fifth.

Observe also that the last sharp in a given key is $\hat{2}$ of the minor scale and that the last flat is $\hat{6}$. Examples:

G♯ is the last sharp. If $\hat{2}$ is G♯, $\hat{1}$ is F♯.
D♭ is the last flat. If $\hat{6}$ is D♭, $\hat{1}$ is F.

FIGURE 16-1 *Number and names of accidentals for minor key signatures*

(1) Name of minor key	(2) Number of #'s or ♭'s in key signature	(3) Names of #'s or ♭'s						
A minor	none							
E minor	1♯	f♯						
B minor	2♯	f♯,	c♯					
F♯ minor	3♯	f♯,	c♯,	g♯				
C♯ minor	4♯	f♯,	c♯,	g♯,	d♯			
G♯ minor	5♯	f♯,	c♯,	g♯,	d♯,	a♯		
D♯ minor	6♯	f♯,	c♯,	g♯,	d♯,	a♯,	e♯	
A♯ minor	7♯	f♯,	c♯,	g♯,	d♯,	a♯,	e♯,	b♯
(A minor)	(none)							
D minor	1♭	b♭						
G minor	2♭	b♭,	e♭					
C minor	3♭	b♭,	e♭,	a♭				
F minor	4♭	b♭,	e♭,	a♭,	d♭			
B♭ minor	5♭	b♭,	e♭,	a♭,	d♭,	g♭		
E♭ minor	6♭	b♭,	e♭,	a♭,	d♭,	g♭,	c♭	
A♭ minor	7♭	b♭,	e♭,	a♭,	d♭,	g♭,	c♭,	f♭

**EXERCISES
16-1, 16-2**

Minor Key Signatures on the Staff

The order of accidentals of the key signature on the staff is the same for minor as for major. In Figure 16-2, the lowercase letter *m* is the commonly used abbreviation for *minor*.

FIGURE 16-2 *Minor key signatures*

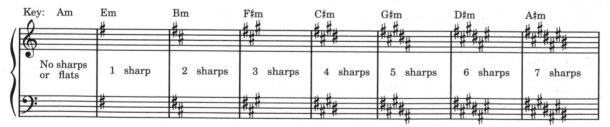

With practice, you should be able to reproduce the circle of fifths for minor keys (from memory) in *one minute*. Compare your results with Figure 16-3.

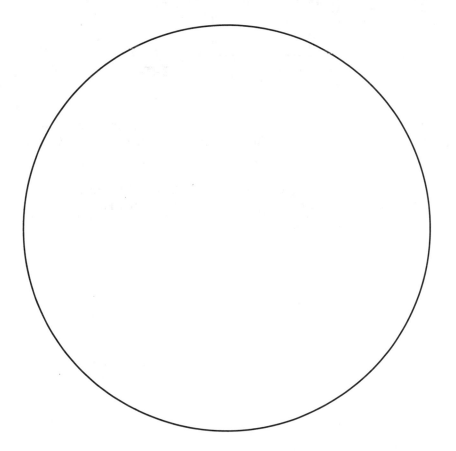

CHAPTER SUMMARY

1. The function of the key signature is the same in minor as it is in major. As in major, the terms *keynote* and *tonic* refer to the first note of the scale.

2. The three forms of the minor scale (natural, harmonic, and melodic) use a variety of accidentals, but the minor key signature is determined solely by those sharps or flats in the natural (pure) form of the scale.

3. The order for minor keys is:

	Em	Bm	F#m	C#m	G#m	D#m	A#m
Am	1#	2#	3#	4#	5#	6#	7#

	Dm	Gm	Cm	Fm	B♭m	E♭m	A♭m
Am	1♭	2♭	3♭	4♭	5♭	6♭	7♭

4. The order of accidentals of the key signature and their position on the staff are the same whether major or minor.

5. The circle of fifths for minor keys enables us to organize knowledge of keys, including relationships of keys, number of accidentals required for each signature, and enharmonic keys.

6. The circle of fifths for minor keys is built exactly like that for major, except that the starting point of no sharps or flats is Am instead of C.

CHAPTER SEVENTEEN

Major and Minor Key Relationships

The Circle of Fifths for Major and Minor Keys Together
Relative Keys
Parallel Keys
Solmization in Relative Major and Minor Keys

Although major and minor keys have been covered in two separate presentations, certain relationships exist between the two systems. The fact that there are seven sharp keys, seven flat keys, and one key without accidentals in each of major and minor is evidence that such a relationship exists. This evidence can be demonstrated graphically through further study of the circle of fifths.

The Circle of Fifths for Major and Minor Keys Together

We have already built one circle of fifths for major keys and another circle of fifths for minor keys. Each started with the key signature of no sharps or flats at the top of the circle and progressed clockwise by fifths up (sharp keys) and counterclockwise by fifths down (flat keys). This being so, we should be able to place major and minor keys in the same circle. Figure 17-1 shows such a circle, with the major keys outside the circle and the minor keys inside the circle.

At each point in the circle are two keys that share the same accidentals (including the pairs at the bottom of the circle); these are known as *relative keys*.

Relative Keys

A pair of keys, one major and one minor, located at the same point in the circle of fifths will each have the same accidentals; these keys are known as *relative keys*—for example, G major and E minor, each with one sharp. Each key of any pair of relative keys will have the same key signature.

Three locations at the bottom of the circle show the enharmonic pairs of keys, major enharmonic keys outside the circle and minor enharmonic keys inside the circle. The relative keys are connected by a bracket—for example, B major and G# minor (five sharps).

FIGURE 17-1 *The circle of fifths for major and minor keys together*

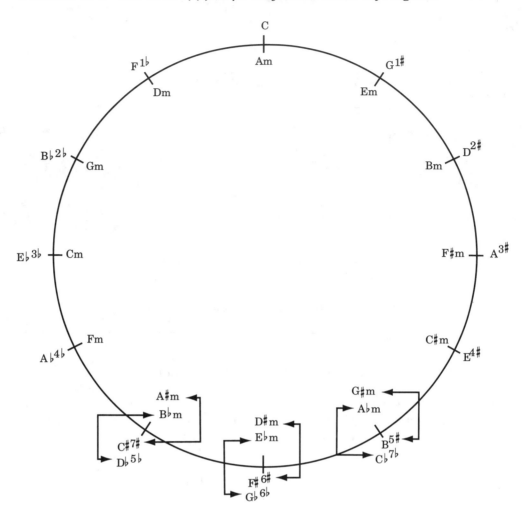

EXERCISE
17-1

Figure 17-2 shows the relationship between the tonic notes of each pair of relative keys. From a given tonic note, the tonic of its relative key can be located as follows.

1. From $\hat{1}$ in a major key, $\hat{6}$ of that key will be $\hat{1}$ of the relative minor key. For example, when C is $\hat{1}$ in major, $\hat{6}$ of C major (A) will be $\hat{1}$ of A minor.
2. From $\hat{1}$ in a minor key, $\hat{3}$ of that key will be $\hat{1}$ of the relative major key. For example, when A is $\hat{1}$ in minor, $\hat{3}$ of A minor (C) will be $\hat{1}$ of C major.

The resulting interval between the tonic notes of relative keys is always a *minor third,*[1] three half steps encompassing three letter names, as shown in Figure 17-3a. Notice also that when $\hat{1}$ in major occupies a line, $\hat{1}$ in the relative minor occupies the next lower line (with an appropriate accidental if needed), and when $\hat{1}$ in major occupies a space, $\hat{1}$ in the relative minor occupies the next lower space, as seen in Figure 17-3b and c, and in any pair of tonic notes in Figure 17-2.

[1]Intervals, including the minor third, will be studied in Chapters Eighteen and Nineteen.

FIGURE 17-2 *Identical signatures for relative major and minor keys*

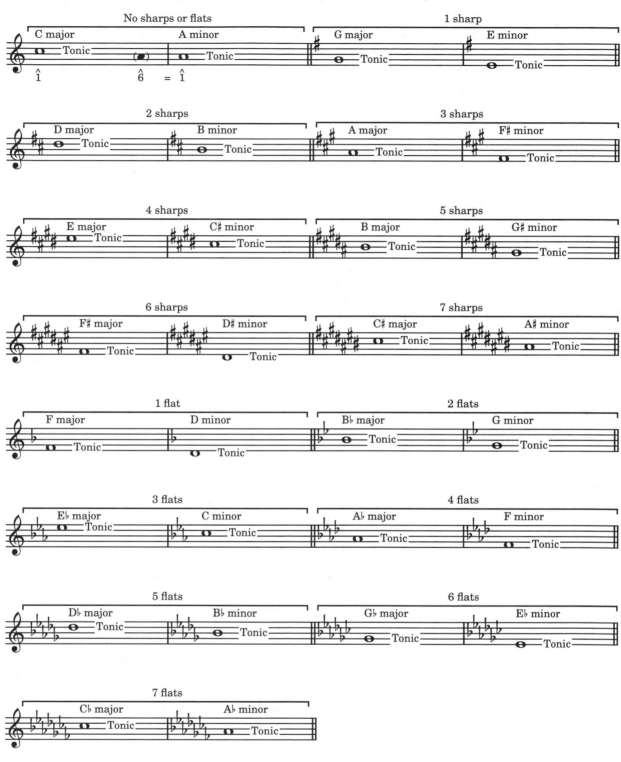

FIGURE 17-3   *Locating tonic notes of relative keys*

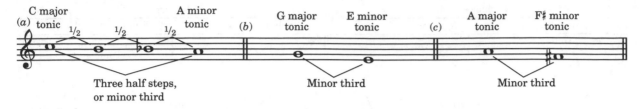

EXERCISES
17-2, 17-3

In an additional type of relationship, two keys are referred to as *parallel keys*.

Parallel Keys

Parallel keys are keys with the same tonic note but with completely different key signatures. For example, C major and C minor are parallel keys: They share C as tonic but have different key signatures. Here are two other examples:

FIGURE 17-4   *Parallel keys*

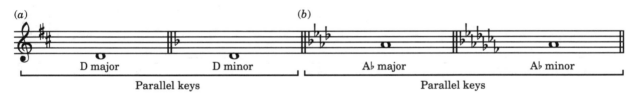

EXERCISE
17-4

Solmization in Relative Major and Minor Keys

Relationship between major and minor keys is further revealed in the application of syllables to the scales. When the system of the seven basic syllables was formulated, the intention was for *mi-fa* and *ti-do* to represent half steps and for any other pair of adjacent syllables to represent whole steps in both major and minor scale formations. For these pairs of syllables to coincide with their corresponding half steps and whole steps, the minor scale necessarily starts on *la,* as shown in Figure 17-5. Observe also that $\hat{1}$ *(do)* of the major scale is identical to $\hat{3}$ *(do)* of the relative minor scale and that $\hat{1}$ *(la)* of the minor scale is identical to $\hat{6}$ *(la)* of the major scale.

208

FIGURE 17-5 *The syllabic relationship between major and minor scales*

C Major and Its Relative Key, A Minor

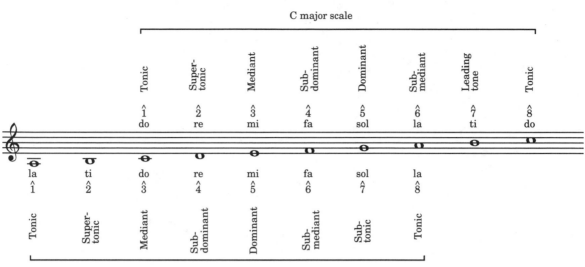

The syllables *fi* (fee) for ♯$\hat{6}$ and *si* (see) for ♯$\hat{7}$ are used as required in minor scales other than the natural form, as shown in Figure 15-11.

***EXERCISE
17-5***

FIGURE 17-5 *The syllabic relationship between major and minor scales*

C Major and Its Relative Key, A Minor

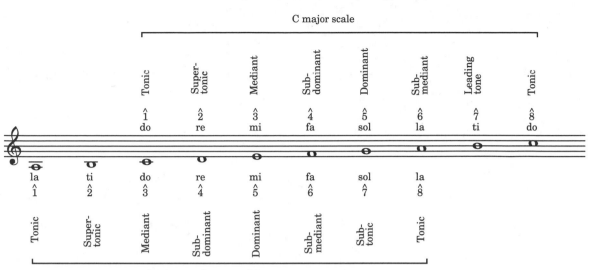

A minor scale, natural form

The syllables *fi* (fee) for ♯$\hat{6}$ and *si* (see) for ♯$\hat{7}$ are used as required in minor scales other than the natural form, as shown in Figure 15-11.

EXERCISE
17-5

(11) 3 flats   _____ _____

(12) 4 sharps   _____ _____

(13) 6 sharps   _____ _____

(14) 7 sharps   _____ _____

(15) 5 flats   _____ _____

(*Return* to page *208.*)

EXERCISE 17-4

Naming key signatures of parallel keys

State the key signatures for both the major and the minor keys that have the given pitch as tonic.

	Major	*Minor*
(1) A♭	4♭	7♭
(2) E	_____	_____
(3) F♯	_____	_____
(4) G	_____	_____
(5) C	_____	_____
(6) E♭	_____	_____
(7) C♯	_____	_____
(8) B	_____	_____
(9) D	_____	_____
(10) A	_____	_____
(11) F	_____	_____
(12) B♭	_____	_____

(*Return* to page *208.*)

EXERCISE 17-5

Solmization of major and minor scales

(*a*) Starting on any pitch as *do,* sing a major scale ascending and descending. Then sing down from *do* to *la* and sing the natural form of the relative minor scale.

(*b*) Starting on any pitch as *la,* sing the natural minor scale. Then, sing up from *la* to *do,* and sing the relative major scale.

213

CHAPTER SUMMARY

1. Major and minor systems can be combined on one circle of fifths. This device enables us to organize knowledge of keys, including relationships of major and minor keys, number of accidentals for each key signature, and enharmonic keys.

2. At the top of the circle, both C major and A minor occupy the position for no sharps or flats. A feature of this circle is that at any given point the number of accidentals serves both the major and the minor key.

3. *Relative keys* share the same signature—for example, G major and E minor (one sharp)

4. The circle of fifths (combined) readily shows relative keys occupying the same point on the circle. Another method to determine relative key is to count down three half steps from a major tonic to find the relative minor tonic, or vice versa. Still another method is to consider that the submediant of a major scale is identical to the tonic of the relative minor, or vice versa.

5. *Parallel keys* are keys with the same tonic but with different key signatures—for example, C major and C minor.

CHAPTER EIGHTEEN

Intervals: Major and Perfect

Interval
Naming the Interval
Major and Perfect Intervals in the Major Scale
Analysis of Major and Perfect Intervals in the Major Scale
Simple and Compound Intervals

At various times in the preceding chapters, we have had occasion to refer to *intervals;* the term itself was identified as early as Chapter Two, page 20. We have used intervals of the half step, the whole step, and the octave to help us in constructing the scale, the perfect fifth to help us understand the circle of fifths, and the minor third for locating relative keys. We will now make a more complete study, beginning with a review of the definition of the term *interval.*

Interval

An *interval* is the distance or difference between two pitches. A *harmonic interval* is the sounding of two pitches simultaneously; a *melodic interval* is the sounding of two pitches consecutively.

FIGURE 18-1   *Harmonic and melodic intervals*

Harmonic   Melodic interval   Melodic interval
interval   ascending   descending

Since any combination of two different pitches will produce an interval, it follows that many types of intervals exist, requiring a system for *naming intervals.*

Naming the Interval

The name of an interval is made up of two parts: a noun of *quantity* and an adjective of *quality*.

1. The *quantity* of an interval is determined by counting the number of staff degrees or the number of letter names encompassed. For example, the interval G–B is a third because it encompasses three staff degrees and also three letter names.

FIGURE 18-2   *The quantity of an interval*

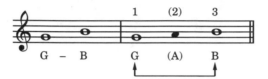

The names that indicate quantity are *prime, second, third, fourth, fifth, sixth, seventh,* and *octave.*[1]

2. The *quality* of an interval distinguishes its special characteristic. The significance of quality is demonstrated in Figure 18-3. The intervals G–B and G–B♭ are both thirds, but G–B consists of four half steps, whereas G–B♭ contains only three half steps. The quality of *major* or *minor* indicates the difference.

FIGURE 18-3   *Difference in interval quality*

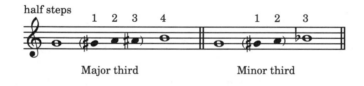

The adjectives of quality are *major, minor, perfect, diminished,* and *augmented.*

Every interval is named by the combined terms for quality and quantity, such as *major third* or *perfect fifth.* These are the possible combinations:

major and minor[2]	refer only to	seconds, thirds, sixths, and sevenths
perfect[2]	refers only to	fourths, fifths, and octaves
diminished and augmented	refer to	any interval

---

[1]Intervals larger than an octave are *compound* intervals. See page 219.

[2]The terms *major* and *minor* when applied to intervals simply mean larger or smaller. For an explanation of *perfect,* see footnote 6 on page 250.

Other combinations, such as "major fourth" or "perfect third," do not exist.

We will begin our study of intervals with those found above the tonic tone of a major scale.

Major and Perfect Intervals in the Major Scale

In a major scale, distance from the tonic note up to each of the other scale tones provides seven intervals. The following table gives these, with their interval names.

from	up to	the interval name is	abbreviated
$\hat{1}$	$\hat{2}$	Major Second or whole step	M2
$\hat{1}$	$\hat{3}$	Major Third	M3
$\hat{1}$	$\hat{4}$	Perfect Fourth	P4
$\hat{1}$	$\hat{5}$	Perfect Fifth	P5
$\hat{1}$	$\hat{6}$	Major Sixth	M6
$\hat{1}$	$\hat{7}$	Major Seventh	M7
$\hat{1}$	$\hat{8}$	Perfect Octave	P8
$\hat{1}$	$\hat{1}$	Perfect Prime or Unison[3]	P1 (PP)

FIGURE 18-4   *Intervals in the C major scale*

These intervals are found in the same order in any major scale—for example, D major.

FIGURE 18-5   *Intervals in the D major scale*

[3]The perfect prime, although not an interval by previous definition, is the name given to two notes of the same pitch. When the two pitches sound together (for example, a soprano and an alto singing the same pitch), the PP is commonly called a *unison*.

In the major scale, only major and perfect intervals occur above the tonic note.

FIGURE 18-6 *Specific major and perfect intervals in the major scale*

Major Intervals		Perfect Intervals	
M2	$\hat{1}$–$\hat{2}$	P4	$\hat{1}$–$\hat{4}$
M3	$\hat{1}$–$\hat{3}$	P5	$\hat{1}$–$\hat{5}$
M6	$\hat{1}$–$\hat{6}$	P8	$\hat{1}$–$\hat{8}$
M7	$\hat{1}$–$\hat{7}$		

EXERCISE
18-1

Intervals that will be studied later use the adjectives *minor, diminished,* and *augmented.*

Analysis of Major and Perfect Intervals in the Major Scale

In analyzing an interval, assume the lower note to be $\hat{1}$ (tonic) and count the scale degrees to the upper note. The number of scale degrees will determine the name of the interval. For example, D up to A:

A appears as $\hat{5}$ in the D major scale; therefore, D up to A is a perfect fifth.

Also, B♭ up to G:

G appears as $\hat{6}$ in the B♭ major scale; therefore B♭ up to G is a major sixth.

This procedure for analysis, where the lower note is assumed to be $\hat{1}$, is the same for harmonic intervals. For example, G and B:

B appears as $\hat{3}$ in the G major scale; therefore, the interval is a major third.

The procedure is the same for descending melodic intervals. Calculate from the lower note of the interval. For example, to determine the name of the interval A down to E, calculate from E, the lower note, up to A.

A appears as $\hat{4}$ in E major. Since E up to A is a perfect fourth, it follows that A down to E, the same interval, is also a perfect fourth.

EXERCISE
18-2

Simple and Compound Intervals

Intervals encompassing a perfect octave or less are known as *simple* intervals. Intervals larger than a perfect octave are called *compound* intervals because they include an octave and an additional *simple* interval. Like simple intervals, compound intervals are designated by the number of scale degrees spanned.

FIGURE 18-7 *Simple and compound intervals in the C major scale*

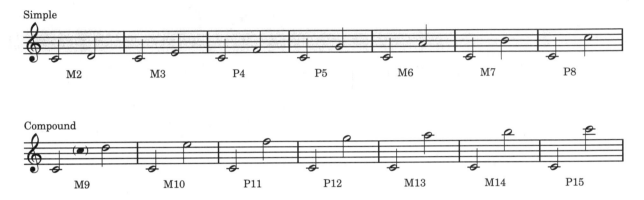

The compound interval is often computed as the addition of the quantity 8 (the octave) and the quantity of the simple interval. In Figure 18-8a, the octave C–C (P8) has been added to C–D (M2). Since the upper C has been counted twice, the intervallic sum of the two intervals is one number less than the arithmetical number (P8 + M2 = M9, not M10).

Compound intervals larger than the ninth are often reduced to simple terminology. The perfect twelfth (P12) of Figure 18-8b and c may be called a perfect fifth when distinction between the two intervals is not critical.

FIGURE 18-8 *Analysis of compound intervals*

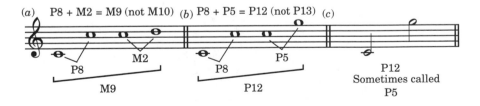

EXERCISE
18-3

CHAPTER SUMMARY

1. An interval is the difference or distance between two pitches.

2. A *harmonic interval* is the sounding of two pitches simultaneously; a *melodic interval* is the sounding of two pitches consecutively.

3. An interval is named by *quality* and *quantity*. *Major, perfect, diminished,* and *augmented* are terms of quality; quantity is determined by the *number* of staff degrees spanned by the interval.

4. Major and perfect intervals occur between tonic and other degrees of the major scale.

5. Because scales are constructed on consecutive staff degrees and intervals are named by number of staff degrees spanned, the scale-step numbers and the quantity number of an interval are the same.

6. *Major* modifies numbers 2, 3, 6, and 7; *perfect* modifies 4, 5, and 8 (and 1).

7. The intervals from tonic up to each of the major scale tones are M2, M3, P4, P5, M6, M7, and P8.

8. In analyzing an interval, assume the *lower note* to be $\hat{1}$ (tonic) and count the scale degrees to the upper note.

9. *Simple* intervals encompass a perfect octave or less; larger intervals are called *compound* intervals, meaning an octave plus a simple interval. In musical analysis, compound intervals are frequently reduced to simple terminology.

CHAPTER NINETEEN

Intervals (continued)

Minor Intervals
Diminished Intervals
Augmented Intervals
Modification of Intervals
Analyzing and Writing All Types of Intervals
Intervals in Inversion

In the previous chapter, we measured the distance from the tonic tone to each note of the major scale and obtained either major or perfect intervals. To measure any other interval, each will be compared with a major or a perfect interval. The three remaining types of intervals are these:

Minor (abbr. *m.* or *min.*)
Diminished (abbr. *dim.* or sometimes °)
Augmented (abbr. *aug.* or sometimes +)

Minor Intervals

A *minor* interval is one half step smaller than a major interval. Column 3 of Figure 19-1 shows that minor intervals are one half step smaller than the major intervals of column 1.

Diminished Intervals

A diminished interval is one half step smaller than a perfect interval (compare column 4 with column 2 in Figure 19-1) and also is one half step smaller than a minor interval (compare column 4 with column 3). By comparing column 4 with column 1, you will see that diminished intervals are one whole step smaller than major intervals.

FIGURE 19-1 *Intervals above C*

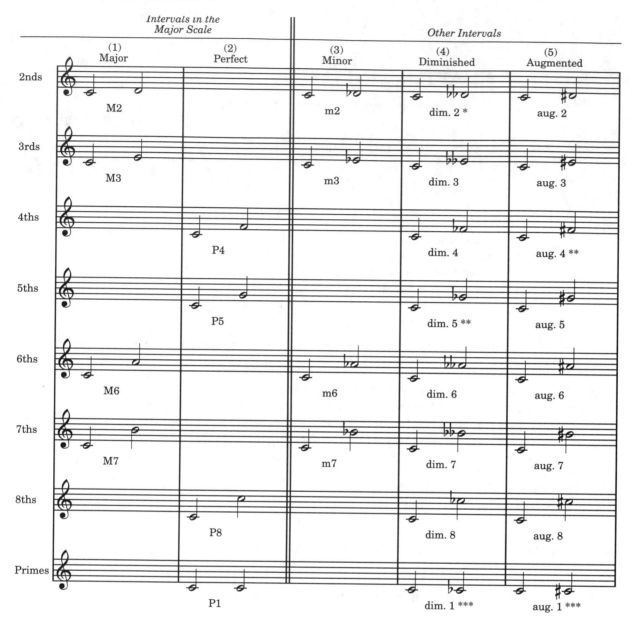

*Enharmonic with the Perfect Prime (C–D♭♭ = C–C).
**Also called *tritone*. The dim. 5 and aug. 4 each encompass *three whole steps* and thus are enharmonic with each other.
***Usually called a *chromatic half step*. As a dim. prime, the second note is lower than the first note.

Augmented Intervals

The augmented interval is one half step larger than a perfect interval (compare column 5 with column 2) and also is one half step larger than a major interval (compare column 5 with column 1).

Modification of Intervals

In Figure 19-1, you can see that any type of interval (M, m, P, dim., or aug.) is a modification by one half step of some other type of interval. This is shown in Figure 19-2.

FIGURE 19-2 *Modification of intervals*

Type of Interval Before	Modification		Type of Interval After
M	− 1/2 step	=	m
m	− 1/2 step	=	dim.
P	− 1/2 step	=	dim.
dim.	− 1/2 step	=	(doubly dim.)[1]
aug.	− 1/2 step	=	P or M
M	+ 1/2 step	=	aug.
m	+ 1/2 step	=	M
P	+ 1/2 step	=	aug.
dim.	+ 1/2 step	=	P or m
aug.	+ 1/2 step	=	(doubly aug.)[1]

Modification by half step may be applied to *either* the upper note *or* the lower note of an interval. Figure 19-3*a* shows the major third C–E; at *b*, it becomes the minor third C–E♭ when its upper tone (E) is lowered one half step; or, at *c*, it becomes the minor third C♯–E when its lower tone (C) is raised one half step.

FIGURE 19-3 *Modifying a major third*

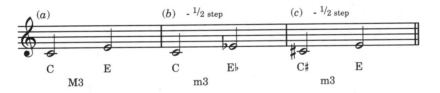

EXERCISE 19-1

Analyzing and Writing All Types of Intervals

You can analyze and write any interval by using the information in Chapter Eighteen and in Figures 19-1 and 19-2. The application of this information follows.

1. When the Lower Note of an Interval Is Tonic of a Major Scale

Locate the lower note of the interval, assume it to be tonic ($\hat{1}$) of a major scale, and count the scale degrees to the upper note. If the upper note appears in the major scale, it is either a *major* or a *perfect* interval. If the upper note does not belong to the major scale, then it is a *minor,* a *diminished,*[2] or an *augmented* interval, according to its alteration as shown in Figure 19-1.

For example, consider the interval G up to E♭: G up to E is a M6; therefore, G up to E♭, a decrease of one half step, is a m6.

---

[1]Doubly diminished and doubly augmented intervals are uncommon in musical practice and will not be considered further in this text.

[2]In scales with a key signature of four or more flats, some of the intervals in column 4 (dim.) would require a "triple flat" (♭♭♭)—for example, G♭ up to B♭♭♭. This type of notation is impractical. If such an interval were needed in actual music (and that would be rare), it would be spelled enharmonically.

M6   decrease by 1/2 step
m6

Analyze the interval B up to F✕: B up to F♯ is a perfect fifth; therefore, B up to F✕, an increase of one half step, is an aug.5. Observe that F♯ was raised to F✕, which uses the *same letter name,* rather than to its enharmonic equivalent, G, which is a minor sixth.

P5   increase by 1/2 step
aug. 5

Analyze the interval A♯ down to E: Since E is the lower note, count up the E major scale to A, a P4; A♯ is an increase of one half step; therefore, E up to A♯, or A♯ down to E, is an augmented fourth.

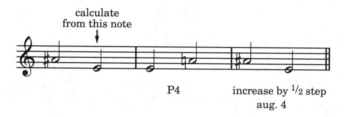

calculate from this note

P4   increase by 1/2 step
aug. 4

EXERCISE 19-2

To write an interval above a given note, use the same process applied in analyzing an interval. For example, to write a minor sixth above F, consider F as the tonic of F major and count up six scale steps to D. F up to D is a major sixth, so by lowering D one half step to D♭, you have F up to D♭, which is a minor sixth.

m6   M6   m6

EXERCISE 19-3

2. When the Lower Note of an Interval Is Not the Tonic of a Major Scale

By changing the ♯ or the ♭ of the lower note to natural (♮), we can easily find an interval based on the lower note as tonic of a major scale. If we replace the ♯ or the ♭ and observe the increase or decrease in the size of the interval, according to Figure 19-2, the name of the original interval will become apparent. Consider the interval D♯ up to A: D-natural up to A is a P5; therefore, D♯ up to A, a decrease by a half step, is a dim.5.

P5   decrease by 1/2 step
dim. 5

Consider F♭ up to B♭: Since there is no scale of F♭, calculate the interval from F-natural up to B♭, a P4; therefore, F♭ up to B♭, an increase by a half step, is an aug.4.

P4 increase by ½ step
aug. 4

The analysis of a few uncommon spellings of intervals may be more complex:

aug. 3 M3
(M3 + ½ step) (aug. 3 - ½ step)

The student's power of reasoning, however, might supply a simpler solution: Since D to F♯ is a M3, then D♯ to F𝄪, with both notes raised a half step, is also a M3.

M3 M3

EXERCISE
19-4

To write an interval above a given note, use the same process—for example, a dim.5 above F♭:

1. Change F♭ to F♮.
2. In the scale of F major, F up to C is a P5.
3. A dim.5 above F is C♭.
4. Lower both notes of F–C♭ to F♭–C♭♭.

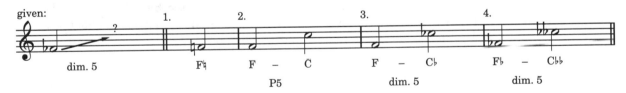

given: 1. 2.   3.   4.

dim. 5 F♮ F – C F – C♭ F♭ – C♭♭
       P5   dim. 5   dim. 5

Enharmonic intervals are frequently obvious, especially when related to the keyboard. In fact, any diminished or augmented interval is enharmonic with some perfect, major, or minor interval, except the diminished fifth and the augmented fourth (tritone), which are enharmonic with each other. For example, C up to G♯ is an aug.5 and C up to A♭ is a m6; G♯ and A♭ are enharmonic and are the same key on the keyboard. Caution is due in this respect: Proper spellings must be maintained according to the designation of the interval. It is incorrect to say that C up to G♯ is a m6 or that C up to A♭ is an aug.5, even though the intervals are enharmonic.

FIGURE 19-4   *Enharmonic intervals*

aug. 5   m6

EXERCISES
19-5, 19-6,
19-7

Intervals in Inversion

You may have noticed that some pairs of intervals use the same pitch names, yet look and sound different from the other pair. The notes D and F♯, for example, can be used as D up to F♯, a major third, or F♯ up to D, a minor sixth (the same is true when the notes are descending).

Each of the two intervals in this relationship is said to be an *inversion* of the other. An interval can be inverted when its lower note is placed one octave higher, or its upper note one octave lower. In either case, there is a change in size of the interval but no change in the pitch names used.[3]

FIGURE 19-5   *Inverting an interval*

(*a*) Moving the lower tone up an octave

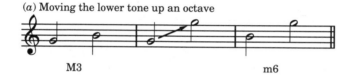

M3   m6

(*b*) Moving the upper tone down an octave

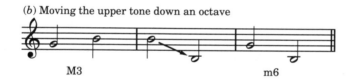

M3   m6

Any interval built on any pitch can be inverted by this process, as seen in Figure 19-6, where, for illustration, the C is the lower note in each interval and is placed an octave higher in the inversion.

[3]Jean Philippe Rameau, theorist and composer, noted in 1722 that any pitch and its octave sounded the same, except that one was an octave higher. Therefore, he reasoned, one note of the octave represents the other, and in that sense, one is the same as the other. Thus, an interval differing from another interval only by octave transposition of one note is merely a different expression of the same sound.

FIGURE 19-6 *Inversions on the staff*

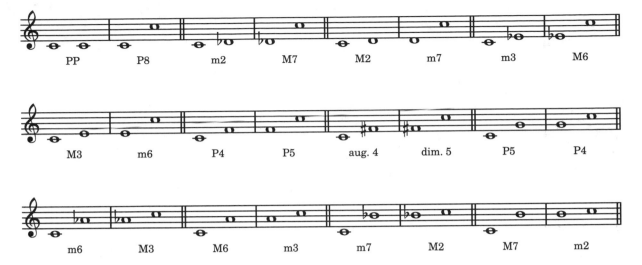

FIGURE 19-7 *Table of inversions*

Interval	Inversion	Interval	Inversion
PP	P8	dim.5	aug.4
m2	M7	P5	P4
M2	m7	aug.5	dim.4
aug.2	dim.7	m6	M3
dim.3	aug.6	M6	m3
m3	M6	aug.6	dim.3
M3	m6	dim.7	aug.2
dim.4	aug.5	m7	M2
P4	P5	M7	m2
aug.4	dim.5	P8	PP

Observe the following in Figures 19-6 and 19-7:

A *perfect* interval inverts to a *perfect* interval.

A *minor* interval inverts to a *major* interval.

A *major* interval inverts to a *minor* interval.

A *diminished* interval inverts to an *augmented* interval.

An *augmented* interval inverts to a *diminished* interval.

*EXERCISES
19-8, 19-9*

EXERCISE 19-1

Modification of intervals

(a) *Major to minor.* Supply the second note of the minor interval as indicated. For this exercise (all parts, *a–e*), use a natural sign (♮) if the second note is natural. Use half notes.

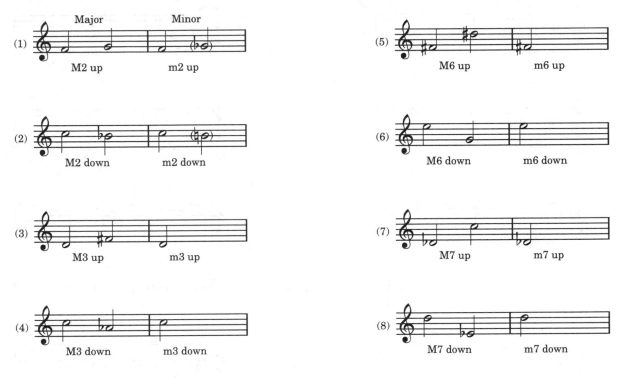

(b) Minor to diminished. Supply the second note of each diminished interval as directed. Use half notes.

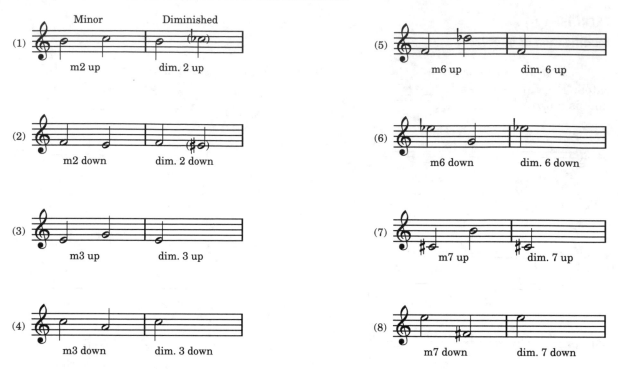

(c) Perfect to diminished. Supply the second note of each diminished interval. Use half notes.

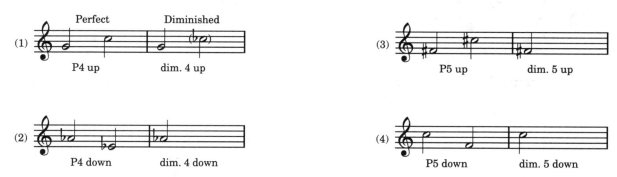

(d) Major to augmented. Supply the second note of each augmented interval. Use half notes.

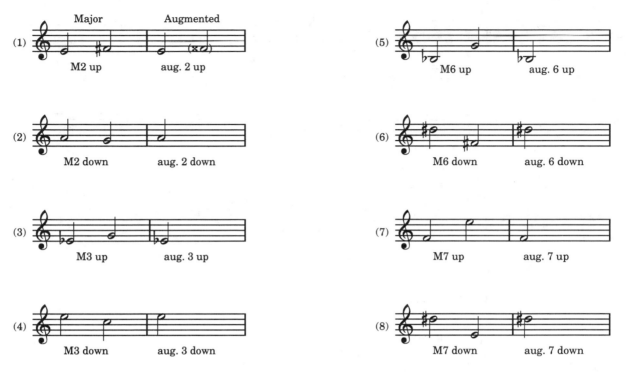

(e) Perfect to augmented. Supply the second note of each augmented interval. Use half notes.

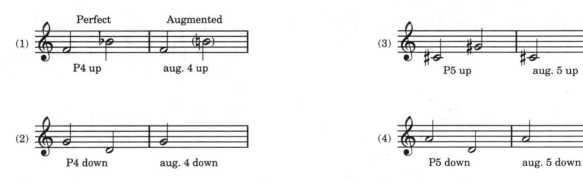

(*Return* to page 227.)

EXERCISE 19-2

Analyzing minor, diminished, and augmented intervals

Below each interval, write the interval name.

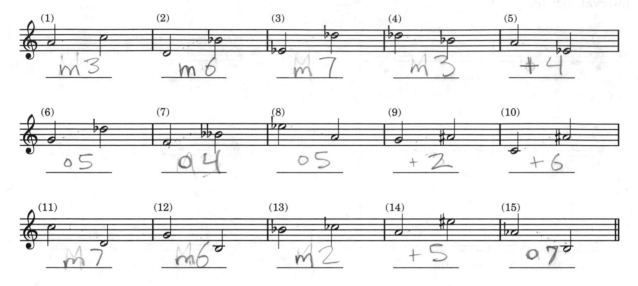

(1) m3 (2) m6 (3) m7 (4) m3 (5) +4

(6) o5 (7) o4 (8) o5 (9) +2 (10) +6

(11) m7 (12) m6 (13) m2 (14) +5 (15) o7

(*Return* to page *228.*)

EXERCISE 19-3

Writing minor, diminished, and augmented intervals

Write on the staff the second note of these ascending intervals. Use half notes.

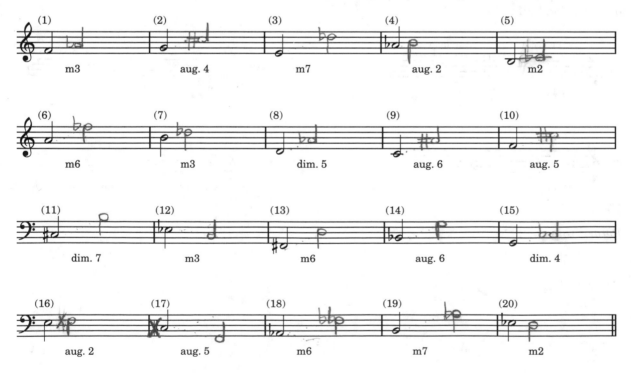

(1) m3 (2) aug. 4 (3) m7 (4) aug. 2 (5) m2

(6) m6 (7) m3 (8) dim. 5 (9) aug. 6 (10) aug. 5

(11) dim. 7 (12) m3 (13) m6 (14) aug. 6 (15) dim. 4

(16) aug. 2 (17) aug. 5 (18) m6 (19) m7 (20) m2

(*Return* to page *228.*)

EXERCISE 19-4

Analyzing all types of intervals above notes that cannot be tonics of major scales

Below each interval, write the interval name.

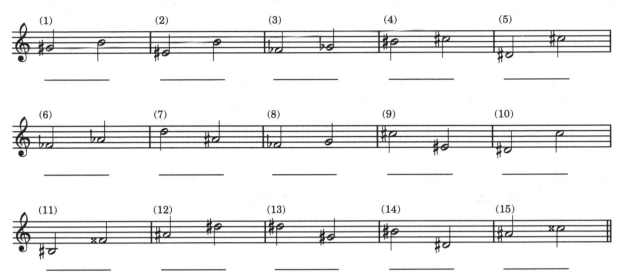

(*Return* to page *229.*)

EXERCISE 19-5

Writing intervals above notes that cannot be tonics of major scales

Write on the staff the second note of these ascending intervals. Use half notes.

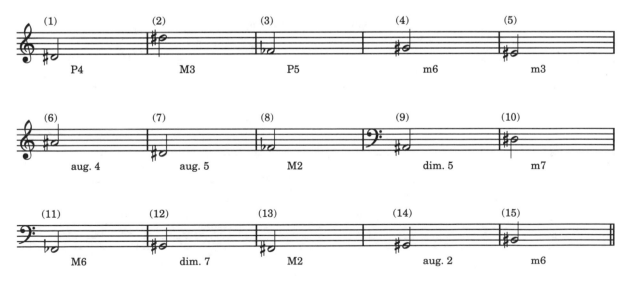

237

EXERCISE 19-6
Analyzing all types of intervals

Identify interval by name. Write abbreviation below each interval given.

EXERCISE 19-7
Spelling all types of intervals

Write the letter name of the second note of each interval given.

Example: m3 above D♯ is _____F♯_____

(1) M3 above B is _____

(2) Dim.5 above A is _____

(3) P8 above E♯ is _____

(4) m7 above G is _____

(5) Aug.2 above G is _____

(6) P4 above F♯ is _____

(7) Dim.7 above F♯ is _____

(8) P5 above D♯ is _____

(9) M2 above G♭ is _____

(10) M6 above C♯ is _____

(11) P4 above F♯ is _____

(12) M7 above E is _____

(13) Aug.6 above B♭ is _____

(14) m2 above C♯ is _____

(15) m6 above D is _____

(16) Aug.5 above E is _____

(17) m3 above D♭ is _____

(18) M3 above G is _____

(19) Aug.4 above F is _____

(20) m6 above F is _____

(21) Dim.4 above E♭ is_____

(22) m3 above A is _____

(23) Aug.2 above E is _____

(24) P5 above G♭ is _____

(25) Dim.3 above E♭ is _____

(*Return* to page *230.*)

EXERCISE 19-8
Inversion of intervals

Name the inversion of each of these intervals.

(1) Perfect fifth   _____

(2) Major second   _____

(3) Minor sixth   _____

(4) Major third   _____

(5) Augmented fourth   _____

(6) Minor second   _____

(7) Major sixth   _____

(8) Minor seventh   _____

(9) Minor third   _____

(10) Perfect fourth   _____

(11) Diminished fifth   _____

(12) Major sixth   _____

EXERCISE 19-9
Inversion of intervals

Place on the staff the inversion of the given interval and state the name of both intervals. Write the inversion of each given interval in two ways:

(a) Move the upper note down an octave.

(b) Move the lower note up an octave (in either order).

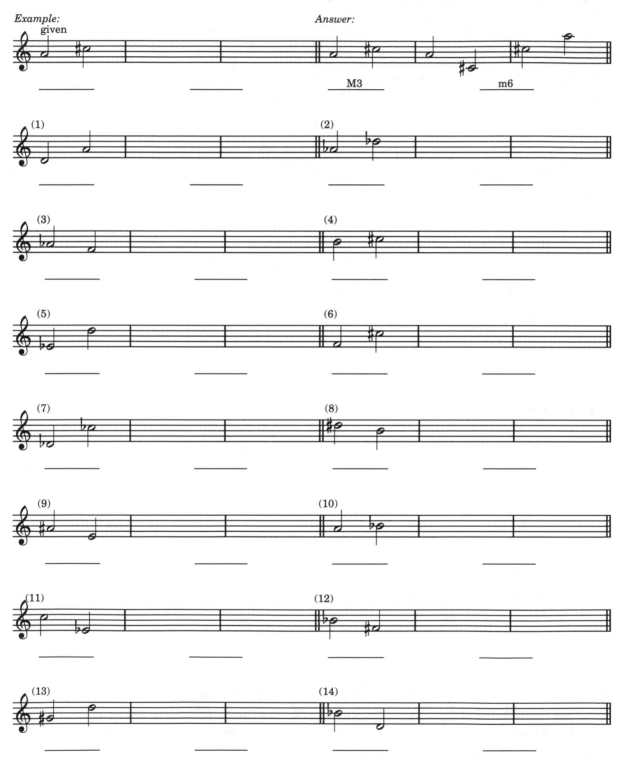

CHAPTER SUMMARY

1. A *minor interval* is one half step smaller than a major interval.

2. A *diminished interval* is one half step smaller than a minor or a perfect interval.

3. An *augmented interval* is one half step larger than a major or a perfect interval.

4. Any type of interval (M, m, P, dim., or aug.) is a modification by one half step of some other type of interval. By using knowledge of major and perfect intervals and modifications, we can calculate any type of interval.

5. Intervals above notes that cannot be tonics of major scales can be lowered or raised to simplify the notation or the spelling. When the interval becomes apparent, return the analysis to the original notation.

6. Although intervals may be enharmonic, each must be spelled according to its own designation. C up to A♭ is a m6, and C up to G♯ is an aug.5. Although enharmonic, one interval cannot be given the name of the other.

7. When an interval is rewritten so that the original bottom note becomes the upper, or vice versa, the interval is said to be *inverted*. The constants of interval inversion are shown below.

Original Interval	Inversion	Original Interval	Inversion
P	P	1	8
M	m	2	7
m	M	3	6
dim.	aug.	4	5
aug.	dim.	5	4
		6	3
		7	2
		8	1

CHAPTER TWENTY

Harmony I: Chords; Major Triads

Chapters Twenty through Twenty-three present an introduction to the study of Harmony, *allowing students to apply in a practical manner much of their acquired knowledge of the basics of music. These chapters will conveniently serve as a transition or link to a formal course in the subject.*

Where keyboard facilities are lacking or too limited, for practical purposes, Chapters Twenty-one and Twenty-three may be omitted. Chapters Twenty and Twenty-two provide all the intended harmonic material plus exercises in harmonic structures and harmonic analysis.

The term *harmony* refers to the simultaneous sounding of two or more pitches. Music in Western culture, especially since about the year 1600, is based to a great extent on the principles of harmony. We have already experienced a simple form of harmony in *harmonic intervals* (page 215), wherein the two tones of the interval sound together. When three or more tones sound together, the result is a *chord*.

Chords

Chords are usually built using intervals of the major and the minor third.[1] A chord structure is most easily demonstrated when, like a harmonic interval, the notes of the chord are placed on the staff in vertical alignment, indicating that all tones sound simultaneously. This configuration is known as a *block chord*. Figure 20-1 shows at (1) a single tone, followed by harmonic structures above that tone: at (2) an interval, and at (3), (4), and (5), three varieties of chords.

[1]This is generally true of music written before the twentieth century. Chords built in thirds are known as *tertian harmony*. Later practice has added chords built in seconds, fourths (quartal harmony), and fifths (quintal harmony).

FIGURE 20-1 *Harmonic structures*

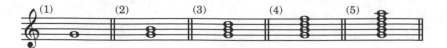

Chord tones also may sound successively, as in Figure 20-2*a;* in this form, chords are known as *broken chords* or *arpeggiated chords,* in contrast to the block chords shown in Figure 20-1. When appearing as a left-hand accompaniment to a melody on the piano (Figure 20-2*b*), the series of broken chords is often known as an *Alberti bass,* named after Domenico Alberti (1710–1740), who was one of the first composers to use the device extensively.

FIGURE 20-2 *Broken chords; Alberti bass*

Mozart, Piano Sonata, K. 545

Our study of harmony will focus on the three-note chord, Figure 20-1 (3), a sonority known as a *triad.*

The Triad

The triad is a very commonly used structure in harmonic music. It consists of two consecutive intervals of the third above a given note, and can easily be built on the staff using three consecutive lines, Figure 20-3*a,* or three consecutive spaces, Figure 20-3*b.*

FIGURE 20-3 *Building a triad*

EXERCISE 20-1

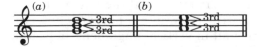

The lowest note of the triad (the note upon which the triad is built) is known as the *root* of the triad. The note immediately above the root is the *third,* since it is at the interval of a third above the root. The remaining note

244

is the *fifth* of the triad, since it is a fifth above the root. The three triad members may also be referred to as 1, 3, and 5.

FIGURE 20-4   *Triad members*

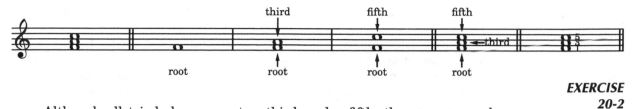

EXERCISE
20-2

Although all triads have a root, a third, and a fifth, there are several *types of triads.*

Types of Triads

If we write a triad above each of the seven letters of the musical alphabet, we produce the seven basic triad spellings (those without sharps or flats).

FIGURE 20-5   *Basic triad spellings*

When these are played on the piano and we listen carefully to each, we will discover that some sound like others even though located at different pitch levels. This is because those that sound the same display the same arrangement of major and minor thirds within the triad.

There are four combinations of major and minor thirds; each combination produces a different type of triad with its own identifying name. The first three of these are included in Figure 20-5.

1. M3 + m3 = major triad, C E G, F A C, G B D.
2. m3 + M3 = minor triad, D F A, E G B, A C E.
3. m3 + m3 = diminished triad, B D F.
4. M3 + M3 = augmented triad. The fifth of this triad is always a pitch name not in the diatonic scale—for example, C E G♯ in C major.

We will investigate each of these triads in the above order, beginning in this chapter with the *major triad.*

The Major Triad

In the major triad, the arrangement of intervals above the lowest note is major third and minor third, and the distance from the root up to the fifth is a perfect fifth.

FIGURE 20-6 *The major triad on C*

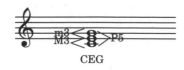

CEG

Any pitch name can serve as the root of a major triad. The most commonly used major triads are those whose root names are the same as the tonic tones of the fifteen major scales (review Chapter Five). If you can spell those scales, you can quickly spell a major triad simply by selecting $\hat{1}, \hat{3},$ and $\hat{5}$ of the particular scale.

Major Key	$\hat{1}, \hat{3}, \hat{5}$
F	F A C
E♭	E♭ G B♭
A	A C♯ E

EXERCISE 20-3

There remain a limited number of possible major triad spellings whose roots cannot be $\hat{1}$. Usually, the root of such spellings is a sharped note, as in the D♯ Fx A♯ of Figure 20-7. Major triads with roots carrying a double sharp or a double flat are uncommon.

FIGURE 20-7 *Major triad built on D♯*

Schubert, Minuet

D♯ Fx A♯

Each of the remaining possible major triad spellings has as its root a chromatic tone. Any such triad, including those described in the preceding paragraph, can easily be spelled by a single method.

1. When the root carries a sharp (♯), lower the sharp to a natural (♮), spell the triad on that pitch, and then raise all pitch names one half step.

   Problem: Spell a major triad on D♯.
   Solution: Spell a major triad on D: D F♯ A.
   Raise all notes one half step: D♯ Fx A♯.

2. When the root carries a flat (♭) or a double flat (♭♭), raise the accidental one half step, ♭ to ♮, or ♭♭ to ♭, spell the major triad on that pitch, and then lower all notes one half step.

246

Problem: Spell a major triad on D♭♭.

Solution: Spell a major triad on D♭: D♭ F A♭.

Lower all notes one half step: D♭♭ F♭ A♭♭.

*EXERCISE
20-4*

If you are fluent in spelling intervals, it is often easier simply to spell any major triad by its intervallic structure. For example, to spell a major triad above A♭:

M3 + m3 = A♭–C + C–E♭ = A♭ C E♭

or,

M3 and P5 = A♭–C + A♭ –E♭ = A♭ C E♭

*EXERCISE
20-5*

Up to this point, we have considered the triad only when the root is the lowest note. Rearranging the notes of the triad so that the third or the fifth is the lowest note results in *inversion of the triad.*

Inversion of Triads[2]

When either the third or the fifth of any triad is found as the lowest note, the triad is said to be in *inversion,* or, put in a slightly different way, the triad is *inverted. First inversion* indicates that the third of the triad is the lowest note, and *second inversion* indicates that the fifth of the triad is the lowest note.

FIGURE 20-8 *Inversions of the C major triad*

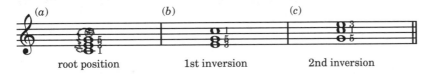

root position   1st inversion   2nd inversion

Notice that intervals that are not found in the root position of the triad appear between triad members in inversion.

FIGURE 20-9 *Intervals in inverted triads*

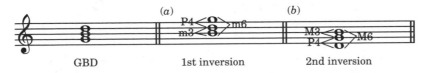

GBD   1st inversion   2nd inversion

---

[2]The discussion in this section and the following two sections (*triad position* and *doubling*) apply equally to all types of chords.

These inversions do not alter the identification of the triad. When the three tones of the inverted triad are rearranged in thirds, the lowest note of these thirds is always the root. In Figure 20-9*a*, although the first inversion reads B D G from the lowest note up, these notes can be rearranged in thirds to become G B D; likewise, in Figure 20-9*b*, D G B is recognized as a G B D triad.[3]

In addition to variation by inversion, triads can be varied by *position*.

Triad Position

Any triad (or any other chord) whose notes are as close together on the staff as possible is said to be in *close position*. In *open position*, the tones are placed farther apart from each other. You can easily recognize a chord in open position because there will be one or more places in its structure where a chord member could have been inserted, as in Figure 20-10 and in the example from Schubert, Figure 20-7.

FIGURE 20-10   *Close and open position*[4]

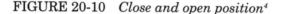

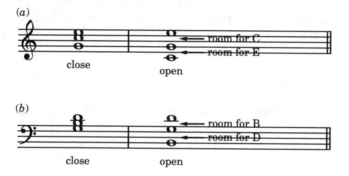

An additional way of varying a triad is through *doubling* of any of its members.

Doubling

In almost all composed music, more than three notes sound simultaneously. Therefore, when a triad is used, one or more of its notes must be *doubled;* that is, a given pitch spelling will be used two or more times.

---

[3]Inversion of triads is based on the same principle as inversion of intervals (review footnote 3, page 230). When the lowest note of the triad is placed an octave higher, this octave represents the original note, and the triad remains unchanged except for the arrangement of its members.

Prior to Rameau's theory (1722), analysis of vertical sonorities was based solely on the intervals above the lowest note. Thus, the three triads in Figure 20-9 were considered three different sonorities.

[4]Also called close/open structure; close/open harmony; close/open voicing.

FIGURE 20-11 *Doubled tones*

(a) Doubling at the octave   (b) Doubling at the unison

Doubling is most frequent when the great staff is used. Figure 20-12 shows a series of triads, each written using four notes, requiring one note in each triad to be doubled.

FIGURE 20-12 *Doubling in triads on the great staff*

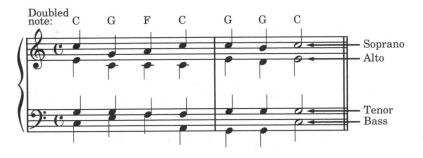

EXERCISE 20-8

Figure 20-12 is written in the *four-part* (or *four-voice*) *chorale* style that is commonly used in church hymns and in patriotic and community songs, such as "America" and "Auld Lang Syne." The names of the four voices are indicated at the right of the figure. Each person performs his or her part by reading from left to right, guided (in Figure 20-12) by the stem direction on the notes of each part: soprano, stems up; alto, stems down; tenor, stems up; bass, stems down.

This example demonstrates with extreme simplicity the dual concept basic to music composition in the period ca.1600–ca.1900, as well as much of the music of the twentieth century. The horizontal aspect of music composition is the sounding of melodic lines[5] (sometimes several simultaneously, as in Figure 20-12). The vertical aspect is the harmonic structure (chords) at any point, and the use of these chords in succession. The horizontal and the vertical aspects are of equal importance, and special skills are required to combine them successfully; these are presented in more advanced studies in Harmony.

We have seen in the preceding material a number of ways in which triads are used, all illustrated with abstract examples. When we look at most any example of "real" music, we will find the use of one additional feature that is not part of the triad itself; this is *dissonance*.

Dissonance and Consonance

Looking at the next example, Figure 20-13, we see a simple folk song with an accompaniment of only two triads, G B D and D F♯ A (the D F♯ A C chord will be discussed shortly). Measure 1 shows a triad, G B D, and, in the melody, another pitch, A (circled), that is not part of the triad. The pitch A as used here is an example of *dissonance,* in contrast to the *consonance,* G B D, with which it sounds. In the example, other dissonances are also circled.

---

[5]The simultaneous sounding of two or more melodic lines, usually displaying more melodic and rhythmic contrast than shown here, is known as *counterpoint.*

FIGURE 20-13 *Harmony with dissonance*

Poland

Traditionally, *consonance* refers to a pleasant sound, and *dissonance* refers to a harsh or unpleasant sound. For the present purpose of definition, a harmony is consonant when it contains only those intervals found in a triad and its inversions.[6] Any additional tone sounding simultaneously with the triad is therefore dissonant to that triad.

Music written early in the history of the art (ca. A.D. 1000) used dissonance sparingly. The history of music is, in part, a history of the increasing use of dissonance and the increased tolerance of the ear for such sounds. The words "consonance" and "dissonance" are used today only as identifying terms; they do not necessarily describe the effect of any sound upon any particular listener.

Dissonant tones may be found in one of two ways:

1. The *nonharmonic tone.* Any tone that is not part of a triad but that sounds simultaneously with it, except as in "2" following, is known as a *nonharmonic tone.*[7] In Figure 20-13, each circled note in the melody is not part of the triad with which it sounds. Each is therefore dissonant and identified as a nonharmonic tone.

2. *Chords larger than a triad.* In the next-to-the-last measure of Figure 20-13, we see the chord spelling D F♯ A C. Here, the pitch C is an additional third placed above the major triad D F♯ A. D F♯ A C, though built in thirds, is dissonant because it includes the dissonant interval of a minor seventh, D up to C, shown at (3) in Figure 20-14. With this particular arrangement of thirds, the chord is known as a major-minor seventh chord (major triad plus interval of a minor seventh).

[6]These are: major and minor thirds, major and minor sixths, the perfect fourth, the perfect fifth, and the octave. Of the consonant intervals, those that cannot in any context suggest a major or a minor key are called *perfect.*

[7]Some of the other names in current usage are: nonchord tones, foreign tones, accessory tones, and bytones. Nonharmonic tones can be identified and named more specifically based on the way they are approached and left in the melodic line, and are described in most harmony texts. In Ottman, *Elementary Harmony,* fourth edition, see Chapters 11 and 12.

In the still-larger chord D F♯ A C E (ninth chord), shown at (4) in Figure 20-14, both C and E are dissonant. Such chords will not be considered further in this text.

FIGURE 20-14   *Chords larger than a triad*

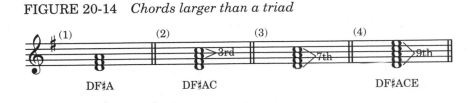

DF♯A   DF♯AC   DF♯ACE

Like triads, seventh chords can be inverted. Since the seventh chord is a four-note chord, there are three inversions.

FIGURE 20-15   *Inversions of a seventh chord*

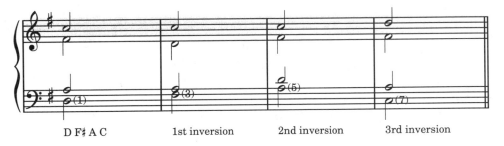

D F♯ A C   1st inversion   2nd inversion   3rd inversion

Figure 20-16 shows nonharmonic tones (circled) and seventh chords in the four-voice chorale style. Notice in particular the chords marked (1), (2), and (3).

FIGURE 20-16   *Dissonances in four-voice chorale style*

Bach, "Nun danket alle Gott" ("Now Thank We All Our God")

1. The seventh chord, D F♯ A C, is in first inversion, since the third of the chord (F♯) is the lowest tone.
2. When the apparent seventh (here, C in the bass) appears on a weak part of a beat, it is usually considered a nonharmonic tone. This use is common. This "seventh" is often called a "passing seventh."
3. The seventh chord, D F♯ A C, in root position is temporarily obscured by nonharmonic tones on the first beat of the measure, but its construction becomes clear when the nonharmonic tones resolve to F♯ and C on the second beat.

EXERCISES
20-9, 20-10

In the previous music examples, we have identified chords by their spellings. More useful is the identification of a chord by its relationship to a key.

Chords in a Major Key

Any triad in a key can conveniently be identified by the scale-step number of its root, using roman numerals, or by the scale-step name of its root. A triad built on the fifth (dominant) scale step, for example, can be called a "V triad" (spoken: "five triad") or a "dominant triad." The triads of Figure 20-17 are known as *diatonic* triads, that is—triads consisting exclusively of scale degrees. (Chords with tones not in the scale are known as *altered* chords.)

FIGURE 20-17   *Triads in a major key*

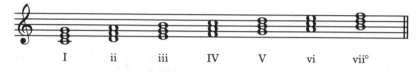

The roman numerals may also indicate chord quality:

> An uppercase roman numeral (I, IV, V) indicates a major triad.
>
> A lowercase roman numeral (ii, iii, vi) indicates a minor triad.
>
> A lowercase roman numeral with an added ° (vii°) indicates a diminished triad.
>
> An uppercase roman numeral with an added + (I+, IV+, and so forth) indicates an augmented triad, studied in Chapter Twenty-two.

The triad number, then, tells us

1. The location of its root in the scale
2. The quality of the triad

For purposes of the present chapter, harmony in a major key, we will study three commonly used triads, I, IV, and V, and one seventh chord, V^7. You should be able to spell the three triads easily in all major keys—for example, in B♭ major.

EXERCISES
20-11, 20-12

> I: $\hat{1}$ is B♭; the I triad is B♭ D F
>
> IV: $\hat{4}$ is E♭; the IV triad is E♭ G B♭
>
> V: $\hat{5}$ is F; the V triad is F A C

In examining "real" music, we will find the V^7 (dominant seventh) chord used much more frequently than the V triad. As mentioned before, the V^7 is constructed simply by adding a minor third above the fifth of the V triad. This added tone, incidentally, is $\hat{4}$ of the key and at the interval of a minor seventh above its root.

FIGURE 20-18 *Spelling the V⁷ chord*

C: GBD   GBDF
      V   V⁷

To spell a V⁷ chord in E♭ major, for example:

> V = B♭ D F
> m3 above F = A♭ (or, $\hat{4}$ of E♭ major is A♭)
> V⁷ = B♭ D F + A♭, or B♭ D F A♭

*EXERCISE
20-13*

Examples of music may now be analyzed using chord numbers instead of chord spellings. Here are selected measures of music examples presented earlier, this time with roman numeral symbols.

FIGURE 20-19 *Use of roman numeral symbols*

(a) from Figure 20–13, measures 5–8

G: I   I   V⁷   I

(b) from Figure 20–16, measures 1–2

G: I   I   IV   I

(c) from Figure 20–2b, showing broken chords and a V⁷ chord in inversion

I   V⁷   I

*EXERCISE
20-14*

EXERCISE 20-1
Writing triads

Complete each triad by placing two notes on successive lines or spaces above the given note.

(*Return* to page *244*.)

EXERCISE 20-2
Locating chord members

Place the identification of the chord member, shown above the triad, alongside the appropriate note of the triad.

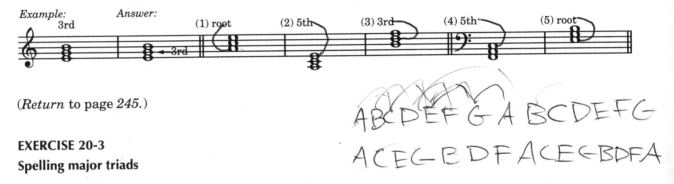

(*Return* to page *245*.)

EXERCISE 20-3
Spelling major triads

Spell the major triad built on the tonic note of each of the fifteen major scales.

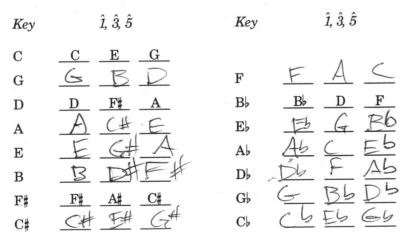

Key	1̂, 3̂, 5̂			Key	1̂, 3̂, 5̂		
C	C	E	G				
G	G	B	D	F	F	A	C
D	D	F♯	A	B♭	B♭	D	F
A	A	C♯	E	E♭	E♭	G	B♭
E	E	G♯	A	A♭	A♭	C	E♭
B	B	D♯	F♯	D♭	D♭	F	A♭
F♯	F♯	A♯	C♯	G♭	G♭	B♭	D♭
C♯	C♯	F♯	G♯	C♭	C♭	E♭	G♭

Handwritten: ABCDEFG A BCDEFG / ACEG BDF ACEG BDFA

(*Return* to page *246*.)

EXERCISE 20-4

Spelling major triads

Spell major triads whose roots are chromatic tones, but not tonic tones listed in Exercise 20-3.

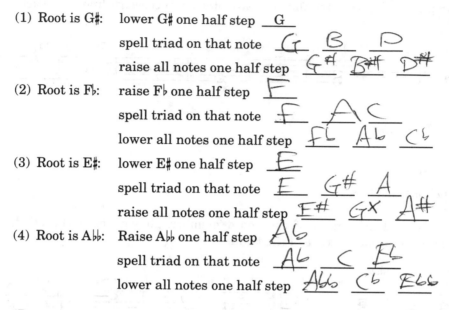

(1) Root is G♯: lower G♯ one half step __G__

spell triad on that note __G__ __B__ __D__

raise all notes one half step __G♯__ __B♯__ __D♯__

(2) Root is F♭: raise F♭ one half step __F__

spell triad on that note __F__ __A__ __C__

lower all notes one half step __F♭__ __A♭__ __C♭__

(3) Root is E♯: lower E♯ one half step __E__

spell triad on that note __E__ __G♯__ __A__

raise all notes one half step __E♯__ __G𝄪__ __A♯__

(4) Root is A♭♭: Raise A♭♭ one half step __A♭__

spell triad on that note __A♭__ __C__ __E♭__

lower all notes one half step __A♭♭__ __C♭__ __E♭♭__

(*Return* to page *247*.)

EXERCISE 20-5

Spelling and writing major triads

Spell a major triad from a given root and place the triad on the staff. Use any convenient method of spelling.

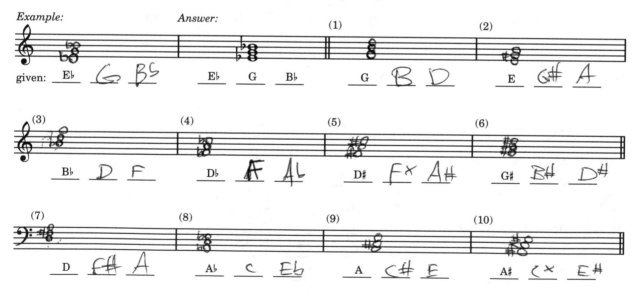

Example: *Answer:*   (1)   (2)

given: __E♭__ __G__ __B♭__   __E♭__ __G__ __B♭__   __G__ __B__ __D__   __E__ __G♯__ __A__

(3) __B♭__ __D__ __F__   (4) __D♭__ __F__ __A♭__   (5) __D♯__ __F𝄪__ __A♯__   (6) __G♯__ __B♯__ __D♯__

(7) __D__ __F♯__ __A__   (8) __A♭__ __C__ __E♭__   (9) __A__ __C♯__ __E__   (10) __A♯__ __C𝄪__ __E♯__

(*Return* to page *247*.)

EXERCISE 20-6

Identifying triads in inversion

A triad in inversion is given. Rearrange the notes on the staff to form a triad in thirds. Spell the triad in thirds, and then indicate first or second inversion for the given triad.

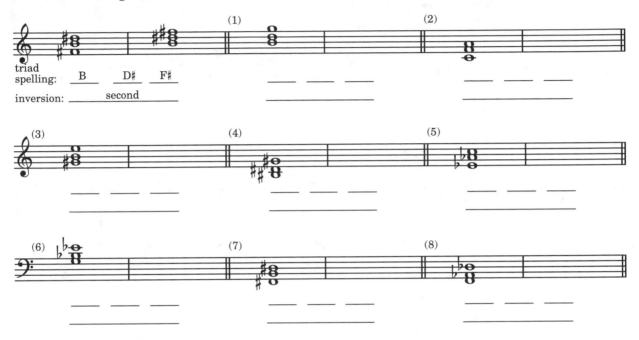

triad
spelling: __B__ __D#__ __F#__

inversion: _____second_____

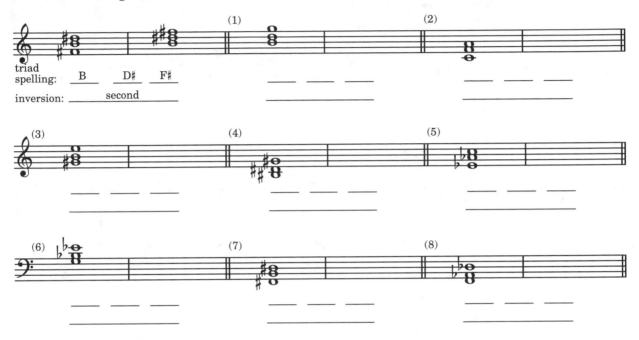

(Return to page 248.)

EXERCISE 20-7

Reducing triads in open position to close position

Rearrange the notes of the given triad so that the position is changed from open to close (the highest note is unchanged). Also, spell the triad in the order of thirds.

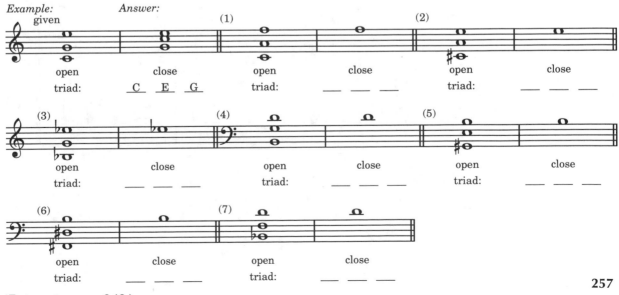

Example: *Answer:*
given

open   close   open   close   open   close

triad: __C__ __E__ __G__   triad: __ __ __   triad: __ __ __

open   close   open   close   open   close

triad: __ __ __   triad: __ __ __   triad: __ __ __

open   close   open   close

triad: __ __ __   triad: __ __ __

(Return to page 248.)

EXERCISE 20-8

Locating doubled notes in four-voice triads

Above the staff, write the name of the doubled note.

(1) Doubled note:

(2) Doubled note:

(*Return* to page *249*.)

EXERCISE 20-9

Triads and dissonance

Place the spelling of each triad below the staff, spelling each triad from its root even if its third or fifth appears as the lowest note. Circle all tones that are not part of the triad spelling. Chord spellings other than major triads are provided.

Bach, "Herzlich lieb hab ich dich, O Herr"

ACE   EGB

*Two nonharmonic tones sound simultaneously. Others will be found in these examples.

Bach, "Was Gott tut, das ist wohlgetan"

ACEG ___ ___

EXERCISE 20-10

Triads, chords, and dissonances

Place the spelling of each chord below the staff. Circle each dissonance, including the seventh of any seventh chord.

Beethoven, *Piano Sonata, Op. 49, No. 2*

(1) Tempo di Menuetto

GBD   DF♯AC

*

*Incomplete chord. What pitch is missing?

(2) Andante

Gluck, *Orfeo* (1762)

Live with-out   my Eu - ri - di - ce?   Can I   live   with-out   my   love?

Dvořák, Humoresque, Op. 101, No. 7

(3) Poco lento e grazioso

p

repeat (dim.)

(*pp*)

1.

2.

p

C♯ E G♯

(*Return* to page *252.*)

EXERCISE 20-11
Spelling the I, IV, and V Triads

Spell the I, IV, and V triads in the keys indicated.

Key	I			IV			V		
C	C	E	G	F	A	C	G	B	D
D	___	___	___	___	___	___	___	___	___
G	___	___	___	___	___	___	___	___	___
E	___	___	___	___	___	___	___	___	___
F	___	___	___	___	___	___	___	___	___
E♭	___	___	___	___	___	___	___	___	___

EXERCISE 20-12
Spelling the I, IV, and V Triads

Spell the given triad in the key indicated.

V in the key of C:	G	B	D
IV in the key of B♭:	___	___	___
V in the key of A:	___	___	___
IV in the key of E♭:	___	___	___
I in the key of A♭:	___	___	___
V in the key of E:	___	___	___
IV in the key of F:	___	___	___

(*Return* to page 252.)

EXERCISE 20-13
Spelling V⁷ chords

Spell the V⁷ chord when the key is given.

Key	V triad			+	m3 above (or 4̂)	=	V⁷			
C	G	B	D	+	F	=	G	B	D	F
F	___	___	___	+	___	=	___	___	___	___
A	___	___	___	+	___	=	___	___	___	___
D	___	___	___	+	___	=	___	___	___	___
B♭	___	___	___	+	___	=	___	___	___	___

Key	V triad	+	m3 above (or $\hat{4}$)	=	V^7
E	___ ___ ___	+	___	=	___ ___ ___ ___
A♭	___ ___ ___	+	___	=	___ ___ ___ ___
E♭	___ ___ ___	+	___	=	___ ___ ___ ___

(*Return* to page *253*.)

EXERCISE 20-14
Analysis

Write chord numbers below the staff. Circle each nonharmonic tone and the seventh of each seventh chord. Also, review Exercise 20-10, adding chord numbers.

Haydn, Piano Sonata, H. XVI:6

Chopin, Mazurka, Op. 17, No. 1

This example does *not* open with a tonic triad.

CHAPTER SUMMARY

1. A *chord* consists of three or more pitches, these found as consecutive intervals of the third.

2. A *triad* is a chord of three notes.

3. From its lowest note when spelled in thirds, the notes of the triad are identified as *root, third,* and *fifth.*

4. *Root position:* The root of the triad is the lowest note.
   First inversion: The third of the triad is the lowest note.
   Second inversion: The fifth of the triad is the lowest note.

5. Triads are of four varieties, dependent upon the type and distribution of the thirds used. These, identified by interval construction from the root up, are
   Major triad: major third plus minor third
   Minor triad: minor triad plus major third
   Diminished triad: minor third plus minor third
   Augmented triad: major third plus major third

6. A triad or another chord whose notes are as close together as possible is said to be in *close position.* In *open position,* chord tones may be farther apart.

7. One or more tones of a triad are frequently *doubled,* since most music is written in more than three voices.

8. Traditionally, *consonance* refers to a pleasant sound, and *dissonance* refers to an unpleasant sound. For descriptive purposes, consonance refers to sonorities made up only of intervals from the triad, and dissonance refers to other tones sounding simultaneously with the triad.

9. Chords larger than the triad (seventh chord, ninth chord, and so forth) are built by adding thirds above the triad.

10. Triads are identified by roman numeral symbols:
   Uppercase numeral = major triad   (I, V)
   Lowercase numeral = minor triad   (i, v)
   Lowercase numeral with ° = diminished triad   (ii°, vii°)
   Uppercase numeral with + = augmented triad   (I+, III+)

CHAPTER TWENTY-ONE

Keyboard Harmony I

Melody Harmonization
Playing the Chord Progression I V⁷ I
Procedure for Harmonizing a Melody at the Keyboard
Playing Chord Progressions Using I, IV, and V⁷

The preceding study of chords and nonharmonic tones leads to the immediate application of that material at the keyboard in *melody harmonization.* As a brief preliminary, however, we should bring into focus the two systems of chord symbolization that we will encounter in our procedures. The elements of these systems were covered in Chapter Twenty.

1. *Roman numerals.* The traditional system of chord symbolization by roman numerals tells the relationship of chords to each other and provides means for codifying chord progressions.

2. *Lead sheet symbols.* Another system of chord symbolization is found in public school music, popular sheet music, "fake-books," jazz, and professional lead sheets, from which the term *lead sheet symbols* is derived. This system uses the root letter (uppercase) of a chord to stand alone representing a major triad. Any other type of chord is symbolized by adding the appropriate modification to the root letter.

FIGURE 21-1   *Chord symbolization*

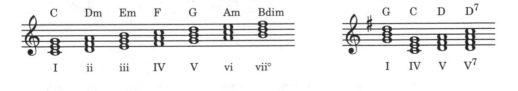

Melody Harmonization

Choosing a series of chords to accompany a given melody is one aspect of the skill of *melody harmonization,* sometimes called "chording." There exists in music literature a virtually countless number of melodies, including large numbers of folk songs, that can be harmonized by I, IV, and V (V⁷) only, or even by I and V (V⁷) only. In many of these, a satisfactory choice of chords is provided by clues in the melody itself. A familiar folk tune, "Red River Valley," is a good example (Figure 21-2).

FIGURE 21-2   *Harmonized folk melody*

"Red River Valley" (measures 1–4 only)

The clues helping to determine chord choice in this melody, and in most other simple melodies, are

1. *Notes on the strong beat(s) of the measure.* In measure 1, B on the first beat and G on the third beat suggest G B D, the I triad.
2. *Intervals of a third or larger.* In measure 2, the interval E up to G suggests C E G, the IV triad.
3. *Broken chords.* In measure 3, the notes B-G-B-D are a broken form of G B D.
4. *Long-held notes and repeated notes.* In measure 4, the note A, held for three beats, suggests D F♯ A, the V triad.
5. *Upbeats.* These are usually left unharmonized (indicated in Figure 21-2 by dashes).

With the facility on the keyboard gained from previous work in this text (or from private piano lessons), and with a satisfactory system of chord progression established, could you harmonize this melody at the keyboard? In the simplest way, play the block triad in the left hand at the place indicated, while you sing the tune and/or play the melody with the right hand.

If what you play is placed on staff paper, it will look like Figure 21-3.

FIGURE 21-3   *Melody with block chord accompaniment*

Playing block chords, all in root position, is cumbersome and ordinarily requires visual guiding of the left hand. The chords of Figure 21-3 can also be played without the large leaps through the use of inversions, shown in an easy keyboard formula in Figure 21-4.[1] You can play chords in this manner more or less kinesthetically (by muscular memory), without the distraction at each chord change of having to shift the focus of the eyes from the music down to the keyboard.

[1]Neither of these methods of harmonization can produce a professional or artistic performance (as presented in more advanced study), but both are most useful for exploring harmonic patterns and for the achievement of personal pleasure in keyboard activity.

FIGURE 21-4 *Formula for playing I, IV, and V⁷ chords*

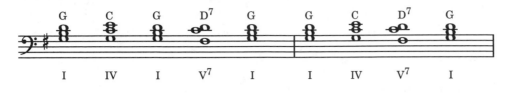

In this formula, V⁷ (with the fifth of the chord omitted) is used instead of the V triad because it simplifies the fingering and, at the same time, furnishes a richer sound. This formula can be used for any major key, since you already know how to spell a chord from its roman numeral symbol.

Here is how the complete version of "Red River Valley" looks with the style of chordal accompaniment shown in Figure 21-4, this time in the key of E♭ major, where

I	=	E♭	G	B♭
IV	=	A♭	C	E♭
V⁷	=	B♭	D	F	A♭

FIGURE 21-5 *"Red River Valley" in the key of E♭*

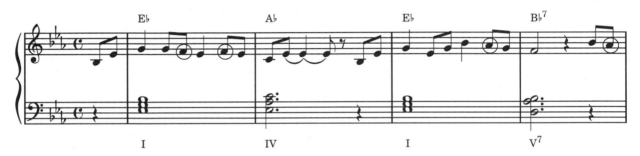

If, based on experience and skills already developed in chording, you can easily harmonize and play "Red River Valley" and similar melodies, *you may skip directly to Exercise 21-5.* If you wish to develop this ability, continue with the following study.

Now that we have completed a harmonization of "Red River Valley," which system of chord symbols should we use? Compare Figures 21-3 and 21-5. The roman numeral symbols are the same for both keys, and they will indicate the same harmonization no matter what other major key is chosen. When lead sheet symbols are used, the letter names in these two figures are different, and will be different for each of the remaining thirteen major keys.

Music examples in this chapter include both systems. In the exercises where you devise a harmonization, the use of roman numeral symbols is preferred, but either system may be used.

Playing the Chord Progression I V⁷ I

The most used chord progression in traditional music is V⁷ I. The following illustration includes this progression in a simple arrangement showing the smoothest connections between chords.

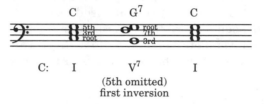

In Figure 21-6, the number before each note indicates the recommended fingering, the thumb being "1" and the little finger "5." Arrows indicate step-wise movement.

FIGURE 21-6   *Fingerings for the progression I V⁷ I, left hand*

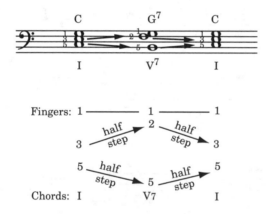

In playing the progression I V⁷ I, notice that the thumb repeats its key, whereas the other connections are by half step. In the V⁷ chord, the thumb plays the root letter name and, a whole step below, the 2nd finger plays the seventh. This harmonic interval of a whole step between thumb and 2nd finger, as well as the half-step connection played by the 5th finger, can easily be felt on the keyboard. Identical fingering is applicable to the progression I V⁷ I in any major key.

EXERCISE 21-1

For harmonizing a melody at the keyboard, a systematic approach is most effective. The following procedure is recommended.

Procedure for Harmonizing a Melody at the Keyboard

Study:

1. *Key.* Recognize the key of the melody. Spell the I and V⁷ chords (later, when assigned, I IV V⁷) and visualize the notes on lines and spaces of the treble staff. This will help you to determine which melody notes are chord tones.

2. *Chord Choice.* Find clues in the melody (review page 266) that will suggest an appropriate chord choice. Notice any segments of the melody that reappear and will use chords already determined. Write the chord symbols (see Figure 21-2).

Play:

(If necessary, repeat any step until you can play without hesitation, in tempo.)

1. *Left hand alone.* Play the chords you have written.
2. *Right hand alone.* Practice the melody.
3. *Hands together.* Play both melody and chords. Sound a chord on the downbeat of each measure, even though it may be a repeated chord.

For an example, the procedure is applied to the following melody.

FIGURE 21-7 *Melody for harmonization*

Study:

1. *Key.* F major. I = FAC; V7 = CEGB♭

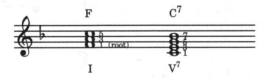

2. *Chord Choice.*
   Measure 1: **F,** the first note, is the root (1) of I.
   CHOOSE I.
   Measure 2: **G** is 5 of V⁷.
   CHOOSE V⁷.
   Measure 3: **A** and **C** on the strong beats suggest F A C (I).
   C down to **F** is 5 down to 1 of I.
   B♭, second note of the measure, is a nonharmonic tone.
   CHOOSE I.

Measure 4:   **E** and **G,** on the strong beats, are 3 and 5 of V⁷.
             G down to **C** is 5 down to 1 of V⁷.
             F, the second note, is a nonharmonic tone.
             CHOOSE V⁷

Measures 5, 6, and 7:   These are the same as measures 1, 2, 3.

Measure 8:   **G** down to **E** is 5 down to 3 of V⁷.
             CHOOSE V⁷ FOR THE FIRST BEAT.
             F, the last note, is 1 of I.
             CHOOSE I FOR THE LAST BEAT.

FIGURE 21-8   *Melody with chord symbols*

Play:

(Use Figure 21-8.)

1. *Left hand alone.* Play the series of chords.

2. *Right hand alone.* Practice the melody.

3. *Hands together.* Play both melody and chords.

You have now completed the procedure for harmonizing a melody at the keyboard. Compare your finished performance with the written-out version in Figure 21-9.

FIGURE 21-9   *Melody with chordal accompaniment*

*When the lowest note of the melody coincides as a unison with the highest note of the left-hand chord, the left-hand thumb should release this key momentarily, allowing the right hand to continue with the melody.

In other cases, if the melody overlaps the left-hand chord tones, the left hand should play the progression an octave lower (or, less preferred, the right hand could play the melody an octave higher). Advanced study of inversions, beyond the scope of this book, would enable the performer to choose from a variety of positions for the left hand.

**EXERCISE
21-2**

An added dimension of chording will be found in the use of the IV chord in combination with I and V⁷.

270

Playing Chord Progressions Using I, IV, and V⁷

Playing the Progression I IV I

Of all the possible progressions using the chords I, IV, and V⁷, the progression I IV I is the easiest to play. The following illustration shows the smoothest connections between chords.

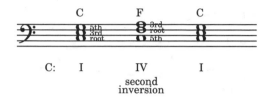

In Figure 21-10, fingerings are shown before each chord. As before, arrows indicate stepwise (whole- or half-step) movement.

FIGURE 21-10   *Fingerings for the progression I IV I, left hand*

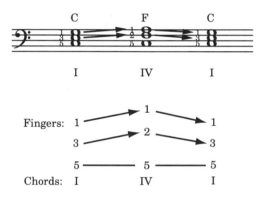

In playing the progression, notice that the little finger repeats the same key; in the IV chord, the thumb and the 2nd finger form the interval of a major third.

EXERCISE 21-3

Playing the Progression I IV V⁷ I, Left Hand

The remaining chord connection to be studied occurs in the progression IV V⁷.[2]

---

[2]The reverse of the IV V⁷ progression, V⁷ to IV (sometimes called *retrogression,* as opposed to *progression*), will not be studied in this text. Though commonly used in popular "rhythm and blues," the progression V⁷ IV is uncommon in composed music and traditional folk music.

FIGURE 21-11 *Fingerings for the progression I IV V⁷ I, left hand*

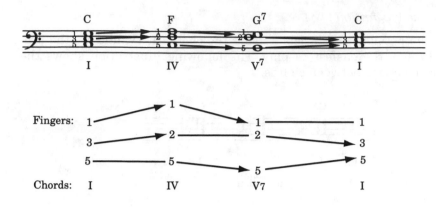

In playing the chords IV V⁷, notice that the 2nd finger repeats the same key while the thumb and the 5th finger move stepwise.

EXERCISES
21-4, 21-5

EXERCISE 21-1

Playing the progression I V⁷ I (left hand)

(a) Play the written progressions. Use recommended fingerings for all keys. Repeat until you can play without hesitation.

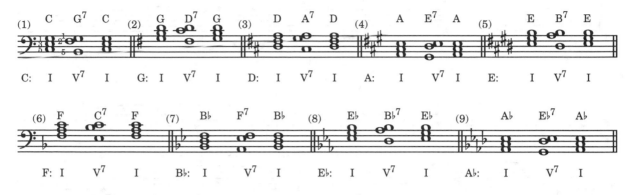

(b) Without looking at the music, play I V⁷ I in these keys: (1) C; (2) G; (3) D; (4) A; (5) E; (6) F; (7) B♭; (8) E♭; (9) A♭.

(To extend this exercise, practice the progression in the remaining keys: B; F♯; C♯; D♭; G♭; C♭.)

(*Return* to page 268.)

EXERCISE 21-2

Harmonizing melodies using I and V⁷ only

Harmonize each of the following melodies. Use the procedure outlined on pages 269–270.

*Use the same chord throughout the bracket.

273

(3)

(4)

(5)

Mozart, Symphony No. 39 in E♭ Major, K. 543

(6)

"Oh Dear, What Can the Matter Be?"

For additional practice, use these melodies from *Music for Sight Singing*, fourth edition: 85, 87, 99, 100, 101, 117, 119, 155, 195, 239, 242, 290, 296.

(*Return* to page *270.*)

EXERCISE 21-3

Playing the progression I IV I (left hand)

(a) Play the written progressions. Use recommended fingerings for all keys. Repeat until you can play without hesitation.

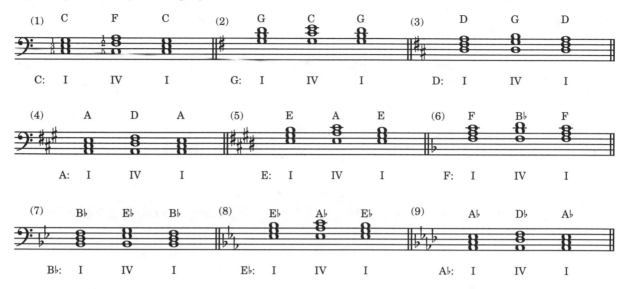

(b) Without looking at the music, play I IV I in these keys: (1) C; (2) G; (3) D; (4) A; (5) E; (6) F; (7) Bb; (8) Eb; (9) Ab. (To extend this exercise, practice the progression in the remaining keys: B; F#; C#; Db; Gb; Cb.)

(*Return* to page *271*.)

EXERCISE 21-4

Playing the progression I IV V⁷ I (left hand)

(a) Play the written progressions. Use recommended fingerings for all keys. Repeat until you can play without hesitation.

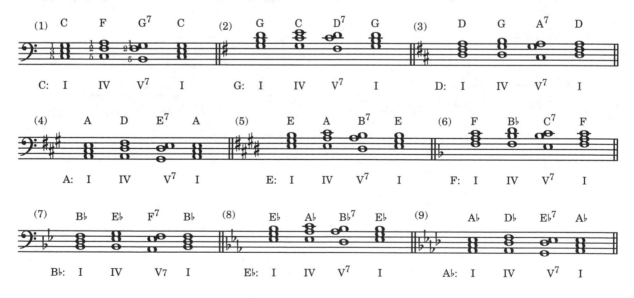

(b) Without looking at the music, play I IV V⁷ I in these keys: (1) C; (2) G; (3) D; (4) A; (5) E; (6) F; (7) B♭; (8) E♭; (9) A♭.

(To extend this exercise, practice the progression in the remaining keys: B; F♯; C♯; D♭; G♭; C♭.)

EXERCISE 21-5
Harmonizing melodies using I, IV, and V⁷

Harmonize each of the following melodies at the keyboard. Use the procedures outlined on pages 269–270.

(1) "On Top of Old Smokey"

(2) "Jenny Crack Corn"

(3) "When the Saints Go Marchin' In"

For additional practice, use these melodies in *Music for Sight Singing*, fourth edition: 90, 156, 157, 191, 280, 332, 333, 348, 357.

CHAPTER TWENTY-TWO

Harmony II: The Minor, Diminished, and Augmented Triads

The Minor Triad
Chords in a Minor Key
The Diminished and Augmented Triads

The Minor Triad

The minor triad consists of a minor third and a major third, with the order of the thirds above the root reversed as compared with the major triad; the interval of the fifth is the same in major and minor.

FIGURE 22-1 *Major and minor triads compared*

(a) Major triad
M3 + m3
M3 and P5

(b) Minor triad
m3 + M3
m3 and P5

Spelling the minor triad can be accomplished in several ways:

1. If the spelling for a major triad above a given root is known, simply lower the third of that triad by one half step, as in Figure 22-1, F A C to F A♭ C.

EXERCISE 22-1

2. As with major triads, fifteen minor triads can be spelled by selecting 1̂, 3̂, and 5̂ of each minor scale; for example:

Minor Key	1̂, 3̂, 5̂
A	A C E
F♯	F♯ A C♯
C	C E♭ G
B♭	B♭ D♭ F

EXERCISE 22-2

3. Uncommon spellings on chromatic roots can be spelled in the same manner as those in major (review page 246).

> *Problem:* Spell a minor triad on E♯
> *Solution:* Spell a minor triad on E: E G B
>   Raise each note one half step: E♯ G♯ B♯
> *Problem:* Spell a minor triad on G♭
> *Solution:* Spell a minor triad on G: G B♭ D
>   Lower each note one half step: G♭ B♭♭ D♭

4. Spell the minor triad by interval, as shown in Figure 22-1*b*.

There are other respects in which features ascribed to the major triad also apply to the minor triad: triad inversion (review page 247), triad position (review page 248), triad doubling (review pages 248–249), and use of dissonance in conjunction with the triad (review pages 249–250). A new consideration arises when using *chords in a minor key*.

Chords in a Minor Key

Although the system of numbering chords in a minor key follows the same principles used in major keys, there are differences:

1. The quality of a triad on a given scale step in minor will differ from that on the same scale step in major; for example, in C major, I = C E G, whereas in C minor, i = C E♭ G.
2. The melodic form of the minor scale includes ♯$\hat{6}$ and ♯$\hat{7}$ ascending and $\hat{7}$ and $\hat{6}$ descending. Since all triads except the tonic (i)[1] include one of these scale steps, it follows that each triad can be found in two forms, as seen in Figure 22-2.

FIGURE 22-2   *Use of $\hat{6}$ and ♯$\hat{6}$, or $\hat{7}$ and ♯$\hat{7}$, in triad spellings from minor keys (example in C minor)*

Triads using		Triads using	
$\hat{6}$ (A♭)	♯$\hat{6}$ (A)	$\hat{7}$ (B♭)	♯$\hat{7}$ (B)
D F A♭	D F A	E♭ G B♭	E♭ G B
F A♭ C	F A C	G B♭ D	G B D
A♭ C E♭	A C E♭	B♭ D F	B D F

In a composition, the choice from each pair is determined by the direction in which the sixth or the seventh scale step progresses. Figure 22-3 shows that each $\hat{6}$ and $\hat{7}$ descends, whereas each ♯$\hat{6}$ and ♯$\hat{7}$ ascends, just as in the melodic form of the scale. Observe that the triads using ♯$\hat{6}$ or ♯$\hat{7}$ are considered diatonic, since these two tones belong to the melodic form of the scale.

[1]The *final* tonic triad is sometimes found as a major triad, especially in music written before ca. 1750. The third is often called a "Picardy third." The source of the name is unknown. See Exercise 22-7, example 3.

EXERCISE 22-3
EXERCISE 22-4

FIGURE 22-3 *Uses of $\hat{6}$, $\hat{7}$, $\sharp\hat{6}$, and $\sharp\hat{7}$*

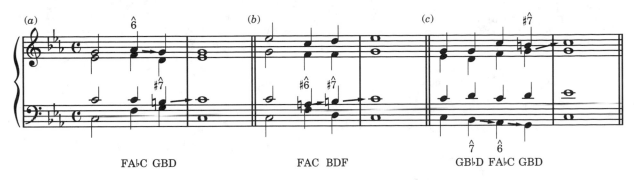

FAbC GBD   FAC BDF   GBbD FAbC GBD

We will work in detail only with the most commonly used chords, as shown in Figure 22-4: the i triad, the iv triad (using $\hat{6}$), and the V and V⁷ chords (using $\sharp\hat{7}$). Note that V and V⁷ are used in parallel major and minor keys because the third ($\sharp\hat{7}$) of each chord usually ascends.

FIGURE 22-4 *Chords in a minor key*

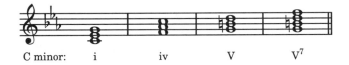

C minor: i   iv   V   V⁷

EXERCISES
*22-5, 22-6,
22-7*

The Diminished and Augmented Triads

Compared with major and minor triads, the use of the diminished triad is infrequent, and the use of the augmented triad could almost be considered rare. Here are the distinguishing features of these triads.

The Diminished Triad

1. The triad is composed of two minor thirds. The interval from its root up to its fifth is a diminished fifth (dim.5). See Figure 22-5a.
2. The triad is used almost exclusively in first inversion. In this inversion, the interval from the fifth of the triad up to its root is an augmented fourth (aug.4). See Figure 22-5b.
3. The symbol for a diminished triad is a lowercase roman numeral with an added °, as in vii°. Used as a diatonic triad, the diminished triad is found on the leading tone in both major and minor keys (vii°) and on the supertonic tone in minor keys (ii°). See Figure 22-5c.
4. The intervals of the diminished fifth and its inversion, the augmented fourth, equally divide the octave. Each interval includes the equivalent of three whole steps, which is why both intervals are known as a *tritone*. See Figure 22-6.

FIGURE 22-5 *The diminished triad*

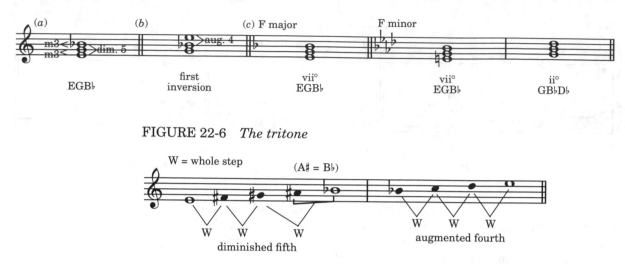

FIGURE 22-6 *The tritone*

Figure 22-7 shows the use of the two diminished triads in a minor key.

FIGURE 22-7 *vii° and ii° in a minor key*

The Augmented Triad

1. The triad is composed of two major thirds. The interval from its root up to its fifth is an augmented fifth. See Figure 22-8*a*.

2. The triad is used in root position and in first inversion. In first inversion, the interval from its fifth up to its root is a diminished fourth. See Figure 22-8*b*.

3. The symbol for an augmented triad is an uppercase roman numeral with an added +, as in I+. It exists as a diatonic triad only on the third degree of a minor scale as III+ (C minor, E♭ G B). See Figure 22-8*c*. In a major key, it is always an altered chord, such as C E G♯ or F A C♯ in C major. See Figure 22-8*a*.

FIGURE 22-8 *The augmented triad*

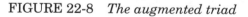

Figure 22-9 shows an augmented triad used as V+, an altered chord A C♯ E♯ in D major. This excerpt has been transposed from its original key of C♯ major, where V+ is spelled G♯ B♯ D×.

FIGURE 22-9 *V+ in a major key*

D: I   V+   I
    AC♯E♯

EXERCISES
22-8, 22-9

EXERCISE 22-1

Spelling minor triads

Major triads are shown on the staff. After each, write a minor triad by lowering the third of the major triad one half step. Spell each major and minor triad below the staff.

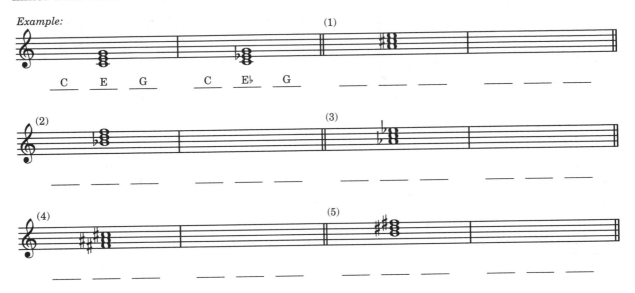

Example: (1)

C   E   G   C   E♭ G   ___ ___ ___   ___ ___ ___

(2)   (3)

___ ___ ___   ___ ___ ___   ___ ___ ___   ___ ___ ___

(4)   (5)

___ ___ ___   ___ ___ ___   ___ ___ ___   ___ ___ ___

(*Return* to page *279*.)

EXERCISE 22-2

Spelling minor triads

Spell the minor triad built on each of the tonic notes of the fifteen minor scales.

Minor Key	$\hat{1}, \hat{3}, \hat{5}$			*Minor Key*	$\hat{1}, \hat{3}, \hat{5}$		
A	A	C	E				
E	E	G	B	D	___	___	___
B	___	___	___	G	___	___	___
F♯	___	___	___	C	___	___	___
C♯	___	___	___	F	___	___	___
G♯	___	___	___	B♭	___	___	___
D♯	___	___	___	E♭	___	___	___
A♯	___	___	___	A♭	___	___	___

(*Return* to page *280*.)

EXERCISE 22-3

Spelling minor triads

Spell less common minor triads built on chromatic notes.

(1) Root is B♯:   lower B♯ one half step   ____

                         spell minor triad on that note   ____ ____ ____

                         raise all notes one half step   ____ ____ ____

(2) Root is F♭:   raise F♭ one half step   ____ ____ ____

                         spell minor triad on that note   ____ ____ ____

                         lower all notes one half step   ____ ____ ____

(*Return* to page *280*.)

EXERCISE 22-4

Spelling minor triads

Spell a minor triad from each of the given roots. Use any convenient method of spelling. Place the triad on the staff.

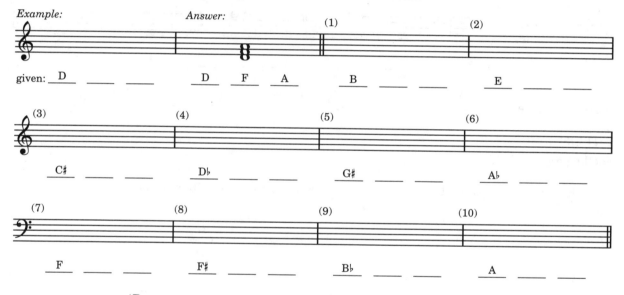

(*Return* to page *280*.)

EXERCISE 22-5

Spelling minor triads in a key

Spell the i, iv, V, and V^7 chords in minor keys.

Key	i			iv			V			V^7			
A	A	C	E	D	F	A	E	G#	B	E	G#	B	D
D	—	—	—	—	—	—	—	—	—	—	—	—	—
E	—	—	—	—	—	—	—	—	—	—	—	—	—
G	—	—	—	—	—	—	—	—	—	—	—	—	—
B	—	—	—	—	—	—	—	—	—	—	—	—	—
F#	—	—	—	—	—	—	—	—	—	—	—	—	—
C	—	—	—	—	—	—	—	—	—	—	—	—	—
F	—	—	—	—	—	—	—	—	—	—	—	—	—

EXERCISE 22-6

Placing the i, iv, V, and V^7 chords on the staff

The key name is given. Place its signature on the staff and then place the indicated triads on the staff. Be sure to place the appropriate accidental, ♯ or ♮, before the third of the V and V^7 chords.

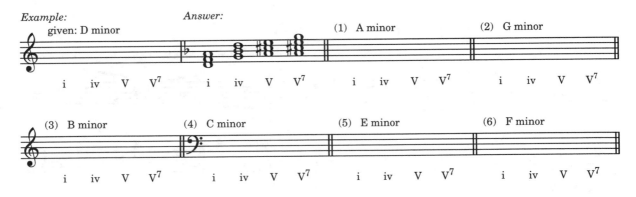

EXERCISE 22-7
Harmonic analysis

Place chord numbers below the staff as appropriate. Circle nonharmonic tones and the sevenths of seventh chords (a few have been circled for you).

(1) Andante

Verdi, *La Forza del Déstino*

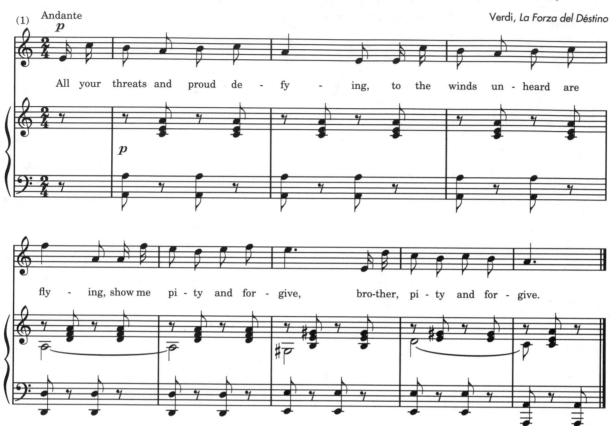

All your threats and proud de - fy - ing, to the winds un - heard are

fly - ing, show me pi - ty and for - give, bro-ther, pi - ty and for - give.

Schumann, *Album for the Young*, Op. 68, "The Wild Rider" (original key, A minor)

(2)

Bach, "Christe, du beistand und deiner Kreuzgemeinde"

*Review footnote 1, page 280.

(*Return* to page *281*.)

EXERCISE 22-8

Spelling diminished and augmented triads

(a) From the given root, write two successive minor thirds to complete a diminished triad.

(b) From the given root, write two successive major thirds to complete an augmented triad. One of the spellings includes both a sharp and a flat.

(a) Diminished			(b) Augmented		
B	D	F	C	E	G♯
F♯	A	C	A♭	C	E
E	⎯	⎯	F	⎯	⎯
G♯	⎯	⎯	G	⎯	⎯
A	⎯	⎯	E♭	⎯	⎯
D	⎯	⎯	B♭	⎯	⎯
G	⎯	⎯	A	⎯	⎯
C♯	⎯	⎯	D♭	⎯	⎯

EXERCISE 22-9
Harmonic analysis

Each of these music excerpts contains one example (except as noted) of either a diminished or an augmented triad. Circle the triad, write "dim." for diminished or "aug." for augmented above the triad, and write the triad spelling below the staff.

(1) "Good King Wenceslas"

(2) Munter   Schumann, *Myrthen*, Op. 25, "Sitz' ich allein"

(3) Allegro molto   Beethoven, Piano Sonata, Op. 10, No. 1

Look for two triads, one of which is diminished and one is augmented.

(4) Bach, "O Ewigkeit, du Donnerwort"

CHAPTER SUMMARY

1. Among several ways, a minor triad may be spelled simply by lowering the third of a major triad.

2. The quality of any triad in a minor key except the tonic is affected by use of $\hat{6}$ and $\hat{7}$ or $\sharp\hat{6}$ and $\sharp\hat{7}$. In C minor, the subdominant triad is iv (using $\hat{6}$) and IV (using $\sharp\hat{6}$). Which triad is used is determined by whether the $\hat{6}$ or the $\hat{7}$ in the melodic line ascends or descends.

3. The diminished triad is composed of two minor thirds and is usually found in first inversion, and as vii° in major and minor, and as ii° in minor.

4. The interval of the *tritone* consists of three whole steps, commonly in the diminished triad as root up to fifth (diminished fifth) or as fifth up to root (augmented fourth). The two versions of the tritone are enharmonic.

5. The augmented triad consists of two major thirds (C major, C E G$\sharp$). It always requires an accidental. Its use is uncommon.

CHAPTER TWENTY-THREE

Keyboard Harmony II

Playing the Chord Progression i V⁷ i
Harmonizing Melodies in Minor Keys
Playing Chord Progressions Using i, iv, and V⁷

In Chapter Twenty-two, you studied the spelling, notation, and analysis of i, iv, and V⁷. Is your keyboard skill sufficient to use these chords in melody harmonization? Test yourself by chording the following melody.

FIGURE 23-1   *Melody for keyboard harmonization*

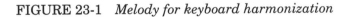

Brahms, Hungarian Dance No. 4 (original key, F♯ minor)

If your performance compares favorably with Figure 23-2 and you are confident of your ability to harmonize similar melodies, skip to Exercise 23-5. Otherwise, continue the study following Figure 23-2.

FIGURE 23-2   *Harmonized melody*

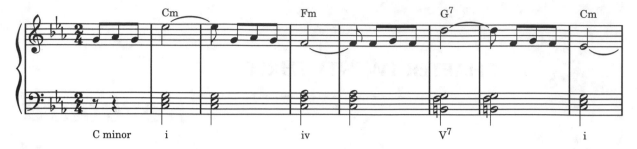

Playing the Chord Progression i V⁷ i

Playing the progression i V⁷ i is made easy by the finger control you have developed as a result of playing chords in major keys. A few observations are sufficient to ensure correct playing in any minor key.

In this progression, shown in Figure 23-3, the thumb repeats the same key; the little finger moves a half step from tonic to leading tone; and in the V⁷ chord, the 2nd finger is a whole step below the thumb. These points of reference are exactly the same for major and minor keys, the only difference in the progression being in the tonic chord, either major (I) or minor (i).

FIGURE 23-3   *Fingerings for the progression i V⁷ i, left hand*

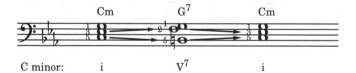

EXERCISE 23-1

Harmonizing Melodies in Minor Keys

Having practiced the keyboard progression i V⁷ i, we can now apply these chords in a musical way. Refer to page 269, "Procedure for Harmonizing a Melody at the Keyboard." With the substitution of minor tonic for major, follow all procedures for *Study-Play* to harmonize melodies in minor keys.

EXERCISE 23-2

294

Playing Chord Progressions Using i, iv, and V⁷

Playing the Progression i iv i

In playing this progression, shown in Figure 23-4, the little finger repeats the same key; in the iv chord, the thumb and the 2nd finger form the interval of a minor third.

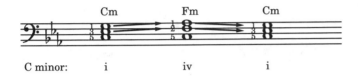

C minor: i   iv   i

EXERCISE
23-3

FIGURE 23-4   *Fingerings for the progression i iv i, left hand*

Playing the Progression i iv V⁷ i, Left Hand

When connecting iv V⁷ in this progression, shown in Figure 23-5, the 2nd finger repeats the same key while the thumb and the 5th finger move stepwise.

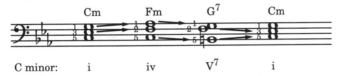

C minor: i   iv   V⁷   i

FIGURE 23-5   *Fingerings for the progression i iv V⁷ i, left hand*

EXERCISES
23-4, 23-5

EXERCISE 23-1

Playing the Progression i V⁷ i (left hand)

(a) Play the written progressions. Use recommended fingerings for all keys. Repeat until you can play without hesitation.

(b) Without looking at the music, play i V⁷ i in these keys: (1) A minor; (2) E minor; (3) B minor; (4) F♯ minor; (5) C♯ minor; (6) D minor; (7) G minor; (8) C minor; (9) F minor. (To extend this exercise, practice the progression in the remaining keys: G♯ minor; D♯ minor; A♯ minor; B♭ minor; E♭ minor; A♭ minor.)

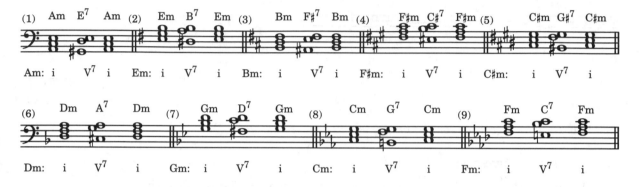

(*Return* to page *294*.)

EXERCISE 23-2

Harmonizing melodies using i and V⁷ only

Harmonize each of the following melodies. Use the procedure outlined on pages 269–270.

Sweden

(*Return* to page *295.*)

EXERCISE 23-3

Playing the progression i iv i (left hand)

(*a*) Play the written progressions. Use recommended fingerings for all keys. Repeat until you can play without hesitation.

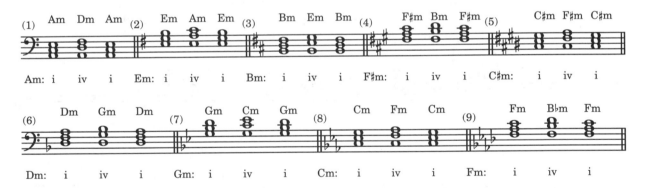

(*b*) Without looking at the music, play i iv i in these keys: (1) A minor; (2) E minor; (3) B minor; (4) F♯ minor; (5) C♯ minor; (6) D minor; (7) G minor; (8) C minor; (9) F minor. (To extend this exercise, practice the progression in the remaining keys: G♯ minor; D♯ minor; A♯ minor; B♭ minor; E♭ minor; A♭ minor.)

(*Return* to page *297.*)

EXERCISE 23-4

Playing the Progression i iv V⁷ i (left hand)

(a) Play the written progressions. Use recommended fingerings for all keys. Repeat until you can play without hesitation.

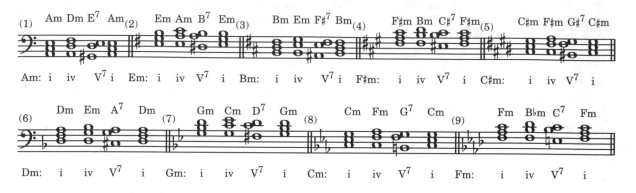

Am: i iv V⁷ i   Em: i iv V⁷ i   Bm: i iv V⁷ i   F♯m: i iv V⁷ i   C♯m: i iv V⁷ i

Dm: i iv V⁷ i   Gm: i iv V⁷ i   Cm: i iv V⁷ i   Fm: i iv V⁷ i

(b) Without looking at the music, play i iv V⁷ i in these keys: (1) A minor; (2) E minor; (3) B minor; (4) F♯ minor; (5) C♯ minor; (6) D minor; (7) G minor; (8) C minor; (9) F minor. (To extend this exercise, practice the progression in the remaining keys: G♯ minor; D♯ minor; A♯ minor; B♭ minor; E♭ minor; A♭ minor.)

EXERCISE 23-5

Harmonizing melodies using i, iv, and V⁷

Harmonize the following melodies at the keyboard. Use the procedures outlined on pages 269–270. Include at least one iv chord in each harmonization.

Slovakia

(4)

England

(5)

Mexico

(6)

Spain

(7)

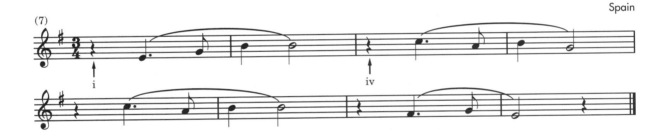

United States

(8)

England

(9)

Fine

D.C.

(10)   Italy

(11)   Russia

300

APPENDIX A

Elementary Acoustics

Hearing is one of the five senses—the others are sight, touch, smell, and taste—through which the body receives stimuli from outside sources. What a person hears is the result of a three-stage process in which (1) an object is set in vibration, (2) the vibrations are conducted through a medium such as air, and (3) the vibrations are received by the ear and transmitted to the brain, which perceives them as sound.

A musical sound combines four qualities that differentiate it from other sounds:

1. *Pitch*, the highness or lowness of a sound
2. *Intensity*, the loudness or softness of a sound
3. *Timbre*, the tone color of a sound, the factor that enables us to distinguish the characteristic sound of a particular instrument or voice (a violin, a trumpet, a bassoon, a bass singer, and so on)
4. *Duration*, the length of time a sound exists

The study of both the production of sound and the qualities of sound is known as *acoustics*.[1]

Creating Sound (Vibrations)

To create *vibrations*, an object must be set in motion. There are many ways to do that in music: for example, striking a drum head, blowing on a reed, or drawing a bow across a string. A vibration is the back-and-forth movement of the object so stimulated. Vibrations are usually measured in terms of their *frequency*—that is, the number of back-and-forth movements per second. Frequencies may range from less than one (but more than zero) to many tens of thousands per second.

The vibrations of the original object and of the surrounding air when counted are expressed in *cycles per second* (abbreviated *cps* or Hz[2]). Figure A-1 shows a simplified diagram of 2 Hz. The horizontal center line represents one second of time, and the undulating curved line represents two back-and-forth movements of air as set into motion by the vibrating object. Actually, 2 Hz cannot be heard (see the next section, "Pitch"), but can you visualize 262 Hz, the number of vibrations for middle C, or approximately 4,186 Hz for the highest note on the piano?

---

[1]Of the four qualities of sound, duration alone does not depend upon acoustical phenomena.

[2]In honor of Heinrich Hertz, 1857–1894, discoverer of radio waves. The abbreviation "Hz" is now more commonly used.

FIGURE A-1 *Demonstrating vibrations*

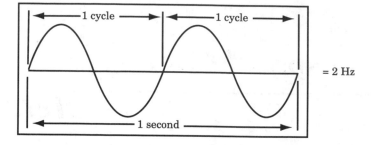

Once established, the created vibrations are only vibrations, and not sound, until passage through a medium and transmission to the brain are accomplished. Thus, if there is a lack of a transmitting medium (a vacuum), there is no sound. Or, if the ear does not pick up the vibrations (because of the weakness of the vibrations or a physical defect in the ear), there is—for that person—no sound.

Pitch

The *pitch* of a sound is specifically related to the frequency of vibrations. The higher the frequency, the higher will be the perceived pitch, and the lower the frequency, the lower will be the perceived pitch. Thus, for example, 3,000 Hz will sound much higher than 1,000 Hz. The human ear responds to frequencies in the approximate range of 16.0–20,000 Hz. The piano produces a range of approximately 28.0–4,000 Hz, from its lowest to its highest tone.

The Relation of Intervals to Frequency

An interval can be expressed by the numerical ratio between its two tones. For the octave, the ratio is 1:2, meaning that the upper tone of the octave will have double the number of vibrations of the lower tone. If the lower tone is 600 Hz, its octave will be 1,200 Hz. For the perfect fifth, the ratio is 2:3. If the lower note of the perfect fifth is 200 Hz, the upper note will be 300 Hz. Similarly, the simplest ratios describe other intervals commonly used in music composition.

FIGURE A-2 *Ratios of simple intervals*

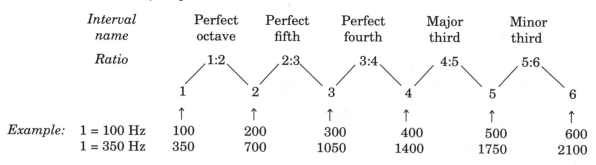

Interval name	Perfect octave	Perfect fifth	Perfect fourth	Major third	Minor third
Ratio	1:2	2:3	3:4	4:5	5:6
	1 2	3	4	5	6

Example: 1 = 100 Hz

| 100 | 200 | 300 | 400 | 500 | 600 |

1 = 350 Hz

| 350 | 700 | 1050 | 1400 | 1750 | 2100 |

The Overtone Series

The series of ratios in Figure A-2 is coincidental with another phenomenon in sound, the *overtone series*. Simply stated, when any pitch is sounded, a series of higher frequencies that is also created vibrates simultaneously. These higher frequencies, usually inaudible, display the same ratios as those in Figure A-2, as well as an indefinite series beyond these. Figure A-3 shows the first sixteen members of an overtone series based on a tone of 88 Hz.

FIGURE A-3 *The overtone series*

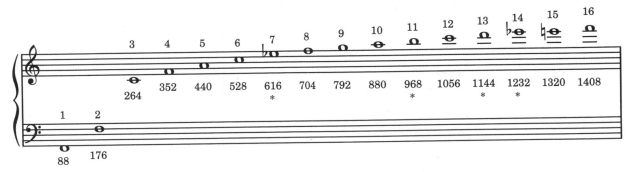

*Out of tune in relation to current tuning systems.

In addition to the intervals from Figure A-2, you can see in the overtone series the ratios of these intervals:

major sixth = 3:5   major second = 8:9
minor sixth = 5:8   minor second = 15:16

Members of the overtone series are named in one of two ways; that marked **(1)** is more generally used.

(1)
1 = first partial or fundamental
2 = second partial
3 = third partial
4 = fourth partial

(2)
1 = fundamental
2 = first overtone
3 = second overtone
4 = third overtone

etc.

Pitch Names

Knowing the relationship of pitches does not explain how individual pitches are named. The naming of pitches has always been arbitrary. For example, many different frequencies, including 435, 440, and 446, have in the past been called the tuning A (the A above middle C). Only as recently as 1937 did an international conference assign the name "A" to the frequency of 440 Hz (as used in Figure A-3), a designation now almost universally used.

Intensity

The *intensity* of a sound, whether it is loud or soft, is determined by the *amplitude* or size of the vibration. The greater the amplitude, the louder, or more intense, the sound will be. In Figure A-4, both *a* and *b* show 2 Hz. At *a,* the distance traveled above and below the line (the amplitude) is much less than at *b.* Therefore, *a* represents a softer sound than *b.* (Understand, of course, that 2 Hz is inaudible at any amplitude, but it is convenient for demonstration.)

FIGURE A-4   *Amplitude of vibrations*

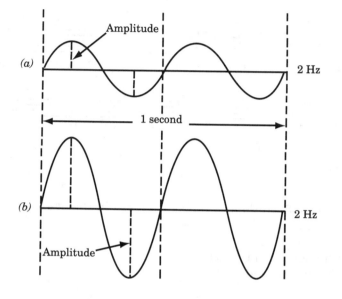

Intensity is measured in units of *decibels* (dB = 1/10 of a *bel*).[3] The greater the amplitude of a sound wave, the higher the dB. Musical sounds range from about 25 dB (a soft tone on the violin) to 100dB (the volume of a full orchestra).

Figure A-5 shows two sounds differing in both pitch and intensity. The pitch at *a* is higher than that at *b* because there are more vibrations per second, but *a* is softer (less intense) than *b* because the vibrations are of a smaller amplitude.

[3]The term *bel* is derived from Alexander Graham Bell (1847–1922).

FIGURE A-5 *Differences in both pitch and intensity*

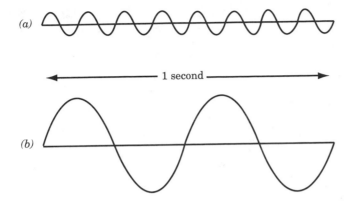

It should be understood that all the preceding diagrams of patterns of vibrations are for demonstration of basic concepts only. A diagram of a real sound is very complex, being a composite of a vibrating rate of the fundamental *and* all its overtones, as well as representing the factor of intensity.

Timbre (Tone Color)

When you hear two different instruments[4] (say, a violin and a trumpet) play the same pitch, you easily recognize that there is a difference in the sound each produces. The characteristic sound of an instrument is known as its *timbre*. Differences in timbre are related to the differences in the strengths and weaknesses of the partials of a given tone. A given partial for a pitch on one instrument may be more or less intense than the same partial in the pitch produced by the other instrument. In some sounds, some partials may be missing entirely. Figure A-6 shows two sets of partials (1–6 only), each set representing the same pitch, but each having partials of differing intensities, as reflected by the height of the vertical lines. Because the two pitches so represented differ in the makeup of their partials, one will differ in timbre from the other.

FIGURE A-6 *Differences in timbre*

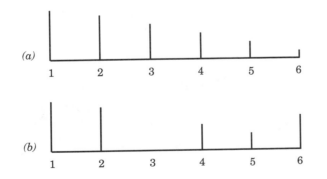

Therefore, even if partials are rarely heard as individual sounds, the ear readily picks them up in their various and multiple combinations and thus allows us to hear a great variety of timbres.

[4]For purposes of this discussion, the voice is included as an instrument.

305

APPENDIX B

Octave Registers, 8va, The C Clef and Other Clef Uses, and Repeat Signs

Octave Registers

Fifty-two white and 36 black keys make up the standard keyboard of 88 keys. In naming the keys, the 7-letter series of the music alphabet is used repetitiously. In fact, for white keys, there are 8 A's, 8 B's, and 8 C's, plus 7 each of D's, E's, F's, and G's. Therefore, there is a need for a system whereby any one pitch can be designated distinctly from any other pitch of the same letter name. The solution is a system called *octave registers,* whereby the entire range of pitches on the keyboard is divided into octaves, each with its own distinguishing identification.

On the keyboard, Figure B-1, *middle C* is designated as c^1 (spoken "c-one" or "one-line c"),[1] and each C higher as c^2 through c^5. Letter names above c^1 and below c^2 are designated d^1, e^1, f^1, and so forth. Each higher octave is treated in the same way; for example, the G above c^3 is g^3.

Octaves below middle C in descending order are *c, C,* and *CC,* with the lowest note designated *AAA.* These octaves are named as marked, and again, any letter name is designated the same as the C below it; for example, the E above CC (spoken "contra C") is EE ("contra E").

---

[1] Instead of c^1–c^5, the octave designations c', c'', c''', and so forth, may be used, hence the spoken designations "one-line c," "two-line c," and so forth.

FIGURE B-1 *Octave registers. From Raymond Elliott,* Fundamentals of
Music, *3rd edition © 1971, p. 15. Reprinted by permission of Prentice-
Hall, Inc., Englewood Cliffs, New Jersey.*

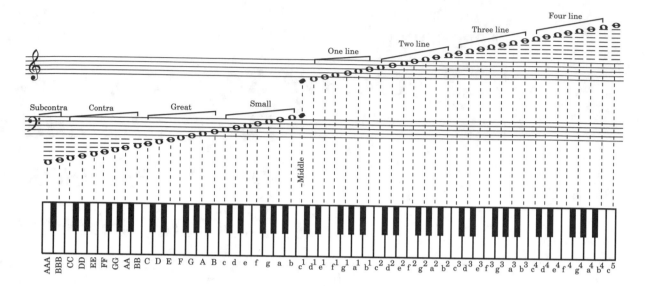

8va

In most music compositions, a large percentage of the pitches are within the
range of the great staff plus one or two ledger lines above or below. On the
other hand, there are compositions that utilize many pitches far above or
below the staff. Such music containing many ledger lines in the notation can
be quite difficult to read. To ease this difficulty, a special sign is used, *8va.*

The sign *8va* or *8,* an abbreviation for the Italian *all' ottava* ("at the
octave"), when used above the treble clef, indicates that the notes are to be
played one octave higher than written. This eliminates the necessity of placing notes many ledger lines above the staff, making the music far easier to
read. The notes of Figure B-2*a* are written in the location of the pitches c^2, d^2,
e^2, f^2, and g^2, over which is placed the sign 8--¬. The passage is performed
as though written in the three-line range (c^3, d^3, and so on), as shown in part
b of Figure B-2. Observe that the "8" is placed over the first note affected, the
dotted line continues to the last note affected, and the sign ends with a vertical line down from the dotted line.

FIGURE B-2   *8va above treble clef*

(*a*) written

(*b*) played

FIGURE B-3   *Use of 8va*

Chopin, Waltz, Op. 64, No. 3

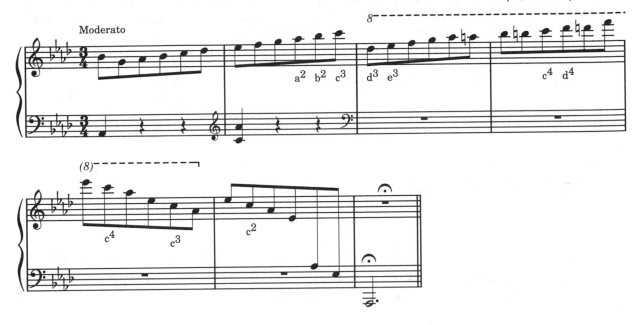

This sign is also used below bass notes to indicate that they are to be performed an octave lower than written. The sign is identical to that used with the treble clef, except that the final vertical line proceeds up from the dotted line: 8---⌐ .

FIGURE B-4   *8va below bass clef*

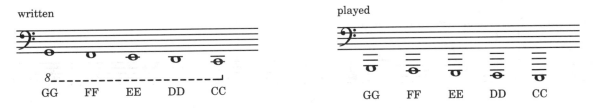

Following the same principle, the 8va sign is sometimes used above the bass clef, but rarely below the treble clef. Although the sign is most frequently found in connection with a series of pitches as in the preceding illustrations, 8va may also be used with but a solitary note. An "8" at the last note of a composition may be used without the horizontal line.

The C Clef and Other Clef Uses

The C clef sign (𝄡) is one of three used in notation, the other two being the more familiar G (𝄞) and F (𝄢) clef signs. All clef signs work by the same principle: Each has a distinctive design with a focal point that establishes its letter name on a particular line of the staff. Once the sign is placed, the clef is given its own name, such as "treble clef" or "bass clef."

Theoretically, a clef sign can be placed on any line of the staff, justified by avoiding excessive ledger lines in the notation. In common practice, the C clef sign appears in two locations: on the middle line as *alto clef* and on the fourth line as *tenor clef*. Music for viola is written in the alto clef; tenor clef is often used for cello, bassoon, and trombone.

Figure B-5a shows the commonly used clefs. Those shown in B-5b are rare. Any or all of these clefs can be found in editions of early music and in modern publications of pre-nineteenth-century music.

FIGURE B-5 *Names of clefs*

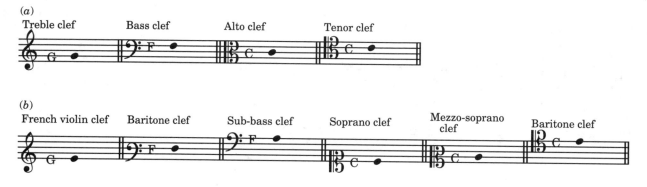

Repeat Signs

Double Bar and Dots

A repeat sign consists of a double bar preceded by two dots around the third line, and indicates a repetition of the music preceding the sign. Upon reaching the repeat sign the second time, continue to the next measure.

FIGURE B-6 *Repeat sign at end of a measure*

When the section to be repeated ends before the end of the measure, the repeat sign (double bar with dots) will be found between the two single bar lines of the measure.

FIGURE B-7 *Repeat sign (double bar and dots) within a measure*

If the section to be repeated begins after the beginning of the composition, the section is enclosed by double bars, the first with dots to the right of the double bar and the second with the dots to the left of the double bar.

FIGURE B-8 *Indication of repetition of a section within a composition*

First and Second Endings

The first ending ([1.   ]) indicates a return to the beginning, or to a previous repeat sign (‖:). During the repetition, the music of the first ending is skipped and the piece continues with the second ending ([2.   ]).

FIGURE B-9 *First and second endings*

D.C., D.S., and Fine

Da capo (It., *da capo,* literally, "from the head"), abbreviated *D.C.,* indicates a repeat from the beginning of the composition. See Figure B-10.

Dal segno (It., *dal segno,* "from the sign"), abbreviated *D.S.,* indicates a repeat from the sign 𝄋. See Figure B-11.

Fine (It., *fine,* "end," pronounced *fee´-nay*) indicates the place where the composition ends after using *D.C.* or *D.S.* A double bar is used with the *fine.* See Figures B-10 and B-11.

FIGURE B-10 *The da capo*

FIGURE B-11 *The dal segno*

APPENDIX C

The Medieval Modes and Other Scale Forms

The Medieval Modes

Our present-day major and natural minor scales are identical to two scales in earlier music history. Eight-note scale systems evolved as early as the eighth century A.D., and by 1600 music was written in a system of six scales, called *modes*. These can be found on the keyboard by playing up an octave from each letter name using only white keys. Any mode consists of five whole steps and two half steps. The half steps are always E–F and B–C, but each mode differs from the others because of the varying locations of the half steps. These differences, and the name of each mode, are shown in Figure C-1.

FIGURE C-1 *Modes*

First Note	White-Key Scale	Mode
A	a $\hat{2}$b—c$\hat{3}$ d $\hat{5}$e—f$\hat{6}$ g a (½ at b–c, ½ at e–f)	Aeolian
(B)[1]		(Locrian)
C	c d $\hat{3}$e—f$\hat{4}$ g a $\hat{7}$b—c$\hat{8}$ (½ at e–f, ½ at b–c)	Ionian
D	d $\hat{2}$e—f$\hat{3}$ g a $\hat{6}$b—c$\hat{7}$ d (½ at e–f, ½ at b–c)	Dorian
E	$\hat{1}$e—f$\hat{2}$ g a $\hat{5}$b—c$\hat{6}$ d e (½ at e–f, ½ at b–c)	Phrygian
F	f g a $\hat{4}$b—c$\hat{5}$ d $\hat{7}$e—f$\hat{8}$ (½ at b–c, ½ at e–f)	Lydian
G	g a $\hat{3}$b—c$\hat{4}$ d $\hat{6}$e—f$\hat{7}$ g (½ at b–c, ½ at e–f)	Mixolydian

[1]Theoretically, a mode called Locrian can be constructed on B, but it was not used in musical practice.

Through evolutionary processes, the number of scale systems was reduced to two by the mid-seventeenth century. The Ionian mode became the pattern for the major scale. The Aeolian mode became the pattern for the basic minor scale: the pure, or natural, form of the minor scale.

The medieval modes, including Locrian, with their unique sound resources, are frequently employed by twentieth-century composers and in the study of jazz improvisation.

Other Scale Forms

1. The *chromatic scale* is a twelve-note scale utilizing only half steps within its octave. No complete compositions (except short novelties or descriptive pieces) are based on this scale, but a series of half steps in a melodic line, a chromatic passage, is often said to be derived from the chromatic scale. The ascending form generally uses sharp signs, and the descending form uses flat signs.

FIGURE C-2 *The chromatic scale with solmization*

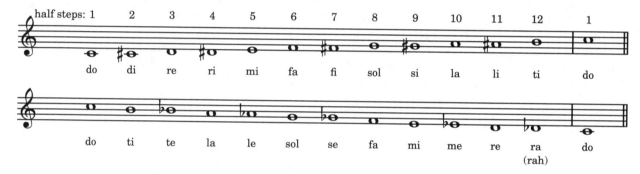

FIGURE C-3 *A chromatic passage*

Glinka, *Russlan and Ludmilla*

2. The *pentatonic scale* is a five-note scale, easily found by playing only the black keys on the piano. Its structure, M2, M2, m3, M2, m3, can be found with 1̂ on any black or white key: Three possibilities are shown in Figure C-4*a, b,* and *c.* In Figure C-4*d,* the scale is indicated by the bracket below the bass clef. Four-note segments of the scale can be seen in the first measure, treble clef: E♭ D♭ B♭ A♭ in the highest voice, and B♭ A♭ E♭ D♭ in the inner voice.

FIGURE C-4 *The pentatonic scale*

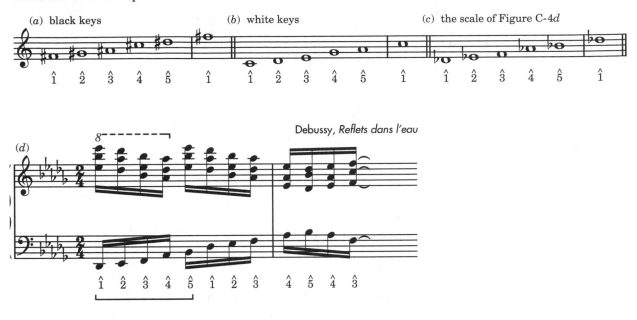

3. The *whole-tone scale* is a six-note scale using only whole steps. When written, the scale includes the interval of a diminished third, shown in Figure C-5a as C♯–E♭ or D♯–F. Figure C-5b shows the scale G A (B)C♭ D♭ E♭ F G.

FIGURE C-5 *The whole-tone scale*

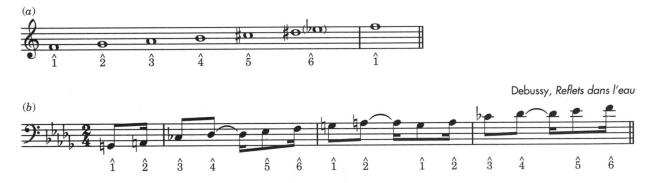

4. The *Gypsy* or *Hungarian scale* is a seven-note scale using the interval of the augmented second between 3̂–4̂ as well as between 6̂–7̂, as shown in Figure C-6. Scale patterns using augmented seconds (other than the harmonic minor) are frequently found in Eastern Europe, the Near East, and North Africa. The melody in Figure C-6b is based on a Slovakian folk song in which the augmented second can be seen descending between 4̂–3̂.

FIGURE C-6   *The Gypsy scale*

5. The *tone row* is a twelve-note series using all the tones of the chromatic scale, without duplication, in an order chosen arbitrarily by the composer. The row is not a scale by definition; yet, it provides organization of the pitch structure of a composition, just as a traditional major or minor scale affords organization of tonal music. Music composed with a tone row is called *twelve-tone music* or *serial music.*

Developed chiefly by Arnold Schoenberg (1874–1951), the twelve-tone technique has profoundly influenced the craft of composition in the twentieth century. An example of a row, as devised by Anton Webern (1883–1945) for his Concerto for Nine Instruments, is shown in Figure C-7. In this particular row, each three-note grouping contains the intervals of a minor second and a major third, although each group is in a different melodic configuration.

FIGURE C-7   *Example of a tone row*

316

APPENDIX D

Keyboard Scale Fingerings

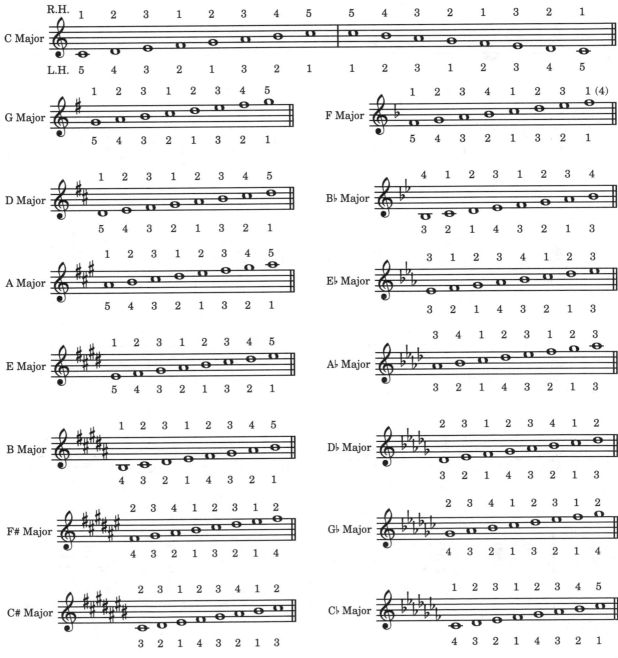

All forms of A minor use the same fingering.

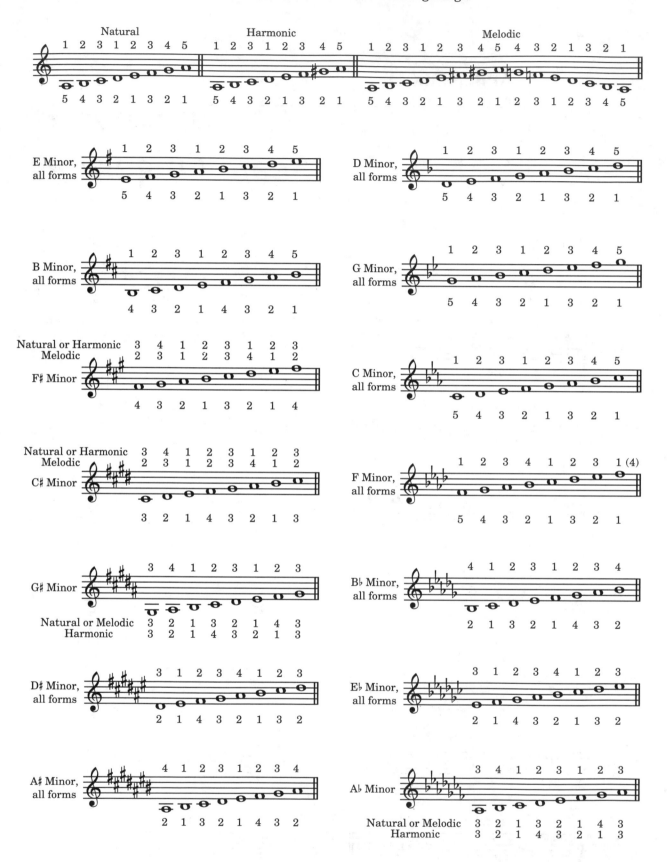

APPENDIX E

Foreign Words and Musical Terms

Most music commonly performed at the present time contains directions for performance, particularly in reference to tempo and dynamics. These markings were first added to music scores by a few Italian composers in the seventeenth century. As this procedure became more widespread, directions in Italian became standard in all languages. In the late nineteenth century, composers began using terms from their native languages, such as French, German, and English, though the older Italian terms continue to be commonly used to the present time.

This list presents a selection of terms frequently encountered in music, including all terms found in *Music for Sight Singing*. Unless otherwise indicated, the language is Italian (Fr. = French, G. = German, L. = Latin).

A

a, à (Fr.)   by
accelerando   getting faster
adagietto   slightly faster than adagio
adagio   slow, leisurely
ad libitum (L.)   at will (abbr. *ad lib.*)
affetto   emotion, passion
affettuoso   very expressively
affretti   hurried
agitato   agitated
al   to
all', alla   to the, at the, in the, in the style of
allant (Fr.)   stirring, bustling
allargando   growing broader, slowing down with fuller tone (abbr. *allarg.*)
allegretto   moderately fast; slower than allegro
allegro   lively, fast
all'ottava   perform an octave higher (when above the notes); perform an octave lower (when below the notes)
all'unisono   in unison
amoroso   amorous, loving

andante   moderately slow
andantino   somewhat quicker than andante
animando   with growing animation
animato   animated
animé (Fr.)   animated
a piacere   freely
appassionato   with passion
assai   very
assez (Fr.)   enough, rather
a tempo   return to the original tempo after a change
attacca   begin next section at once
aussi (Fr.)   as

B

belebter (G.)   lively
ben   well
bewegt (G.)   moved
bien (Fr.)   well, very
brio   vivacity, spirit, fire
brioso   with fire, spiritedly

C

cantabile   in a singing style
coda   end of piece
col', coll', colla, colle,   with
comodo, commodo   comfortable tempo
con   with
coulé (Fr.)   smoothly
crescendo   increasing in volume (abbr. *cresc.*)

D

da capo   from the beginning (abbr. *D.C.*)
dal segno   from the sign (abbr. *D.S.*)
deciso   with decision
declamato   in declamatory style
decrescendo   decreasing in volume (abbr. *decresc.*)
diminuendo   decreasing in volume (abbr. *dim.*)
dolce   soft
dolcissimo   as soft as possible
dolendo   doleful, sad
dolore   pain, grief
doloroso   sorrowful
doppio   double
douce, doux (Fr.)   soft, sweet

E

e   and
einfach (G.)   simple, plain
energico   energetic, vigorous
ernst (G.)   earnest, serious
erregeter (G.)   excited
espressivo   expressive (abbr. *espress.*)
et (Fr.)   and
etwas (G.)   somewhat

F

feierlich (G.)   solemn
ferocé (Fr.)   wild, fierce
fine   end
flebile   tearful, plaintive
forlane   Italian dance; fast tempo, $\frac{6}{4}$ or $\frac{6}{8}$ meter
forte   loud (abbr. *f*)
forte-piano   loud, then immediately soft (abbr. *fp*)
fortissimo   very loud (abbr. *ff*)
forzando   with force (abbr. *fz*)
frisch (G.)   brisk, lively
frölich (G.)   glad, joyous
fuoco   fire

G

gai (F.)   gay, brisk
gaiment, gayment (Fr.)   gaily, briskly
gavotte   French dance; moderate tempo, quadruple time
gesangvoll (G.)   in a singing style
geschwind (G.)   swift, rapid
giocoso   playful
giojoso   joyful, mirthful
gioviale   jovial, cheerful
giusto   correct
gracieusement (Fr.)   graciously
gracieux (Fr.)   gracious
grandioso   grand, pompous
grave   slow, ponderous
grazia   grace, elegance
grazioso   graceful
gut (G.)   good, well
gut zu declamiren (G.)   clearly declaimed

H

heimlich (G.)   mysterious
herzlich (G.)   heartily, affectionate

I

im (G.)   in
immer (G.)   always
innig (G.)   heartfelt, fervent
innigkeit (G.)   deep emotion
istesso   same
istesso tempo   same tempo (after a change of time signature)

J

joyeuse, joyeux (Fr.)   joyous

K

klagend (G.)   mourning
kurz (G.)   short, crisp

L

ländler   Austrian dance; slow, in triple time
langoureuse, langoureux (Fr.)   langourous
langsam (G.)   slow
langsamer (G.)   slower
languido   languid
largamente   broadly
larghetto   not as slow as largo
larghissimo   very slow

largo   slow and broad, stately
lebhaft (G.)   lively, animated
legato   smoothly connected
leger (Fr.)   light
leggiero   light (abbr. *legg.*)
leicht (G.)   light
leise (G.)   soft
lent (Fr.)   slow
lentement (Fr.)   slowly
lenteur (Fr.)   slowness
lento   slow
liberamente   freely
lieblich (G.)   with charm
l'istesso tempo   same as *istesso tempo*
lustig (G.)   merry, lusty

M

ma   but
mächtig (G.)   powerful
maestoso   with majesty or dignity
malinconico   in a melancholy style
marcato   marked, emphatic
marcia   march
marziale   martial
mässig (G.)   moderate
même (Fr.)   same
meno   less
mesto   sad
mezzo   half (mezzo forte, *mf*, mezzo piano, *mp*)
minuet (menuet)   French dance; moderate tempo, triple time
misterioso   mysteriously
mit (G.)   with
moderato   moderately
modéré (Fr.)   moderate
modérément (Fr.)   moderately
molto   much, very
morendo   dying away
mosso   "moved" (*meno mosso,* less rapid; *più mosso,* more rapid)
moto   motion
munter (G.)   lively, animated
mutig (G.)   spirited

N

nicht (G.)   not
niente   nothing
non   not
non tanto   not so much
non troppo   not too much
nobilimente   with nobility

O

ossia   or
ottava   octave

P

parlando   singing in a speaking style
pas (Fr.)   not
pas trop lent (Fr.)   not too slow
pesante   heavy
peu (Fr.)   little
peu à peu (Fr.)   little by little
piano   soft (abbr. *p*)
pianissimo   very soft (abbr. *pp*)
più   more
plus (Fr.)   more
poco   little
presto   fast, rapid
prima, primo   first

Q

quasi   as if, nearly (as in *andante quasi allegretto*)

R

rallentando   slowing down (abbr. *rall.*)
rasch (G.)   quick
rhythmique (F.)   rhythmic, strongly accented
rigaudon   Provençal dance; moderate tempo, quadruple time
rinforzando   reinforcing, sudden increase in loudness for a single tone, chord, or passage (abbr. *rfz*)
risoluto   strongly marked
ritardando   slowing down (abbr. *rit.*)
rubato   perform freely
ruhig (G.)   quiet

S

sanft (G.)   soft
sans (Fr.)   without
sarabande   Spanish dance; slow tempo, triple time
scherzando   playfully
schnell (G.)   fast
sec, secco   dry
segue   follows; next section follows immediately; or, continue in a similar manner
sehr (G.)   very
semplice   simple

semplicemente simply

sempre always

sentito with feeling

senza without

sforzando forcing; perform a single note or chord with sudden emphasis (abbr. *sfz.*)

siciliano Sicilian dance; moderate tempo, $\frac{6}{8}$ or $\frac{12}{8}$ meter

simile similarly; continue in the same manner (abbr. *sim.*)

slancio impetuousness

sostenuto sustained

sotto under

sotto voce in an undertone; subdued volume

spirito, spiritoso spirit

staccato detached; with distinct breaks between tones

stark (G.) strong

stentando slowing down (abbr. *stent.*)

stringendo pressing onward

subito suddenly

T

tant (Fr.) as much

tanto so much

tempo time

tempo giusto correct tempo

tendrement (Fr.) tenderly

teneramente tenderly

tenuto held

tranquillo tranquil

traurig (G.) sad

très (Fr.) very

trio In a minuet or scherzo, the middle section between the minuet (scherzo) and its repetition

triste (It., Fr.) sad

tristement (Fr.) sadly

tristezza sadness, melancholy

trop (Fr.) too much

troppo too much

U

un, uno one, a, an

una corde one string; on the piano: use soft pedal (abbr. *u.c.*)

und (G.) and

unisono unison

V

vif (Fr.) lively

vite (Fr.) quick

vivace very fast

vivamente very fast

vivo lively

W

waltz Austrian-German dance; moderate tempo, triple time

walzer (G.) waltz

Z

zart (G.) tender, delicate

zartlich (G.) tenderly

ziemlich (G.) somewhat, rather

zierlich (G.) delicate, graceful

Index

Triad *(cont.)*
    altered, 252
    augmented, 282
    diminished, 281
    doubling in, 248–49
    inversion of, 247
    major, 245
    minor, 279
Triad position, 248
Tritone, 226, 281
Twelve-tone music, 316

U

Unison, 217
Upbeat, 130

V

Vibration (acoustics), 301

W

White keys, 18
Whole note, 39
Whole step, 48, 217
Whole-tone scale, 315